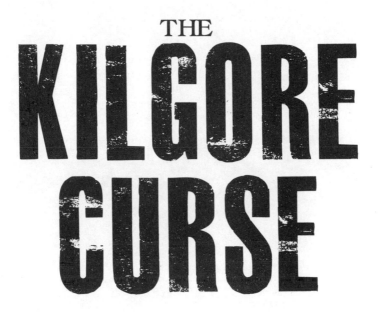

THE
KILGORE
CURSE

THE
KILGORE
CURSE

A Historical Thriller

LARRY PIVNICK MD, JD

BROWN BOOKS
PUBLISHING GROUP

The Kilgore Curse

Brown Books Publishing Group
16250 Knoll Trail Drive, Suite 205
Dallas, Texas 75248
www.BrownBooks.com
(972) 381-0009

A New Era in Publishing™

ISBN 978-1-61254-147-1
LCCN 2014932430

Printed in the United States
10 9 8 7 6 5 4 3 2 1

For more information or to contact the author, please go to
www.LarryPivnick.com

For Linda, my lifelong Muse.

This stoic woman sustained me through medical school as a young man, cheered me during law school in a somewhat excessive mid-life crisis, and gracefully endured the countless hours needed for me to author this novel. Through it all, she managed our medical practice efficiently and raised two astonishing offspring. With her by my side, everything has been possible; without her, this book would never have come to fruition. Sweet wife, you are my inspiration and true companion. I love you always.

In Flanders Fields the poppies grow
Between the crosses row on row,
That mark our place.

We are the dead. Short days ago
We lived, felt dawn, saw sunset glow,
Loved and were loved. And now we lie
Within the earth, in ashes.

Take up our quarrel with the foe:
To you with failing hands we pass
The torch; be yours to hold it high.

Excerpted from "In Flanders Fields," 1915.
Lt. Col. John McCrae MD (1872–1918)

PROLOGUE

Kilgore's Tavern
Dallas, Texas
Saturday, March 20, 1948

Canuto Cortez approached Kilgore's Tavern, bloody murder deep in his heart. The ex-Golden Gloves champion brought along his sturdy son Ramón, as good a man in a brawl as anyone in the Dallas barrio. This time he'd not be bounced from the place like some dirty wetback by his estranged neighbors, the Kilgores, as they'd done just a few hours earlier. This time he'd force them to listen and to make amends.

Outside the tavern, a torrential Dallas thunderstorm bombarded the roof and windows. Wind whipped trees into a frenzy of lashing boughs, and water spume stung pedestrians' eyes. A cold chill penetrated even the hardiest clothing.

Inside though, the heat of a potbellied stove warmed the patrons' frigid bones. A brightly lit bar dominated the narrow tavern, stretching from the front door almost to the back. Barstools lined one side, and two Irish bartenders held court on the other, perched atop a bright red, Coca-Cola cooler, dispensing their oddball version

I

of Celtic wisdom. On this soggy March evening, only a few hardy souls lingered around the warmth of that inviting stove.

Over the bartenders' heads presided a large square clock and flanking that a sign advertising *Falstaff* and *Southern Select* beers at ten cents per bottle. The walls showcased tiered rows of cheap whiskey. Henry Kilgore and his two sons, William and Michael, owned the place.

"Shame you had to put old Canuto out the door, William."

"Yeah, the old fart didn't give me no trouble."

William was a brute of a man, strong as an ox with a like amount of brainpower. The distorted nose and cheekbones of his face had collapsed from one too many fistfights. Scars too numerous to count jigsawed across his cheeks and Neanderthal brow. Few people had the temerity to challenge William to a fight.

With wavy hair, square jaw, and striking blue eyes, Michael, the younger of the two brothers, possessed a combination of intelligence and good looks. He soon returned to the back office to tend to the tavern's books and to a certain lady friend. William resumed his place behind the bar, stationed atop the cooler. After a while, moans and muffled sighs emanated from the back office.

The Cortez and Kilgore families shared the same neighborhood. Both were Catholic, but mutual distrust between Irish and Mexican immigrants guaranteed they'd have little interaction except in essential matters. For Canuto, that time was tonight, so he and Ramón sloshed into Kilgore's tavern like stranded fish washed ashore during high tide.

"Canuto. Ramón. What brings you back to Kilgore's on such a miserable night?" William pressed an alarm button underneath the counter. "Can I offer you boys a brew, on the house?"

"No, gracias, Señor Bill." They straddled a couple of bar stools in front of William. "Me an' Ramón come to talk business." While Canuto talked, Ramón sat mute, black eyes challenging William.

In the back room, Michael heard the buzzer. He hustled out front, leaving one very frustrated señorita behind. "Well, if it ain't the Cortez boys again. Why'd you come back, Canuto?"

"You know why, Señor Mike. An' I no leave here 'til you make things right."

"Nothing to make right. We already discussed that. Now run along before there's trouble."

"This is no good enough. You owe us."

"Canuto, I already said it's outta my hands." He made a slapping motion with his palms to reinforce the point. "Anything else I can do for you before you leave?"

"Sí. There is the question of family honor."

"That's enough. Better leave now before someone gets hurt. And don't come back." Michael motioned for William to escort the Cortezes out.

But Canuto wouldn't budge. "You got no cojones, Señor." He slipped a razor out of his pocket; Ramón flipped open a switchblade. William deployed an evil-looking, serrated knife of his own, while Michael drew a revolver strapped underneath the bar.

For a time, the two clans blustered oaths and insults, neither side wanting to make the first move. Customers stopped their chatter and turned warily to watch. Eventually the bellowing subsided, and the place became silent as a tomb. For a few tense moments, there was an edgy standoff between the four combatants. No one flinched.

The back door cracked open to reveal a pair of almond eyes peering from an olive face, concealed partly by jet black hair. She scanned the tavern, the scent of her perfume wafting through to the bar. No one could say for sure who was back there, or else they turned a blind eye, but several remembered that distinctive perfume. No one saw the door open wider either. A gun grasped in a slim hand poked through the slit.

Two wild shots rang out from the back, one of them clanging off the chandelier overhead. It sprayed shards of glass onto the floor and plunged the entire tavern into semi-darkness. The other bullet shattered the front window pane, which collapsed in a slow-motion waterfall of glass. The patrons dove for cover underneath tables or hid behind the stove.

Whether those shots were meant as a warning to halt the fight or were aimed at anyone in particular, they failed abominably. The four men bolted into action, and the situation quickly unraveled. Canuto swiped at William across the counter, slicing open his abdomen. Ramón leapt over the counter, knifing Michael and producing a red mist from a superficial chest wound. The men cursed, slashed, kicked, and punched each other in the dim light. The Cortezes held the initial advantage, inflicting heavy damage on the Kilgores.

Michael finally managed to level his gun and fire at Ramón, who collapsed to the floor. Seeing his eldest son dying, Canuto fought like a much younger man, utilizing his boxing skills to back William against the mirrored wall. William managed to fend him off long enough for Michael to shoot Canuto too, puncturing his neck.

By the time the sounds of conflict drifted away, Ramón lay dead, slumped over a bar stool. Canuto clung precariously to life, propped against the bar, while pulsating jets of arterial blood gushed from his neck. He choked and gurgled and cursed foul oaths in Spanish at the Kilgores in a barely audible voice. Finally the threats faltered, and he lay inert in an expanding pool of blood.

A patron later translated Canuto's words: "You Kilgores will never live to enjoy your filthy money. God will give you blood to drink. I piss on every Kilgore grave, and I curse your seed for three generations."

The place was in shambles. Tables and chairs were upended, broken glass everywhere. The floor ran crimson with fresh blood, and its cloying, sickly smell clashed with the sulfur stink of gunpowder. An eerie silence engulfed the tavern once more, broken only by the groaning of the wounded survivors, William and Michael, who lay side by side next to the unfortunate Cortezes.

Thus began a series of events that would hold the Dallas community in thrall for the next two years. The *Dallas Morning News* frequently reported the story and its aftermath to the apprehension and titillation of its readers. Who had started the feud? Why? The morning after the melee, the front page headline read

Murder Victims Bring Knives to a Gunfight;
Missing Female Witness Sought by Police.

CHAPTER
I

Calvary Hill Cemetery
Dallas, Texas
Sunday, January 13, 2008

L ife can change in a heartbeat. Between beats comes a peaceful calm, a moment not for rest but for deliberate action—the lull when elite snipers are trained to time their shots. One of many things I could never unlearn. Between heartbeats, everything can end or begin again.

On that crisp winter day, I thought of my last tour in Iraq as I left the freeway and turned toward the cemetery. A bright sun burned through wisps of clouds above, and naked trees lined the roadside. Beside me, my thirteen-year-old son leaned his head against the window and stared sullenly through it in silence. His heartbeats had captured my attention. I could see an artery pulsating on the side of his neck as his mother's used to do. It thrummed faster the closer we got to the cemetery.

"Maybe we can catch a Mavs game soon," I said. "Or see a movie."

He didn't take the bait, just lifted his head clear of the glass only to let it fall back again. I tried to remember myself at his age, but it wasn't much use; this was more than teenage moodiness. I think he would have preferred not to come on these visits, and though I understood, his hesitation bothered me.

My aging BMW glided into Calvary Hill, the largest Catholic cemetery in Dallas, where we had been coming for four years. Monsieur Dumont had founded it in 1880 when his three children died of diphtheria. Now its grounds hold about fifty thousand graves.

"I know it's hard," I said.

"Right."

Danny lived with my late wife's parents up north, in Plano. "Do Ninna and Poppy ever bring you out here?"

"No."

"I'll talk to them about it."

"Don't. It's fine."

I only had him on the weekends, but I told myself it was better this way—better school system in Plano, nice neighborhoods. Nothing to feel bad about, my schedule was full, working in the busy real estate section of the law offices of Shipwright and Chandler, a medium-sized Dallas firm. Whenever I had him, though, I wanted every moment to count.

"We should go to the range next Saturday." This was a peace offering. Danny loved shooting my guns, mostly because it gave him a chance to pelt me with questions about how and when I'd used them in the service. I rarely gave him more than three-word answers. To me, the range was important training for him and skill maintenance for me, nothing more.

"I want to use that Sig forty-five again." He lifted his head off the window and turned to watch me. "And you can tell me about Fallujah."

"I'm pretty sure I finished that story."

He frowned, laying his head against the glass again. "Mom always said you should be proud of your service over there."

"I am."

"You don't act like it."

"We're here."

I steered the car through wrought iron gates and slowed onto the main driveway. In every direction, thousands of headstones, footstones, flower arrangements, and desolate trees dotted the rolling landscape. Though the original cemetery had been tiny, the fenced borders now enclosed about a hundred acres of chalky earth.

We parked the car, and Danny snagged a dozen peach-colored roses from the back seat. We trudged up a gentle rise to a solitary grave beside a wizened live oak tree. I filled my lungs with clean air and exhaled, but despite this effort, one glance at her tombstone caused my chest to constrict. Danny stared off at a distant hill, his hands in his pockets. He had dropped the roses at his feet.

"I hate it here."

I knew how he felt. Four years after she was gone, I still wanted to tear out that tombstone, smash it to smithereens, and tell the world it was only a false alarm. Danny stared at me, a guilty expression on his face. "Because she's not really here."

He looked much older than thirteen at that moment, more careworn, his cheeks rosy from the chill. The rest of him was so pale he clutched his arms around his chest. He was tall and lanky like me with the same wavy black hair, straight nose, bony cheeks, and chin. His normally outgoing personality was exactly like his mother's though, the opposite of my taciturn nature. Lately he had been more and more withdrawn. I knew this place opened old wounds for both of us, but it seemed necessary somehow to come here.

"You're going to be OK," I told him. "We'll get through this. We're tough."

"I am anyway." He tried to smile. "You're a softy now."

"Compared to your mom, I always was. I ever tell you she wanted to be buried with her thirty-eight special? Can't you just see her chasing ghosts around the cemetery with that thing?"

He laughed, and the side of his mouth quirked as it did when he was about to tell a joke, but then he turned away and brushed at his eyes. My heart ached for him.

Four years before, I had come home to find my wife slumped on the couch. A brain hemorrhage, they told me . . . nothing I could have done. She lapsed into a coma and never regained consciousness. We were told that she had no awareness at all, and the neurologist said she might remain comatose forever if we kept her hooked up. She had a living will that took some of the burden away, so she died as she would have wished, without lingering. The worst part had been facing the finality of that decision—asking the doctors to stop her ventilator and let her go. I felt as if I were choosing her last heartbeat; the press of a button changed everything. It haunts me still.

"Your mom would be proud of you." I started to tousle his hair, but he seemed too old for that, so I patted his back. For a moment there was an awkward silence, and I wondered if it was a mistake to keep bringing him out here on the anniversary of her death. Sometimes he seemed to be slipping away from me, like two rafts adrift on the ocean. I didn't know what I would do if I lost him too.

The stone was dark red marble, which always reminded me of her striking, copper hair. The left half was blank, reserved for me at some unknown future date. The right side read *Samantha (Sam) McNamara; born Boston, Mass, April 15, 1969; died Dallas,*

Tex, January 13, 2004; beloved wife of Frank, adored mother of Daniel.

I could hear her voice in my head as if she might step out from behind a tree at any moment. She'd flash me one of her trademark smiles, tilt her head sideways, and say, "Thanks for the visit, Frankie, but why don't you take the boy shooting like he wants, instead of moping around with a bunch of corpses? Don't get me wrong; I do love you for coming."

That was my Sam. I hadn't found anyone who could match her concern for others or her lust for life, and I doubted I ever would. I wished I could express how much I still loved her, how empty I felt without her. Maybe her soul could hear me, could somehow see and understand. I wasn't sure I liked that idea, though—I had put many men to their eternal rest, and I wasn't comfortable with the thought of those evil souls sticking around.

Danny dusted off the roses and placed them carefully at the base of the headstone. My throat tightened. He stepped back and let me put my arm around his shoulders.

"I think she's happy you came today, Danny."

He tried to respond but only managed a sniffling sound.

"If you'd like, I can show you some of our other relatives while we're here. Some of them were pretty notorious." He gave a *whatever* shrug that I chose to interpret as assent, and when I started down the hill, he followed. I guided him past our car and down a tributary off the main road. We avoided treading on any graves as we approached my family's other burial plot.

"Dad, I don't get why Mom wasn't buried with the rest of our family."

"Your mom always wanted her own space, Danny." I drew a deep breath, knowing he wouldn't be satisfied with that answer.

"Truth is, she didn't get along too well with my family, except for Grandma Kate. A few of the old timers had checkered pasts, and your mom didn't approve of some things. They never really accepted her either. I think they thought of her as a stuck-up aristocrat from Boston."

"But she wasn't, right?"

"Well, she was from Boston."

"Hey, who are those people?"

I could barely make out three strangers loitering around one of the headstones in my family's burial plot. One of them gestured wildly, and as I watched, he started kicking clods of dirt onto a grave. I felt my own pulse start to race.

We walked faster while I fought the urge to break into a run and body-slam the stranger off my family's plot and into the bushes.

"Hey, Dad, are those some of our checkered relatives?"

"I don't know, Mr. Wise Guy." I could feel my temper rising, but I was glad to see Danny perking up a bit. "Let's find out, but let me do the talking."

As we approached, we could hear the man raving in Spanish before he spat a wad of phlegm onto the headstone. A gnarled old Hispanic man, he stooped over a wooden cane, continuing to shout. The grave was Henry Kilgore's, my great grandfather on my mother's side, and now spittle dribbled over the names memorialized in stone—Henry and two of his sons, my great uncles William and Michael. Two women were with the man, one much younger than the other, and they nodded with the tired resignation of those who had heard this tirade many times before. Then the doddering fool kicked dirt on the Kilgore graves again.

The women turned to face us as we approached, so I addressed them. "Has the old man got a problem with the people buried here, or is he just off his rocker?"

"I'm sorry," the younger woman said. "My uncle vents like this every time I bring him out here."

"Maybe you should stop bringing him." At this, Danny stopped up short and looked at me. My voice had an edge to it he didn't usually hear.

The woman's arms lightly crossed. "He insists." She softened then, her head tilting toward the spit-drizzled headstone. "Are these the graves of your relatives?" When I nodded, she indicated the older woman and then the man. "These are my great aunt and uncle. His father and two of his brothers are buried here also, in the plot next to your family's. I'm afraid he gets upset every time we visit, but it seems to be a kind of catharsis for him."

"Well, it's offensive to me, and he needs to stop. How would he like it if I kicked dirt and spat all over his family's graves?"

The woman spoke to her uncle in rapid-fire Spanish, but I caught very little of it. As they spoke, he looked past her, his coal-black eyes boring into mine as though he recognized something familiar in my face. He gestured at me and hurled an evil-sounding invective, though I only recognized the word "Kilgore." This was clearly the opposite of an apology, and when he spat in my direction, my fists balled up. Danny gripped my arm.

In Iraq, I learned to be calm—detached from the moment, like an observer merely watching, applying slight pressure on the trigger when called for. But since Sam's death, it had been harder and harder to find that sense of calm and keep my anger in check. I wanted to snatch the man's cane away and beat him with it.

The younger woman stepped between us, hands raised. "Sir, please allow me to start over. I apologize for his rude behavior. I'm Raquel Jennings, and this is Matilda and Alfredo Cortez."

The older woman smiled. "Good to meet you. I am sorry if we have offended you. Please excuse my husband; he can get carried away."

Realizing that my son was watching, I offered my hand to Alfredo, but he refused to take it. His wife's smile turned to acid, and she elbowed him firmly in the ribs. Reluctantly he shook my hand. "I'm Frank McNamara, and this is my son, Danny."

"Normally my uncle's a real gentleman," Raquel said. "But he's obsessed about an injustice he claims was done to our family back in the fifties, and I'm afraid he blames your ancestors."

"What could our family possibly have done that's so terrible he's still incensed about it sixty years later?"

She gave a disarming smile and shrugged. "I don't know the whole story. I've heard bits and pieces ever since I was a little girl. No telling what's true at this point anyway, so best to leave it alone. I apologize again for my uncle's behavior." She began to herd her aunt and uncle toward their car. "A pleasure meeting you and Danny."

My anger was in check, but now my curiosity was up. "Wait a minute. You can't just tell me that my family did something horrible to yours and then simply walk away without an explanation."

She hesitated but then guided her aunt and uncle over to their car, a black sedan parked nearby.

"Guess we'll never know," Danny said.

Once the old couple was seated inside, though, Raquel returned, a little out of breath from trudging back up the hill.

Rather tall for a Hispanic woman, she stood just a bit shorter than Danny. She wore a jet-black, bob haircut, framing an oval, almond-complexioned face. Her incongruous, piercing blue eyes held my gaze. She was undeniably attractive although a good part of her appeal was a clear sense of confidence without the slightest arrogance.

"I can only tell you what I've been told," she began. "Back in 1948, my grandfather, Canuto Cortez, lived with his family on a plot of land near Pearl and McKinney Streets, where the Regency Towers office building is located now. He had three sons and a daughter. Apparently your family, the Kilgores, operated a tavern next door to their land. There was some kind of dispute between the families resulting in bad blood."

"So we don't know who was at fault?"

"According to my uncle, we do. He blames your family for the deaths of his father and brothers. Whenever I heard the story—and listen, you asked—he always called them swindlers and murderers."

"That's ridiculous." At my words, Danny's hand tightened on my arm again, though there was no need this time.

"I'm just telling you why he spits on their graves. That's what you wanted to know, right?"

"But why do you put up with it?"

She straightened, her chin lifting. "Uncle Alfredo has been like a father to me; he and Matilda raised me after my mother died. He's the glue that holds our family together, and I respect his opinion more than most."

"You're saying my family is a bunch of thieving killers while yours were innocent victims, but I've heard family stories too. My family came from Ireland to New York in the late 1800s, and some of them settled in Dallas in the 1930s. They were merchants and restaurant owners, sometimes a bit too fond of the bottle, possibly, but that's it."

"Of course you would have heard a different version of events," Raquel said. "And anyway, I didn't say it was true, only that my uncle believes it."

"But you respect his opinion?"

"Look, it's pretty obvious our relatives had a different interpretation of things. Some were winners, others not so much. We may never know exactly what happened back then, so best to let bygones be bygones, like I said to begin with."

"That's fine, if you can convince your uncle to stop desecrating my family's gravestones every month."

She dropped her arms, the hard lines in her face softening again. "He's a bitter old man, Frank. He's not really angry at you or Danny, but he sincerely believes that he's right. I'll try talking to him again."

"I'd appreciate that." Behind her, I could see Danny had knelt down by the grave and was using a leaf to wipe the spittle from the stone.

"You came today to visit them?" she said, indicating the headstones.

My right hand went to my left, fingering the gold band there. "No."

"Oh." She nodded, then stepped away toward her car. She turned, and as she did, I let go of the ring. "I'm sorry for your loss." Her voice was sincere, and she offered a small smile before descending to the car and slipping inside.

I wasn't sure what I was feeling at that moment. Danny spoke from behind me, where he had stepped to the neighboring family plot. "Dad, did Grandma Kate ever mention the name Cortez to you?"

"Never." My grandmother, Kathleen Kilgore McNamara, was Henry Kilgore's daughter. She would have been about twenty years old when whatever happened first went down. She always maintained that her father was a merchant who worked hard, bought land, and built his tavern. Later, when he sold the tavern in south Dallas to developers, he bought fifty acres of raw land further north and built a ranch on it with his own hands.

"Look at these dates, Dad." We compared the headstones at the Cortez plot with our family's. Two of the Cortez family—Canuto and Ramón—died March 20, 1948. My great uncle Michael died March 21, 1948, only a day later. Enrique "Ricky" Cortez apparently went to meet his maker just a week after that on March 27, 1948. My great-grandfather Henry and my other great uncle, William, both died on the same day two years later—August 5, 1950. I had walked by these headstones many times but never noticed the coincidences.

"How did Grandma Kate say they died, Dad? Henry, Michael, and William."

"Ranching accidents." She had always been a bit vague about this part, but Danny didn't need to hear my doubts. "I was born on that same ranch. When I was three, we moved to Preston Hollow, where your great-grandmother raised me."

"You've never told me that before."

"See what you learn hanging around cemeteries? My parents are also buried somewhere around here. I'll show you another time."

"Hey, Dad, if these families hated each other so much, why would they be buried side by side?"

I looked from one plot to the next. "Good question. Maybe there wasn't enough space in those days. Maybe they buried poor people together at this end, or maybe they attended the same church. Maybe it was someone's idea of a cruel joke. I don't know."

Danny stared at the Cortez plot. "So that Alfredo guy lost his father and both his brothers in a week."

It was hard to imagine the hate-filled old man as anything else, but he would have been roughly the same age Danny was now. Danny had already lost his mother. How would he have reacted if he lost everyone else he loved as well?

"We should find out what happened," he said. "Maybe do something about it."

My legal training kicked in without thought—there was no statute of limitation for murder, but surely no one still alive today had been involved. Still, it was sixty years ago. Nothing could change any of it, could it? Life is meaningless anyway. Just life. We live, we die, we go to heaven…or not. Fate decides, and there's not necessarily any justice involved either.

"What would be the point, Danny? Things happen. There's just chance and the hope you get a winning hand once in a while. I can't change what happened to any of these people."

He started down the hill, and his words barely drifted back to me. "Mom didn't think that way."

"Well she's not here, is she?" The words were out of my mouth before I could reel them back.

He didn't turn around. He just said, "You didn't used to think that way either."

I watched him stride toward our car, feeling anger rising up in me again mixed this time with pride, and guilt too. Here I was concerned about our family's legal culpability, but my young son saw an opportunity to right a past wrong. I couldn't bring his mother back or even the father he once had. And I sure couldn't change what happened four years ago, much less sixty. But maybe small steps would bring us together again.

Plus, a part of me was desperately curious. I heard Raquel's words: "Some were winners, others not so much. We may never know exactly what happened back then." I knew what she meant. I could see her uncle's rheumy, hate-filled eyes, spittle dripping down his chin, still enraged after all these years.

CHAPTER
2

FRANK MCNAMARA'S HOUSE
DALLAS, TEXAS
TUESDAY, JANUARY 15, 2008

I awoke as usual at 6:00 a.m. and looked out the window. Yesterday the temperature had been a mild 75 degrees and people played golf in shirtsleeves, but overnight a "Canadian Front" swept through North Texas in a tidal wave of frigid air, bringing with it freezing rain and snow. Wet roads froze into sheets of solid ice, creating one gigantic hockey rink in the twenty-degree temperatures. Icicles dangled from bowed tree limbs, which in turn dragged down ice-encrusted power lines, causing the entire Metroplex to shut down.

The wintry weather turned Dallas into a ghost town; schools, businesses, and all but essential services closed. The law offices of Shipwright and Chandler, where I worked, had shuttered for the day. Apparently my services weren't all that essential. Outside, it was so cold that the panhandlers had ceased begging at the city's larger intersections; so cold, in fact, that lawyers kept their hands in their *own* pockets. If you can't laugh at yourself, who *can* you laugh at?

Anyone with half a brain and any experience living in Dallas knew to stay home and cancel work for the day. As an attorney, I figured I had at least half a brain, so I stayed home.

I called my devoted paralegal, Sheila Redfern, to warn her not to attempt driving to the office. "If you kill yourself, the firm doesn't want responsibility," I told her, keeping my voice solemn.

"Only a complete nitwit would try to drive to work today," she replied. "So why did you call and wake me up?"

So much for employer concern. I returned to bed but couldn't rest. I tossed and turned and felt guilty. Danny said nothing more, but I knew he wanted me to investigate what happened to the Cortez family. He wanted me to be the type of guy who tried to right a wrong even if he had nothing to gain or even stood to lose. To be fair, I used to be that kind of guy.

I lay in bed and thought about Raquel's story, picturing the unfortunate Canuto Cortez. I imagined him as a hardworking, twenty-something young man who got a job, bought a small house, and succeeded in improving life for himself and his kids, the quintessential American story. There must have been millions like him, but only he had the misfortune of running into my family . . . allegedly.

On the other hand, family lore had taught me that my ancestors also came to America for a better life, only from Ireland. They were diligent people with a strong sense of kinship who succeeded by dint of their resilience, intelligence, and plain hard work. Who was to say that Raquel's family history was right and mine was wrong?

In any case, there were other things to worry about. I had a major project for an important client, and thanks to modern technology, bad weather was no excuse. I stalked into the kitchen to start a pot of coffee. I could at least bill some hours on this miserable day.

Although I worked for the law firm, Forestglen Investments was my largest client and effectively paid my salary. An umbrella corporation wholly owned by the Cannon Family Trust, Forestglen had plans to build a high-rise complex in downtown Dallas with matching residential and office towers. The towers would be joined by a three-story shopping arcade, with the whole complex built atop a six-level underground parking structure.

At a cost of $520 million, the Solar Office and Condominium Towers would easily be the most expensive project of its kind ever undertaken outside of New York, Los Angeles, or Chicago. It remained only to purchase land for the behemoth, and Forestglen had set its sights on the old Regency Tower location. Groundbreaking was scheduled for October if the present building could be demolished in time.

My boss, Donald Chandler, a name partner in the firm, wanted almost my full attention focused on that account. It paid many millions in legal fees each year. As a JD/MBA but still underappreciated associate attorney, my job was to ensure that the transaction went through seamlessly. I say underappreciated because most associates make partner after about seven years or their careers are said to be on downhill trends. I'd already been at Shipwright and Chandler over ten, and people said things even worse about me.

I had returned from the first Iraqi war a decorated veteran and enrolled in law school at Southern Methodist University. Oh, I was cocky then: plenty of money, friends, and a beautiful girl on my arm who later became my wife. I graduated near the top of the class and secured a coveted job with this prestigious firm, but now I was beginning to worry. If I pulled off the Forestglen project, surely I would make partner. I could still make something of myself and make Danny proud.

I had to focus. Chandler had instructed in no uncertain terms that I was to keep the corporation out of trouble and, incidentally, make the law firm lots of money by billing as many hours as possible. If I failed at either endeavor, I'd be out the door, and there went my career, my future, even my chances of paying for Danny's college education. I'd been on a downward spiral long enough.

I poured a cup of black coffee and logged onto my laptop. My cursor hovered over the "forestglen" icon; I could start billing at 6:45. But I kept seeing the disappointment on Danny's face, and I couldn't deny my curiosity. I should clearly leave well enough alone. Still, my mouse crept to the *Dallas Morning News* icon. I opened the site, clicked "archives," and typed "Canuto Cortez; murder; 1948."

Up popped no fewer than fourteen articles relating to Mr. Cortez, all of them between 1948 and 1950. They required only a few seconds to locate and less than an hour to read. By the time I'd finished, Canuto had come to life even more vividly in my imagination. The newspaper described him as only five feet four inches tall, black hair, a round face, and a Pancho Villa moustache. The first article took me back in time to a place that no longer existed, the Kilgore Tavern, in what is now central Dallas.

DALLAS MORNING NEWS, March 21, 1948
Murder Victims Bring Knives to a Gunfight

Two Mexican males were shot to death last night in a blazing barroom brawl when they assaulted the proprietors of the Kilgore Tavern on Belmeade Avenue. The deceased men are Canuto Cortez and his son, Ramón. The Cortezes live next door to the tavern.

When Patrolman E.B. Howard arrived at the scene, the two Cortez belligerents were lying dead on the barroom floor. The two Kilgores nursed knife wounds and writhed on the floor next to their victims. The place was strewn with glass from a shattered chandelier and broken beer bottles; the marble machine was wrecked. A wild shot had punctured a tire on an automobile parked across the road. Witnesses told police that an unidentified woman also fired shots from a doorway in the back.

Both Cortez men were pronounced "Dead on Arrival" at Parkland Memorial Hospital. The coroner will perform autopsies later this week. The Kilgore brothers were also taken to Parkland Hospital where they were treated for minor lacerations to their arms and chests.

After their release from the hospital, the Kilgores were detained briefly by police but later released on their own recognizance. District Attorney Lucius D. Smallbone says he is reviewing police and witness reports and wishes to evaluate the autopsy findings before determining whether to press charges. He indicated he might seek an indictment from the Grand Jury.

I enjoyed the quaint reporting style of those days. Subsequent stories told of the killing of Michael Kilgore the next day; his mutilated body was found in an alley behind the tavern. He had been gagged, arms bound, shot four times, and his throat slit. Detectives wanted to interview Enrique "Ricky" Cortez, another son of Canuto, as a "person of interest" in the case, but they were unable to locate him until a week later.

His decapitated body was discovered near the fairgrounds by a woman walking her dog. Police later located the head in a dumpster behind an abandoned warehouse. Police believed Ricky was killed in retaliation for the murder of Michael Kilgore, who was in turn killed in retribution for the murders of Canuto and Ramón Cortez. The community feared that a blood feud had erupted, a modern version of the Hatfields and McCoys or the Montagues and Capulets. Unfortunately, Raquel's version of the story seemed to more closely coincide with the reports. So far, the Cortezes still seemed more to blame for the feud than the Kilgores. I read on.

District Attorney Smallbone did indict Henry and William for the murders of the three Cortezes. The DMN quoted his high-minded rhetoric: *By this action, I hope to end the back and forth violence that has terrorized our Dallas neighborhoods for the past month. As the duly elected enforcer of the laws of Dallas County, I will not tolerate vigilante justice.*

The Kilgores were represented by the noted criminal defense attorney Lance "Swash" Buckler, whose legal skills were compared to those of Clarence Darrow. He gained a reputation for obtaining "not guilty" verdicts on behalf of the guiltiest of criminals and had never been beaten at trial. Both his steep legal fees and the Kilgores' bail—$5,000 each—were paid by an unknown benefactor.

Unfortunately for Mr. Smallbone's ego and his re-election campaign, Swash Buckler retained his perfect criminal trial record. He proved to the all-white jury's satisfaction that the Kilgores acted in self-defense when they shot and killed the Cortezes, and they were acquitted. After the verdict was announced, some Cortez family members began screaming at the judge and jury in Spanish. Dallas police had to separate them from bystanders hurling racial epithets, and the Cortezes were eventually escorted out of the building.

I wished I'd been able to witness *that* trial. It had all the trappings of high theater: violent crimes of passion, family feuding, and dueling lawyers. Things sure have changed, I thought. You'd never find a jury of twelve white men and women today; it'd be unconstitutional. And when had we last held a murder trial a mere three months after the commission of the crime?

By now I was thoroughly hooked. I found another article written a couple of years later:

DALLAS MORNING NEWS, **August 6, 1950**
Decomposed Bodies Identified as Henry and
William Kilgore

The decomposed corpses of two Caucasian males were discovered at the bottom of the Trinity River by young boys playing in the area. Dental records confirmed the identities of Henry and William Kilgore. They were originally reported missing on December 10, 1949; an unsuccessful search lasted approximately one week. Foul play is suspected.

Authorities reported the bodies were found tethered to the bottom of the river by short chains and cement blocks. This portion of the river normally remains underwater, but recent drought conditions have caused water levels to subside, revealing the rocky bottom with its grisly discovery.

The tally of victims now included Henry, William, and Michael Kilgore, along with Canuto, Ramón, and Ricky of the Cortez clan. Due to this bad blood, no male Kilgores and only one male Cortez survived, Raquel's Uncle Alfredo. Thank God Grandma Kate survived, or I wouldn't be around myself.

I decided I needed a word with dearest Grandma. Why had she lied to me all these years about my great grandfather and my uncles? You don't die of 'an unfortunate ranching accident' tied to a cement block at the bottom of the Trinity River.

While I wondered who killed Henry and William, one last article caught my eye.

DALLAS MORNING NEWS, **September 9, 1949**
New Uptown Development Announced

The construction of a 500,000 square foot office tower was announced today by the Cannon/O'Boyle Corporation of New York City. It will be located at the intersection of McKinney and Pearl Streets in Uptown Dallas. This is the land upon which stood the recently demolished Kilgore Tavern, site of last year's bloodbath between the Kilgore and Cortez families.

Construction will begin next month with the building scheduled for completion in mid-1951. The tower will feature thirty-eight stories of office space, six levels of parking, and a three story shopping arcade. Once completed, the Regency Office Tower will be the tallest building in Dallas.

A chance encounter at a cemetery while visiting my wife's grave was turning into the mystery of a lifetime. More alarming, the Regency Tower's location was the same ground that Forestglen had set its sights on for its massive high-rise project. A little warning bell went off in my head—*leave this old stuff alone, go back to work, and tell Danny I hit a dead end.*

Instead I rummaged through a stack of notes until I located a telephone number I'd scrawled in the margin of a legal pad. A few weeks ago, I had been talking to a shooting buddy of mine, Keith Glenn. He mentioned an old friend who was in his mid-eighties but still sharp and practicing law. He'd been around Dallas a long time, even before construction of the Regency Towers, and might recall something helpful.

I should be worried about making partner, not digging up the bones of the past. I picked up my pen and tapped it against the name I'd written above the digits: *Josue Fuentes.* Outside, a harsh wind kicked up, scraping icy branches against the window. I decided to give Josue a call.

CHAPTER
3

JOSUE FUENTES' HOUSE
SOUTH DALLAS, TEXAS
SATURDAY, JANUARY 19, 2008

I'd been exceptionally busy all week, working mostly on the Forestglen project, and had little time to spend wondering why a bunch of violent Kilgores had set about killing some equally violent Cortezes, and vice versa, sixty years ago. Saturday promised some free time and rekindled my growing fascination with the murders. It was like that old TV show *Family Feud*, except with more bloodshed and fewer prizes.

Josue Fuentes, I had discovered, was a lawyer who appealed an important civil rights case to the Supreme Court in 1954. I called him earlier in the week, and he agreed to meet for breakfast. He thought he remembered something about the feud though I had difficulty comprehending his garbled words. He apologized for the speech impediment caused by his recent stroke. I invited Danny along, and for once he accepted gladly. It made me smile to hear the eagerness in his voice.

Fuentes lived in the strictly Hispanic ghetto of southeast Dallas, where streets formed a confusing crazy-quilt of intersections. He lived curiously close to Grand Park, near the fairgrounds, where the body of Ricky Cortez had been discovered in 1948.

As I pulled the Beemer into Josue's rutted, weed-strewn driveway, I had trouble believing this ramshackle cottage belonged to a noted civil rights attorney. Concrete blocks formed the base of the single-story structure, supporting paint-flecked aluminum siding the rest of the way to the roof. A screened-in porch listed to the left, and a wood and tar-paper roof crowned the whole wondrous arrangement.

Nearby other shacks were in even worse shape, adding to the bedlam. A neighbor across the road had set up a kind of outdoor bazaar, selling food, clothing, and assorted junk on his front lawn. Several decrepit jalopies and pickup trucks clogged the cracked roadway around his home.

The area struck me as rough, to say the least, and I said to Danny, "Tell me again why I asked you to come with me today?"

"Something about a male bonding experience, I think."

"Wise guy. Hand me that .380 from the glove box."

With the gun tucked safely in my back pocket, I approached the door, dodging landmines of bird droppings and glancing over my shoulder. All these years later, I still couldn't help scanning rooftops.

The doorbell was out of order, so I rapped on a rickety wooden door. A moment or two later I heard a wheeze, a cough, and then a distinct tap-shuffle-tap of foot and cane approaching. Danny looked excited as if he were embarking on some grand adventure. On the other hand, I thought there might still be just enough time to get the hell out of Dodge.

No such luck. "Who's there?" barked a raspy voice without any trace of an accent. It commanded attention even though the words slurred together.

"Frank McNamara," I hollered. "We agreed to meet for breakfast. I hope you haven't forgotten."

"I don't forget invitations to a free meal, Mr. McNamara." The door cracked open. "If Keith Glenn says you can be trusted, you must be all right."

He opened the door further, and we exchanged introductions. When I called him "Jose" by mistake, he explained that his name was Spanish for "Joshua," not "Joe," and pronounced like "Ho-sway." A common mistake, he said. His advancing years and the stroke had taken a toll on him. The right side of his face drooped, and his reddened right eye teared continuously. His right arm dangled limply. His good hand clutched a wooden cane with a duck's head handle, allowing his considerable bulk a tenuous balance.

Josue beckoned us inside. We were greeted by a disarray of bedding, mismatched furniture, a few shadeless lamps, and a random lampless shade. Books lay everywhere. Wooden bookcases lined the entrance, filled to overflowing with legal casebooks, and others served as makeshift room dividers. Old, dusty books inundated the entire house with the musty odor of decay. I developed a ticklish cough.

Josue showed me around while Danny made a pit stop, and we finished just as he came out. "Now you've had a tour of my book mausoleum."

I smiled. "Except for the bathroom."

"More books," Danny reported.

"Let's go eat," Josue said. "You drive." He shuffled toward the front door so fast that Danny and I could barely keep up.

Apparently when food was involved, Josue could be quick. I had no idea where Josue would take us, so the gun remained in my back pocket.

Josue arranged his paralyzed leg on the back seat and directed us to a local Mexican eatery, El Taquito. He regaled us with tales of Tex-Mex culture and history as we drove, and he seemed thrilled to have company and be able to get out for a while. He indicated with pride certain prominent citizens and local points of interest along the way.

El Taquito was crowded, and boisterous chatter filled the large room, hardly a word of it in English. The owner treated Josue with great deference and conducted us to a cozy corner table with a good view of the entire place. Apparently Josue was some sort of local hero; he greeted nearly everyone by name as he shuffled by. He hoisted himself onto the bench against the back wall and surveyed his domain.

"Gentlemen, you are about to indulge in the finest Tex-Mex cuisine this side of the Rio Grande," he said. "I recommend the breakfast burritos, but be careful with the salsa. It's got a kick."

"Don't worry, Josue, we're used to salsa."

We placed our orders, and I summarized for Josue my interest in this decades-old case, including what I discovered in the *Dallas Morning News*, the version of history my grandmother always told me, and the conflicting version Raquel described.

"That case sure takes me back, Frank. The Hispanic community was much smaller back then, so we socialized with the Cortez family at church all the time. They seemed like nice enough folks. Pretty daughter too. That case was notorious, as you might imagine. I'm surprised your family succeeded in hiding it from you this long."

"Grandma Kate always fed me some cockamamie story about how her father and brothers were killed in various ranching accidents."

"She was probably trying to protect you." Josue then recounted what he remembered of the case, much of which I'd already learned. He had not been directly involved, he said, as he'd been in his first year of law school at the University of Texas in Austin, graduating in 1951 as one of their first students of Mexican descent. He was born and raised in Dallas, in the very neighborhood where we sat, and after school he came back here to practice. He had been doing so ever since, for fifty-seven years.

Josue mentioned the high-profile defense attorney, Randall Buckler, who had managed to get the Kilgores acquitted. "Everyone wondered how they got the money to pay him or even the bail money for that matter. They weren't especially well off."

"You mean 'Swash' Buckler?"

Josue chuckled at the ancient memory. "Yes, old Swash Buckler. He had quite a reputation, both in court and with the ladies. The Kilgore jury had two women on it as I recall, fairly advanced for those days. This case happened way before the Women's Movement ever began." He pointed at Danny as if he expected the boy to take notes for a history exam. "I still believe the real reason for their acquittal was that all those jurors were *white*. The verdict might've been a lot different if they'd chosen a few Hispanics."

"I'm sure you're right," I said. Danny's stomach rumbled.

Josue kept talking as if transported back in time. "I had a client back in '54, Pete Hernandez. Convicted of rape and murder, also by an all-white jury. Back then, people of Mexican descent were excluded from jury service in Dallas County. I appealed that case to the Court of Criminal Appeals here in Texas and got nowhere. So then I appealed to the US Supreme Court and was granted a writ of cert. Maybe you read about the case in law school, *Hernandez v. Texas?*"

I'd heard of it and should've known more about it, so I avoided his glance. Danny saved me. "I hope this isn't a stupid question, but what's a 'writ of cert'?"

"The only stupid question is the one that's never asked, Danny. A *writ of certiorari* states that the Supreme Court will actually hear a case at its next session. The Justices accept only about 2 percent of the cases appealed to them. For the others, the previous verdict becomes final."

"So the Supreme Court hears only the most important cases?"

"Right. The Court accepts only major cases likely to have an impact on our way of life, or in the case of a conflict between states, or when two Federal Circuit Courts differ on the same issue. We can't have conflicting law in different parts of the country, can we?" Josue had adopted a lecturing tone, and I expected Danny to grimace as he did when it came from me, but instead, he looked fascinated.

"In any event," Josue went on, "while researching the Hernandez case, I came across the Kilgore trial. To the best of my knowledge, the Kilgores and Cortezes killed each other over money or sex; I'm not certain which played a more significant role."

Danny sat up a little straighter as now things were getting interesting. I tried to ignore him. "Money or sex, age-old motives for turning normally peaceful people into killers."

Josue described the financial picture first. In the 1950s, a tightly knit group of wealthy real estate developers controlled zoning issues with two or three huge corporations largely deciding which buildings and roadways got built in Dallas. They are still influential today but were even more so then. They donated vast sums of money to local political candidates, electing whomever they wanted, including the mayor, the councilmen, and every important lower office holder. It was a cozy arrangement with business done in secret at their fancy Dallas Country Club. Needless to say, no Hispanics, blacks, or Jews need apply. The Zoning Commission was the key to their strategy, allowing them to buy land cheaply and have their toadies re-zone it later for tidy profits.

"What does that mean?" Danny asked. The server arrived, and for a moment the question hung in the air as breakfast burritos, salsa, coffee, and water were spread before us.

"Danny, developers would pay a bonus to a homeowner, or 'shill,' to claim that he had already sold his home to them and to encourage his neighbors to do the same. The shill would spread rumors that the city planned to construct a garbage dump nearby or some other such nuisance, and he'd claim he was 'getting out while the gettin' was good.'" Josue shifted his bulk to reach for a burrito, leaning one arm on the table, which creaked. "His neighbors usually sold fast, and the developer could buy residential lots and houses at bargain prices. Then they'd apply to their friends on the City Zoning Commission to have the land rezoned 'Commercial Two,' which increased the land's value by upwards of twenty fold. Then the original shill would sell his property at the higher re-zoned price and make even more money."

"My great-grandfather Henry Kilgore sold his tavern for enough money to buy a fifty-acre ranch in North Dallas," I said. "It might've been around the same time as the Cortez sale. Could the Cortezes have been angry with him because they received a lot less money? Or because he lied to them?"

"Perhaps. But there's another possible explanation."

Danny suddenly began to hack and wheeze, and his face turned red, tears brimming from his eyes. He gulped down an entire glass of water and then drank mine too.

Concerned, I put a hand on his shoulder. "Danny, you OK?"

Josue, on the other hand, laughed so hard he had to clutch his side. Tears streamed from both his eyes too until at last he could control himself. "He's just suffering a minor salsa overdose. Warned you it's potent." He pointedly soaked a morsel of burrito deep in the salsa bowl and gobbled it down. I think he'd been lying in wait for one of us to try the salsa all along.

I nodded to my son and said, "Go ahead, Josue, make us feel inadequate." Danny was still beet-red, but he signaled he was OK. "You were saying something about another possible explanation for the feud?"

"Yes." Josue wiped the tears from his face. "There *was* such a rumor. Do you want Danny to hear the scurrilous details?"

"He's come this far," I said drily. "I think he can handle it, at least better than the salsa, I hope." I glanced at Danny, who was stuffing down burritos again, this time without salsa.

"There might've been a relationship between one of the Kilgore boys and Canuto Cortez's only daughter. Some say the two of them fell madly in love. A father might kill if he didn't approve of his daughter's choice in those days. After the Kilgore boy died, no one ever heard from the Cortez girl again."

"The two families were neighbors, so they would've known each other. You think it's likely Canuto barged into the tavern demanding satisfaction?"

"That or the money, or maybe both. You could check the deeds and tax records for chain of title and the sales prices on those houses. That should be public information, maybe in the basement of the old records building downtown. Might give you a clue as to who sold what, to whom, and at what price. You might find enough resentment to spark a murder."

"I'll do that. We know how the Cortez father and sons ended up, and I've met Alfredo, the surviving son. Any idea what happened to Canuto's daughter?"

"There was a rumor that with all her family dead, she left Dallas and fled back to Mexico. I'm afraid that's all I know about her. Danny, have you recovered your wits?"

"Yes, sir." Danny's voice crackled hoarsely. "I think I learned something today, Mr. Fuentes. Not just about my family."

"Oh, what's that?"

"Better dip your toe in the water before you take the plunge, especially when it comes to Mexican salsa."

Josue hooted. "Smart lad! That lesson will stand you in good stead the rest of your life, young man. You boys about finished?" We nodded, and he signaled for the check. When it came, I snatched it from Josue's grasp over his protests, despite his earlier talk about a free meal.

"It's worth every penny just to pick your brain, Josue. You're a rare bit of living Dallas history, and I appreciate all the information. Maybe we can do this again sometime?"

"I'd love that, Frank. For now, though, please take this old carcass back home. I tire out much too easily these days." As we made our way to the front door, I noticed he'd slowed a step since before breakfast. Maybe he was just full of food, or maybe he didn't relish the idea of returning to his lonely existence at home.

As we exited the restaurant, Josue held his bad arm awkwardly across his chest as if trying to compress his ribs; he looked pale and seemed short of breath. A chorus of good wishes followed us out the door and back to the car, but he didn't acknowledge the accolades with his usual gusto. He only grunted.

"Josue, are you all right?"

"Course I am. Just get a little winded sometimes after a big meal is all."

With Josue's guidance, we retraced our route through the network of twisting streets back to his house. I noticed a cloying, acetone smell inside the car but didn't know what to make of it.

"Give me just a minute, Frank, I've got something for you. Be right back."

He tapped-shuffled-tapped into the house. A moment later he returned, looking happier. He held a folded printout in his semi-paralyzed hand, his cane in the other.

"What have you got there, Josue?" I asked through the car window.

"The p . . . pr . . . ." He opened his mouth to answer, but his twitching lips only stammered, then his hand began to tremble, and he dropped the folded paper through the car window. He slithered down the vehicle's door and hit the ground, hard. His head struck a large rock embedded in the mud, opening a nasty gash. He lay there on the driveway, gasping, his arms and legs askew.

With Josue slumped against the car door, I had to push hard. I squeezed through the opening and dragged Josue away from the car, onto his back. Danny charged around from the other side. It didn't look like Josue was breathing, and as I knelt beside him, this felt all too familiar. Unbidden images flew into my mind; I closed my eyes, trying to shut them out. For a moment I wasn't seeing Josue at all.

I was somewhere else . . . Iraq . . . on overwatch patrol of a barren mountain region near Ramadi as an American convoy passed through the valley a mile below. The young lance corporal with me, Willie Karlsson, and I were nearly invisible in our desert camo gear, seeking enemy targets. We spotted a black-robed insurgent, AK-47 slung over his back, placing a metal object inside a hole he had dug in the roadway. Willie and I began setting up our equipment: his Leupold spotter's range finder and my Barrett sniper rifle. Routine, except in the next moment it wasn't.

Willie stepped on an IED and disappeared in a cloud of shrapnel and smoke, his severed leg pin-wheeling overhead. Dazed from the concussion myself, years of field training automatically kicked in. I rushed to him; blood gushed from his severed right femoral artery. I ripped off my duty belt and cinched it as tightly as possible around the ragged stump of his thigh, reducing the flow to a trickle. Yet he was unresponsive, his face ashen. I could still feel a thready pulse in his neck, so I pumped on his chest until a Medivac helicopter arrived to extract him to the nearest field hospital.

Willie never made it there. My best efforts hadn't been enough. I shook my head, refocusing, and saw Danny's panicked eyes fix on Josue's still form before they shot to me, seeking guidance. I wouldn't fail again, not this time.

"Danny, call 911." He grabbed my cell phone and dialed.

I opened Josue's mouth and found his tongue wedged back in his throat. I dislodged it and heard an ominous rumble. I rotated his head to the side just before a gush of bilious vomit spewed forth. Danny didn't move fast enough and got his brand new Sketchers soaked.

A little air hissed out of Josue's mouth, but his chest barely moved. I could not find a pulse on his neck or wrist. I had seen many corpses in my day and had created more than my fair share, but I'd never seen someone die of natural causes. My own heart thumped wildly.

I whacked him on the chest and began performing chest compressions as a crowd began to gather. The minutes dragged on. My hands and arms started knotting up, and Danny spelled me. The kid was amazingly poised. After what seemed like an eternity, the paramedics arrived to relieve us. They fitted a compression machine over Josue's chest, intubated him, and started an IV, all with split-second efficiency. Then they lifted him onto a mobile gurney and whisked him away in their ambulance.

Only then did I have the chance to catch my breath. Danny let me put my arm around his shoulders and draw him into a sideways hug, and when we got back into the Beemer, we both slumped in our seats, exhausted. On the floor I spotted the pamphlet Josue had dropped into the car just before he'd collapsed. It read: *Hernandez v. Texas, 347 US 475, (US 1954)*. Inside was a summarized version of the case decision that made Josue famous, in which he convinced the Supreme Court of the United States that one Pete Hernandez had been denied his right to equal protection under the Fourteenth Amendment to the Constitution because he'd been judged by an all-white jury, not a real jury of his peers.

After resting a moment longer, I began driving Danny home. On the way there, he closed his eyes, and though I doubted he was sleeping, I let the silence rest as my own thoughts whirled. I knew the message Josue wanted me to absorb: "We have a duty to represent any citizen who needs our help, whether he's indigent or the most heinous criminal imaginable. That's why I represented Pete Hernandez. He sure wasn't popular, and he never paid me a dime. We attorneys have been blessed with unique skills, and this is a sacred duty. Never forget that, Frank."

Maybe so, but I'd seen too much of the dark side of the profession, and in some ways, it jaded me as much as my time in the service. I'd worked hand in hand with covetous lawyers and seen many attorneys' noble quest for justice morph into a zeal for power and the almighty dollar. Lawyers were now seen as part of the problem, not part of the solution as in Josue's day. As a result, the public has lost confidence in our legal system, hence the raw disdain for lawyers in general.

But Josue was a different breed. He reminded me of Atticus Finch, the attorney hero of *To Kill a Mockingbird*, as a rare modern-day example of the dedicated legal idealist. Josue loved his work and helped his community a great deal, and the people revered him for it. Despite his good intentions, though, he ended up in a ramshackle house, partially paralyzed from a stroke and all alone. Then he suffered a heart attack and had to be resuscitated by two strangers in the muddy damp of his driveway. Neither his life nor his career would ever again reach the pinnacle he'd achieved in 1954 when he argued that groundbreaking case before the Supreme Court. Fate is sometimes funny that way.

Though Josue enjoyed a long and distinguished career as a civil rights attorney, he never made much money. Yet I believed he was content with his life, and I envied his happiness. For him, serving others was reward enough. Could I say the same for myself? As we drove north under the bright Texas sun, I sincerely hoped he survived.

CHAPTER
4

LAW OFFICES OF SHIPWRIGHT AND CHANDLER
DALLAS, TEXAS
THURSDAY, JANUARY 24, 2008, 8:00 A.M.

The Petroleum Building is recognizable among the other office towers in downtown Dallas by the garish oil derrick adorning its roof. At one time that derrick symbolized the main source of the city's wealth, but now the insurance, transportation, and financial industries all contribute to the city's affluence as well. Still, the landmark building reeks of prestige. If you can afford the rent, you'd better be able to process a constant flow of wealthy clients. The law firm of Shipwright and Chandler was definitely good at that, and it occupied the entire sixtieth floor.

I exited the elevator and crossed a sumptuously decorated lobby, passing an attractive young receptionist engrossed with the telephone and her fingernails. Down a corridor to the left, my own workplace afforded a magnificent view of nothing but one tedious building after another. My paralegal, Sheila Redfern, greeted me and my smile with her usual degree of sardonic cheerfulness.

"I wouldn't start out real happy today, Mr. McNamara, because it's liable to go straight downhill. Better to just keep to an even keel of deep depression, and then things will stay manageable."

"Does that come from years of experience on the couch, or did you just read a new self-help book? Tell me, why shouldn't I be happy today?"

"Because Mr. Chandler wants to see you ASAP, and he sounded even more peeved than usual. Something to do with Forestglen's Regency Towers purchase. He said to bring the latest info, pronto, so you better go before he sends out a search party. I'm telling you, just start out miserable today and save yourself a whole lotta grief."

"You may be right. When he calls down here personally instead of having the Battleaxe do it, it usually means trouble."

I loved Sheila. Cranky as all get-out and dependent on medication and weekly therapy, yet she had my back when I needed it. She knew office scuttlebutt before anyone else, and she relayed it to me in time to make me appear knowledgeable when I really wasn't. This had proved invaluable on more than one occasion. Needless to say, I took very good care of Sheila at Christmas time and all other times in between.

"Oh, I do have some information that might cheer you up though," she said.

"I wasn't exactly unhappy until I started talking to you." I laid my briefcase on the desk and removed my overcoat. "What is it?"

"I finally got through to the ICU yesterday. Looks like Mr. Fuentes is going to make it."

I had asked Sheila to check on him for me and to keep me updated. The last I had heard, Josue's future was uncertain. At this news, I felt like hugging her. "That's wonderful!"

"He's still intubated, whatever that means, but he's no longer critical. The neurologist says he'll make a full mental recovery. Apparently he suffered a major heart attack. They said he wouldn't have made it if he hadn't received immediate attention. You saved his life, Mr. McNamara."

"Thanks for the good news."

"Just part of the first-class service I provide." She handed me a thick accordion folder. "Here's the latest information on the Regency purchase. I put it together from your notes as soon as I heard Mr. Chandler wanted to see you."

"Sheila, you are a true gem; beautiful inside and out. And that's a statement of fact, not to be construed as sexual harassment."

She blushed and then laughed, a rare sight.

"See you when I get back from the lion's den." I rushed out the door to meet my boss, Donald Chandler. It was unusual to be summoned to his office first thing in the morning, and I wondered what about Forestglen could be so urgent. Normally he barely recognized my existence, certainly not when it came time for salary review or year-end bonuses or promotion. A surge of anger and resentment accompanied this thought, but I suppressed it.

After retracing my steps past the lobby, I crossed to the opposite wing of the building, inhabited by all the higher-ranking attorneys. At the far end of the hallway, I knocked on Donald Chandler's door. His elderly secretary, Barbara Sweeney, known behind her back as "Battleaxe Bobbie," admitted me to the large antechamber of the great one's personal office. Her square face was framed by a bob haircut, and she wore an old-fashioned suit and thick-heeled shoes. She habitually readjusted the spectacles that slid down her hawkish nose until they reached a wart at its tip.

Nobody got past the Battleaxe without permission. She called Chandler on the intercom, and a frustrating interval passed as I waited and waited. Eventually her intercom buzzed. She growled, "He'll see you now."

I entered the private domain of the sole living name partner of Shipwright and Chandler, one of the top five law firms in Dallas. From his corner office, I had a panoramic view of the bustling banking district, downtown skyscrapers, and the superhighways connecting them all. A huge antique English naval desk dominated the room, with an expensive Persian carpet underneath.

As dogs reflect the manner and appearance of their owners, so did the "Battleaxe" reflect that of her boss. Chandler grunted acknowledgment of my presence and bade me take a seat opposite him.

He appeared shriveled, hunched as he was over the paper-work lying on his admiralty desk, but he was actually a tall, bony man. Reading glasses perched low on his nose too, and his long, cadaverous face seemed to collapse inward. His brow creased into a perpetual frown, and his domed skull shone bald as a boiled egg except where it was rimmed by a fringe of silver hair. His Adam's apple bobbed warily as he spoke.

"Frank, we haven't talked in far too long. How are you? How's Danny?" His voice cracked, making his pleasantries sound insincere.

"I'm doing well, Mr. Chandler, busy with work, of course, but managing." He loved to hear I wasn't wasting the firm's money. "Danny's OK, all things considered. How's your family?"

"Everyone's well, thanks. Danny will get through this, don't you worry." He paused. "Let's get straight to the point. I asked you here to find out the status of Forestglen's purchase. Cannon has been on my butt almost daily to get things speeded up. He wants to close no later than the end of the month, and we can't do that until you finish your title search."

Randall Cannon was the CEO of Forestglen, and I knew the reason he was chomping at the bit to complete the purchase of the Regency Office Tower—to begin demolition and start construction of the new Solar Office and Condo Towers. "I'd like nothing better than to assure you and Mr. Cannon that he'll have good title to the property, but I've found a few glitches in the chain of title."

"What kind of glitches?"

I shuffled through the file and passed the offending paperwork across his desk. "Glitch number one: there are three mechanics' and material men's liens outstanding from as far back as 1999. They concern an electrical contractor, an air conditioning company, and roofers who claim they haven't been paid for repairs after some tornado damage. The total is just about $600,000."

"Frank, you know that's small potatoes in a deal of this size. Just settle those claims, will you? Those lien holders ought to be happy to get *some* money, especially after all these years. So, try to get a discount. Cannon and his cronies *love* discounts. What else?"

"Glitch number two: the city of Dallas claims that the present owner owes $922,879 in taxes, penalties, and unpaid interest for the tax years of 2006 and 2007. The owner has filed an appraisal review that's still unresolved, but there's no way the sale can go through until the overdue taxes are paid or a bond is posted pending settlement."

"I'll make a note of that and get the mayor on board. It'll be taken care of, don't worry."

At his words, I wondered if modern real estate developers still had the kind of influence with city government they enjoyed in the fifties.

"What else, Frank? I can read you like an open book. Let's have it."

He could too. I tried to appear inscrutable, but it seldom worked. "What I'm going to say now, Mr. Chandler, is only a *potential* liability." I took a slow breath. "The land has been owned by four different entities. The original developer was the firm of Cannon/O'Boyle, which spent about $3 million to construct the Regency Towers in 1952. When Earl Cannon died, he bequeathed all his assets to his son and daughter, Grant Cannon and Jane Cannon Margolin, at a value of $30 million. Our client, Randall Cannon, is Grant's son, of course. The other partner, Teddy O'Boyle, had no family, so the Cannons inherited everything."

"Get to the point, Frank."

"I'm getting there, sir. Jane sold her share to Grant in 1976, who sold the entire building to Caribbean Investments Inc. for an undisclosed sum. I think he retained a 50 percent ownership, though I can't be sure; Caribbean is an offshore corporation in the Caymans, and secrecy laws there are tight."

"I didn't know he did *that* well from the deal, the shrewd bastard!"

"He sure did. Finally, in 1995, Caribbean Investments sold to the present owners, the Dial/Douglas Real Estate Partnership of New York. Grant Cannon may have retained an ownership interest in that entity too. So now Randall Cannon intends to buy the building from Dial/Douglas for his new Solar Towers development. I'm not sure his own father, Grant, even knows about the purchase if he really does suffer from Alzheimer's disease."

The gravelly voice interjected, "So what's the problem, Frank? How does any of this interfere with the sale?"

"Two problems, Mr. Chandler. First, though the building has changed hands several times, there are no records of any capital gains taxes ever being paid. I found two old tax returns, but they both claimed there hadn't been any profit, so no tax was due. I'm not sure how the sellers managed that with straight faces, considering the building went from $30 million to $55 million to $95 million over the years. Since those returns were never audited, they've gotten away with it so far."

"Why do you say 'so far'? Isn't there a Statute of Limitations of seven years on the audit of tax returns?"

"Yes but not if the IRS suspects fraud. In that case, they can go back as far as they like, and they can slap a tax lien on the property without due process, no matter who the new owner is. So in order to protect our client, we need more information about those sales transactions."

"Fine. I'll talk to Randall to see what he knows about any capital gains. You said there was a second problem?"

"Yes. This one could be potentially damaging to the firm. Since we act for both Grant and Randall Cannon, we may have a conflict of interest if the two of them aren't in agreement about the sale. As well, what is our ethical duty if we discover our clients have continuously broken the law?"

He blustered, "We keep our clients' secrets confidential forever, of course. Our ethical rules require us to report knowledge of future crimes only, not what has already occurred. Lawyers couldn't function if we had to divulge everything the client told us."

"I thought as much, Mr. Chandler. Just wanted to hear it confirmed."

"Good. I'll talk to Randall and make sure he and his father are in agreement. I'll even ask him to sign a waiver absolving Shipwright and Chandler of any conflict. And I'll find out what he knows about potential tax liabilities. You may be worth your salary after all, Frank. Can the deal still be consummated if the problems you've cited get resolved?

"Potentially. But there's one other issue."

"What now?"

"A real question exists as to whether the land for the initial development of the property was legally acquired by Earl Cannon back in 1948."

"My God, man, those events occurred nearly sixty years ago. How is this relevant? There's *got* to be some kind of Statute of Limitations closure on *those* transactions."

I'd obviously lit the fuse on a powder keg, but this only got my adrenaline up, so I forged ahead. "There is. That's why I doubt any *legal* action would prevail though it might if they could prove fraud. But more likely, if the Hispanic community ever got wind of the shenanigans that went on in those days to acquire the land, it'd be up in arms."

"What shenanigans?"

As Josue suggested, I had found the deeds and tax records for chain of title and sales prices on the Cortez and Kilgore properties buried deep in the dusty basement of the old records building downtown. These records confirmed our suspicions—some dirty business had been done—and gave me the confidence and anger to press the issue with Chandler. "Oh, spreading false rumors that the land was to be condemned for a garbage dump, for example, when it was actually intended for a huge office complex; paying shills to encourage their Hispanic neighbors to sell cheaply and then paying the shills far more money to buy them off; bribing city officials to rezone the land after it was acquired to make it much more valuable. What would happen in Dallas if the Hispanic community ever found out how their land was swindled from them in order to make millions for rich, white developers?"

"Frank, I warn you not to speak about these accusations to another living soul. Not only have you no proof, but the Statute of Limitations bars any legal action at this point. The major players are probably all dead by now anyway. If you value your career, you'll forget you ever discovered this. We're dealing with some powerful people who can snuff us out like a candle in a tornado, and they will do so in a heartbeat if we threaten their interests."

Nevertheless, something inside me would not back down. "How about murder, Mr. Chandler? I have reason to believe that at least one of the landowners was murdered along with his son. They were the original shills, and they were killed to keep them quiet." At Chandler's expression, I chose not to reveal my relationship to this landowner. "There's no statute for the crime of murder, is there?"

Chandler's eyes bulged even more than usual, 'til I thought they'd pop right out of his head. I'd gone too far, I knew, but I couldn't stop myself. "How do you think the City Council would change if it became public knowledge that Zoning Board members took money from rich developers? There'd be blood in the streets, that's what, and we'd end up with a lot more minority representation. Then the developers couldn't count on such an accommodating city government to do their bidding, could they? And then the business of Shipwright and Chandler might suffer as well."

"Frank, I don't have to remind you that those same developers you love to hate are some of our biggest clients. They pay your salary . . . and mine." He adopted his most reasonable tone. "Don't

ever forget your responsibility as a lawyer is to preserve attorney/
client confidentiality. Whatever you hear or have learned about a
client during your representation must remain forever secret even
if the representation ceases, even after the client's death. I know
you're aware of that, so I'm going to forget your little outburst
because I believe you're an ethical attorney." Then his voice became
harsh again. "You are to cease any further work on all Forestglen
matters. Please leave that file here; I'll let you know if I need anything else. You may go."

As I trudged out of Chandler's chamber, the Battleaxe greeted
me again, trying to sound pleasant. With her gruff demeanor, she
wasn't quite able to pull it off. "Good-bye, Mr. McNamara. I trust
we'll see you at the firm's annual charity banquet at Dallas Country
Club in a couple of months. It's for the benefit of autism research,
you know."

Of course I'd be there. I had plenty of time on my hands now,
didn't I? Attendance was mandatory anyway, with an obligatory
donation of $500, which I'd already paid. I didn't begrudge the
money for a worthy cause, but I had to wonder why someone
as tight-fisted as Chandler supported this event. Maybe it was to
assuage some personal guilt or for the positive press it brought to
the firm.

I couldn't help feeling resentful after being kicked off the
prize client, but I kept my tone civil. "I wouldn't miss it, Miss
Barbara. See you there."

She fixed me with the same venomous stare Chandler had
given me, as if she were his alter ego, then dismissed me with a
perfunctory nod toward the front door. I thought she must pick
up his vibes through the woodwork or, quite possibly, she'd bugged
his office.

My stride was steady and my face composed as I passed her desk though my battle rage was held barely in check. I was piecing together the past, but now I'd gotten myself removed from my largest project and had probably curtailed any possibility of making partner. By confronting Chandler, I had thrown salt on a festering wound, and I wondered what kind of a mess I'd created for myself this time.

CHAPTER
5

Pappas Brothers' Steakhouse
Dallas, Texas
Thursday, January 31, 2008

Despite Chandler's warning, the deepening mystery surrounding Forestglen's shady origins intrigued me still, and getting kicked off the project only fueled my sense that there must be an injustice worth fighting. Sam had always claimed that there were times when right and wrong went beyond the law. And wasn't this the example Danny looked to me to set—standing up for the voiceless?

I continued to probe, albeit more cautiously. Working at my computer long into the night, I scanned endless pages from historical websites and the *Dallas Morning News*. The more I learned of the dirty dealing of Forestglen's owners, the more I knew I couldn't ignore the corruption even if it threatened my livelihood. I meticulously documented every detail and began to understand the meaning of the word "obsession."

As I learned more about the Cortez family, my thoughts kept turning back to my chance encounter with Raquel at the cemetery.

Everything I discovered affected her too. Surely that was reason enough to contact her, and maybe that would get her off my mind. Of course, there was a good chance I would not even be able to track her down, and that would be that.

To my surprise, a quick search informed me that she was a respected nephrologist at Methodist Hospital who supervised the renal dialysis unit. After several minutes of internal debate, I called the hospital, and after a few minutes on hold, I heard her voice again.

"Dr. Jennings."

"This is Frank McNamara. I don't know if you remember me, but—"

"The cemetery guy. Wants my uncle to stop desecrating his family's graves."

"Uh, right."

"Sorry for being brusque, but I have a patient's kidneys to preserve. What can I do for you?"

I reminded myself that unlike lawyers, who make their living on the telephone, doctors have little patience for lengthy phone conversations. They always claim they're so terribly busy. So I got right to the point.

"I've been investigating the mystery of what happened between our families. I work for a law firm in Dallas, so I had some idea of where to look. I was wondering if you'd like to meet for dinner, and I can tell you what I've found so far."

There was a small pause on the other end. "So this would be strictly business, an informational meeting."

What else would it be? "Yes. Right."

"OK. I have a break at six. Call me then." She gave me her cell number and clicked off. I just sat for a minute or two, looking at the phone in my hand and wondering what I was feeling.

I called her again that evening, and we arranged to meet for dinner at Pappas Brothers' Steakhouse in Dallas. There are usually no half measures in Dallas. Everything's over the top, or it's not worth doing, which is exactly why I chose Pappas. This restaurant is just the opposite—tastefully decorated, comfortable, and quiet. It's the perfect place for a serious business conversation. They also serve thick juicy steaks, of course, grilled to perfection. I pulled in, bypassing the valet, and parked my own car. Five bucks is five bucks after all, especially in this economy.

At the bar, I had to scan the patrons twice before I spotted her, sitting primly and nursing a glass of fizzy water. She looked different in scrubs, still attractive but considerably more professional than the last time I'd seen her. She had pulled her hair into a loose ponytail and wore no makeup or jewelry. I tapped her shoulder, and she nearly vaulted off the barstool.

"Dammit, Frank. You scared the living you-know-what out of me . . ." She held her hand over her chest.

"You all right?"

"With the help of a defibrillator I'll probably recover."

"Next time I'll call to warn you I'm coming."

"Good idea," she laughed. "Or you could just show up when I expect you."

"Sorry about that. I had to handhold a client and couldn't get away."

"Just giving you a hard time. I'm half-harassed myself, didn't even have a chance to go home and freshen up."

It seemed she was still busy, but she was visibly relaxing. "At least you look good in scrubs."

"I'll keep that in mind. How's Danny doing?"

"Griping because he had to go back to school though secretly he loves it. He'd never admit it, wouldn't be cool. He can't wait to get back to the basketball court, and now he claims he wants to become a lawyer one day too. I'd like to believe it's because of my example, but I think it's probably because of a breakfast meeting we had last weekend with a respected Hispanic attorney."

"You mean Josue Fuentes?"

"How'd you know?"

"Word gets around. Josue is a legend in our community; everyone knows someone he's represented. They say you and Danny saved his life, making you two celebrities among us Latinos."

"Latino celebrities? Wonder how I can cash in on that."

She smirked and leaned an arm on the bar. "Don't look at me."

"Did the ambulance bring him to the Methodist Hospital ER?" She nodded, and I slid onto the stool next to her. "Will he be all right?"

"He's going to be fine. He had a large myocardial infarction, what you'd call a heart attack. We doctors call this one the 'Widow maker.' It stopped the blood flow to his brain for a couple of minutes. If you and Danny hadn't given chest compressions and restored the flow, he would've died. He needed a quadruple bypass, and now he's sitting up in bed, cracking jokes. Well done, Frank."

"Thank you. If the law doesn't work out for me, I'm thinking of becoming a paramedic; those guys were good!" The hostess caught my eye. "Like to stay here for a drink, or would you prefer dinner?"

"We better have dinner. I've got to return to the hospital for late rounds. Can't drink anyway—I'm on call."

The pretty hostess guided us to a quiet table in the back where an affable waiter in a starched shirt and white apron greeted us and recited the day's specials. We both came there for steak.

"Frank," she began, "I'm glad you pulled yourself away from your elegant office. I would have thought you'd forgotten all about the insignificant Cortez family."

"Elegant office? Don't make me laugh. All I see from my window are other tall buildings. I've worked for Shipwright and Chandler for more than ten years, but I'm still a lowly associate. I haven't made it to partner yet, so the fancy corner office will have to wait." I realized I was clutching my rolled silverware until my knuckles were white.

Raquel didn't reply as she searched for the right words. I took a breath and forced a smile. "Sorry. Sore subject. No, I haven't forgotten about your family, and they're not insignificant. Do you remember that horrible ice storm the Monday following our visit to the cemetery?"

"Yeah, the hospital had to send out vans fitted with snow tires to pick up most of the staff, including me. The ice melted after a few days, but it sure caused chaos while it lasted. I wouldn't dare drive on those roads."

"Neither would I. I stayed home all day and did some computer research. I should've been working on one of the firm's biggest accounts, but I couldn't stop thinking about Canuto Cortez. I made you some copies of articles I found. Seems a lot of senseless killing took place in those days."

I handed her the articles in their chronological order and recounted the stories, explaining the grim dance of death played out between the two clans. She perused the articles for a few minutes and shook her head. "I knew parts of the story, Frank, but it's even more vicious and gory than I imagined."

Dinner arrived. The waiter allowed us to cut into the steaks to make sure they were to our liking before he left. Perfect. "May I talk while we eat?"

"Please do."

I related how the blood feud, dramatic trial, and dueling lawyers held sway over the city for the better part of two years, then described how the bodies of the two remaining Kilgores, my great-grandfather and uncle, were found in the Trinity River in 1950. "Some people said it was retribution by the Cortez family, through the curse Canuto pronounced as he lay dying, the 'Kilgore Curse.' Others claimed the deaths were the handiwork of the Irish Mafia, but no one could pinpoint a culprit. Most people didn't care much anyway; they just hoped the discovery meant an end to the bloodletting."

"I'm sorry your family members suffered such pitiful deaths, Frank." She didn't really seem overly disturbed. "And I don't want to demean that, but from my point of view, those two had it coming. Knowing my Uncle Alfredo, though, I doubt he had the ability or the cojones to do much about it. Who else could be responsible?"

"Hard to say." I began to notice personality traits in Raquel similar to her uncle Alfredo. She was sawing into her steak with gusto, its juices running red, her appetite undiminished by the conversation. "Let's not be too hasty, Raquel. These events did occur over fifty years ago. Can we agree to disagree about who were the real victims until I've researched a bit further? I promise I'll keep you posted." I wasn't yet prepared to share all of my suspicions.

"OK. I'll try not to be too judgmental, for now. Tell me why you're so interested in this case, Frank . . . really. Your family came out of it smelling like roses, financially speaking at least. Why stir things up now?"

"Maybe because I don't like bullies or maybe I'm a bit of an idealist deep down. Or maybe it's for Danny. I also want to know why my great-grandfather and uncle had to die."

When the waiter brought the check, I reached for it, but Raquel insisted on paying her share. As we walked toward the exit, I thought she looked exquisite from the backside, even in those scrubs, with her dark, braided ponytail swaying beguilingly. We waited while the valet fetched her car. Maybe it was merely the ambience and the wine, but her face seemed to shine in the moonlight, her eyes twinkling.

Her car arrived, a late-model, Japanese import. "I enjoyed seeing you, Frank. Dinner was marvelous, and thanks for all the information. It'd be fun to see you again if anything else turns up." The valet held her door, and she got in.

Did she mean she'd like to go out on a real date? I started toward my Beemer, a short distance away. When Raquel reached the main driveway, she had to swerve to avoid a pickup truck, and I stopped to watch. It fishtailed from the street into the parking lot and barely missed her. Rather than slow down as it entered the lot, the truck seemed to accelerate . . . toward *me*. Its headlights bore down, speed increasing as it hurtled closer.

Too late I realized the driver's intention and threw myself sideways. I was almost clear, but the front bumper clipped my leg and launched me into the air, spinning uncontrollably. I thought of Willie Karlsson's leg cartwheeling overhead after stepping on that landmine in Iraq. I willed myself to land anywhere but on my head, then crashed to the unforgiving pavement with a sickening thud. I heard bones crack. A huge vise seemed to compress my chest. Strangely, there was no pain.

The truck roared away, scattering patrons and other autos in its wake. I saw Raquel's car had the reverse lights on, and I felt confused. Why would she be driving backward? She should be returning to the hospital to care for her patients. And why was ketchup splattered all over my pants? I'd have to get them cleaned.

Then a moment of clarity came, and I thought that I would die here, on this bleak patch of concrete. I thought of Danny with no parents to guide him. Then I saw my wife's smiling face, waiting for me, and a bizarre calm flooded over me.

The pain finally arrived in all its fury. I gasped, but that only increased its intensity. People were talking close to my face, like they were shouting at me, yet I could hear nothing. Lights flashed, red and white, moving nearer, but they too dissolved to inky blackness as I drifted away.

CHAPTER
6

Methodist Hospital ICU
Dallas, Texas
Monday, February 4, 2008

My fate wasn't to meet Sam in heaven just yet. I awoke alone in a stark ICU room crowded with machinery, monitors, wires, and tubes. The place reminded me of fitful childhood nights spent all alone in my darkened bedroom. No grownup was near, only creeping shadows and monster machines snoring alongside my vulnerable body.

The tubes exited most bodily orifices, trapping me. I soon discovered I had to call a nurse if I needed an analgesic shot or to have a bowel movement or if I wanted to roll over. The mechanical ventilator even breathed for me. If I tried breathing on my own, the machine bucked, which resulted in uncontrollable gagging and choking and more racking pain. Then they'd give me more drugs to "stabilize" me. At least I was alive.

When the narcotics wore off as the hours passed, my pain waxed astonishingly intense; when they'd been recently administered, I floated in and out of a stupor. I found out it was my fourth day here in the Methodist ICU and that I'd been irrational up to this point. I'd taken my automatic functions for granted until this accident—though it hadn't seemed much like an accident, had it? And now, being entirely dependent on others depressed me until I felt hopeless even though I heard, through a distant fog, the staff cheerily asserting that my condition continued to improve.

Later in the morning, they removed that damned breathing tube, and my mood perked up. The chipper young nurse described the full extent of my injuries.

"You suffered three fractured ribs, Mr. McNamara, which caused life-threatening bleeding into your chest cavity. The hemo-thorax required a drainage tube to evacuate all the fluid, and you needed several blood transfusions." She consulted a chart and nod-ded. "Six units of whole blood to be exact. You also fractured your left humerus and pelvis, and your bladder ruptured. You needed abdominal surgery to repair that, which is why you're experiencing the joys of a urinary catheter."

"My day is just getting better and better."

"You're lucky to be alive. No vital organs were damaged. The doctor thinks it's due to your extraordinarily strong constitution."

I took this to mean *your very hard head*. I didn't feel that lucky, though; everything hurt too much. The nurse said I'd be back to work in no time, then left to check on another patient. Depression settled in again. Even if she told the truth, I wasn't sure I had a job to go back to or that I'd even want to return to Shipwright and Chandler. Hadn't Chandler relieved me of the Forestglen account, comprising the majority of my workload?

He had seemed defensive and angry at our last conversation, and he definitely didn't appreciate my insinuations. Could our conversation have sparked an attempt on my life? Surely this was paranoia. That speeding car must've been accidental. I'd simply been in the wrong place at the wrong time. I was no longer at war with potential enemies on every rooftop. The firm would probably welcome me back. The question was what kind of drunk or crazy person would steer right for me and stomp on the gas. If not that, then who in this wide world wanted me dead?

"Good morning, Frank. You sleeping?" I recognized the silky, confident voice, and my spirits soared. Amazing how a visit from my doctor could buoy me, if she *were* my doctor.

"Nobody can really sleep in an ICU, Raquel. They're always waking you for something, usually just to give you a sleeping pill."

"I see you're improving by leaps and bounds. Doctors know that when patients start making sarcastic comments, it's a sure sign of recovery."

"Can you tell me anything about Danny? Are you my attending physician or just here socially?

"Both, I suppose. And Danny's fine. He visits you regularly with his grandparents, but until now you've been semi-conscious. He's shook up about all of this, but he's thrilled you're making good progress. I spoke to him myself."

"Thanks for that. The last thing I wondered before I lost consciousness was what would happen to him without me. And the first thing I worried about when I woke up was if he was all right."

"He's a strong kid. Naturally he's worried about you, but he's hanging in there, and you're going to stick around to take care of him. You'll see for yourself when he visits this afternoon, OK?"

"Yes, thanks." I tried to hide the tears of gratitude welling up in my eyes.

"I'm here professionally as well. Someone's got to attend to your kidney function, and you got me. The ruptured bladder didn't help any, but I think your kidneys will heal fine."

"You're the one who saved me, aren't you?"

"God, no. It's taken a regular platoon of people to pull you through. Dr. Anderson's in charge for now. He had to intubate your chest and explore your abdomen. He and an orthopod also fixed your fractures. You're also being treated by a pulmonologist and an intensive care specialist, Dr. Mookerjee. He's here in the ICU full time, keeping a close eye on you." She took a step closer and rested a hand on the bed rail. "But I'm here personally too. I mean, the accident happened right after we finished dinner. It happened on my watch, so to speak."

"Raquel, just before I passed out, I thought I saw you rushing over to me. Did I hallucinate or did that really happen?"

"No hallucination. After that maniac nearly clipped my car, he headed straight for you. I watched him in my rearview mirror and saw him smack into you. I backed up fast to see if I could help. Good thing I did; you hit the pavement hard. He must've been drunk because he just sped away from the scene.

"I dialed 911 on my cell phone and did some basic first aid until the ambulance arrived. As luck would have it, Methodist Hospital is close, so they brought you here."

"You have my eternal gratitude, Raquel. If you hadn't looked back to check on me, who knows if I'd have made it?"

"Believe me, Frank, I'm only a small part of the team responsible."

"Nevertheless, if you hadn't got to me quickly, I could've died. I'd like to repay you in some small way. Would you consider going for dinner again when I'm well enough? This time I'll treat."

"I see you definitely *are* improving. I'll think about it." She gave me a small smile. "OK, I thought about it. When you're well enough, we'll go. You can repay me by doing everything you're told, so you can make a speedy recovery."

"Speedy has got to be relative in this case. How long will it take, really? Don't sugarcoat."

"Well, Frank, it's going to take months, but each day will be a little better. You'll need time to heal and then painstaking rehab to regain full use of your arms and legs. I've seen worse, though, and you're a sturdy individual. Strong-willed too. You're going to need every ounce of that willpower to pull through."

"Oh, oh! I'm starting to relapse already. I can't handle that much candor, Doctor." I couldn't laugh as I said it because my ribs hurt too much.

"Don't you attorneys always want the truth, the whole truth, and nothing but the truth?"

"*Almost* always." I tried to sit up a bit more, but the pain was too great. "I know it'll be tough, but I'll recover. I've got to for Danny's sake."

"Right now you're allowed all the analgesia you need; ask for medication when you need it. Soon enough we'll have to wean you off, and you won't be so happy then."

"Believe me, I'm not having that much fun even with the medicine. Will you be back later on?"

"I'll come by this afternoon. After all, I've got to do right by the patient who saved the life of Josue Fuentes. By the way, he called to ask about your progress. I told him it'd be a HIPAA violation to tell him without your permission, and then I told him anyway. Was that OK?"

"Of course. That stuff seems like just another layer of governmental nonsense, especially if you can't even find out about a friend's progress."

"Preaching to the choir, Frank. Got to go now; see you later."

Once I was alone again, I really did feel morose. Now that I knew the full extent of my injuries, my lengthy recuperation seemed daunting. I couldn't leave Danny without any parents at all, so somehow I'd have to make it. And if I was going to make it, I needed a paycheck. Unfortunately I declined long-term disability insurance because of the outrageous premiums. The thought of asking Grandma Kate for a handout was abhorrent. So I'd get back to work if Shipwright and Chandler would have me. If not, the situation would go from bad to worse.

For the most part, the day passed in tedium and intermittent pain. Nurses came and went, checking vital signs, measuring urine output, and administering medications. I tried to watch television but drifted off to sleep; then I awoke, uncomfortable from the pain again. A nurse gave me another shot.

Dr. Anderson, the trauma surgeon, arrived for rounds about noon. He assured me that all my organs were functioning normally, "considering." My numerous fractures seemed to be stable as well.

The recurring feeling that what happened had been no accident haunted my thoughts. It seemed so unlikely, though, and the last thing I needed was to slip into paranoid delusion, so I pushed it from my mind every time the suspicion arose. Without that to focus on, I was so bored I kept a mental log of everyone's comings and goings. The Intensive Care Specialist, Dr. Raju Mookerjee, rounded about 2:30 p.m. He said my vital signs and lab tests looked normal and wrote orders for the nursing staff, including one for a chest X-ray.

About 3:45 p.m. a radiology technician trundled an X-ray machine into my room. He wore a green gown and rubber gloves, hairnet-style cap, and surgical mask. He said very little as he manipulated the equipment around my bed and over my chest. I paid him scant attention; just another procedure in a lengthy series of scans, tests, and treatments designed to keep my fragile body functioning.

He slid a square, metal-clad sheath containing the X-ray film underneath the bed, briefly disappearing behind the apparatus and fumbling with my intravenous lines for better access. Then he pressed a button on the side of the machine, which buzzed obediently, and that was that.

He began packing up his machinery and thanked me for my cooperation. He folded the arms of the equipment, wheeled out the door, and was swiftly gone. "Thank you," I mumbled, as I drifted once more into narcotic oblivion.

Moments later I woke trembling, anxious, and bathed in a sweat that drenched my sheets. I tried to reach the call button pinned to the bedrail not one foot from my right hand, but I shook too badly. I wretched uncontrollably, wracking my chest fractures with pain, and vomited in my lap. With the next breath, I inhaled vomit into my lungs. My heart pounded until it seemed certain to erupt from my chest.

I tried to cry for help, but my mouth clenched shut, chomping down on my tongue. Then I convulsed in a paroxysm of flopping and guttural grunts. Suddenly two nurses were in the room, attempting to prise open my mouth to insert some sort of padded device and trying to hold onto my flailing arms. I was powerless to stop myself and kept thrashing about.

As consciousness left me, a dreadful demon dragged me over the abyss into narcoleptic stupor. Reality, memory, and nightmare collided somewhere between a cold hospital room and a sun-baked desert. An RPG hit the room, blood and rubble flying, and knocked me into a wall. The rest of the squad was dead. I was alone, saved only by the helmet that had cushioned my head. The stars faded behind storm clouds flashing hot lightning, and I fell unchecked into an ever-narrowing funnel of sand, rock, and smoke. Gravity pulled me past, down into the hole again, but as the blackness tried to overcome me, I fought to retain my wits.

In the distance, I heard Raquel's voice. "What the hell happened in here? He was doing great just a little while ago." Someone placed a mask over my face and ventilated me.

A nurse answered. "At 3:35 he was sitting up in bed, happy as a clam. Not fifteen minutes later, the cardiac monitor showed a tachycardia of 130, with rapid respirations. I ran in here and found him convulsing, gave him five milligrams of IV Valium, and started bagging. The convulsions stopped, but he stayed comatose."

Raquel examined me quickly. "Pupils equal, round, reactive to light and accommodation. Chest clear. No, there's a few crackles in the right upper lobe. Abdomen's soft, no rigidity, and normal bowel sounds; urine output clear. What's the drainage from that chest tube like?"

"Scanty and slightly blood tinged, same as before. Here's his last lab, from about two hours ago."

Raquel glanced through my chart. "Nothing there to suggest a problem. Problem's gotta be an embolus or maybe metabolic. Get stat lab, as in yesterday. Also portable chest, twelve lead EKG, and CT scan of the brain."

The nurse wondered, "Doctor, do you want *another* chest X-ray? The tech just did a portable not twenty minutes ago. The patient's condition deteriorated shortly after he left."

"No, that should be good enough. Get it up here for me to look at, right away! Why's that IV wide open?"

"It shouldn't be. I checked it thirty minutes ago, and it was infusing perfectly." I saw the nurse reach for the clamp on the IV tubing and dial it down. I wanted to say something, anything, to try to help them, but though my brain assimilated what was occurring, I couldn't find my voice.

Dr. Mookerjee arrived. I heard him and Raquel talking urgently.

"Raquel, considering all his fractures and the fact that he's four days post-op, we have to rule out a pulmonary embolus first... But if it's metabolic, the likeliest causes would be acute renal failure, potassium deficiency, or hypoglycemia."

"He shouldn't have any of those, Raj. He's got normal urine output and normal creatinine, so it's probably not renal; normal potassium just two hours ago and the normal EKG I just did, so hypokalemia's unlikely. The glucose was ninety-six, perfect, but what else could change quickly enough to account for his condition?"

"Let's change the IV fluids and infuse him with five percent glucose while we're waiting and add eight milliequivalents of potassium to the IV bag for good measure. Get him down to CT to do some scans: then maybe we'll have some answers."

A bit later the head nurse returned. "Dr. Jennings, I had the radiology department turned practically upside down. They found the X-ray tech unconscious in a storage closet. But we couldn't find Mr. McNamara's chest X-ray anywhere. The portable machine itself disappeared. It finally turned up on the fifth floor near the fire escape. The film cassette was still in it, but it was completely blank. Whoever took the picture hadn't even exposed the film."

"The tech was unconscious and no X-ray was done?" Raquel asked incredulously. "Did you say that Mr. McNamara went downhill shortly after the radiology tech left his room?"

"Yes. Just a few minutes later."

I tried to say, "Yes, you're on the right track. That bastard didn't take any X-ray. He put something in the IV and tried to kill me." But the words sounded only in my mind, and I couldn't move a muscle.

Raquel said, "Do a stat glucose. And draw more blood for a toxic chemical screen. What the hell is going on?" They pricked my finger.

"Dr. Jennings," a nurse interrupted, "maybe this glucometer isn't working right, but the reading I just took says his blood glucose is only thirteen."

"Thirteen? That's incompatible with life," Raquel shouted. "Check it again. Meantime, start another IV, add another bag of glucose, and pump it in as fast as you can. Get that glucose up to a hundred at least. Raj, what happens if your brain's without glucose for more than a few minutes?"

"Damned if I know, Raquel. I've never seen a case like this before. He could have brain damage or might even arrest."

One of the nurses shouted, "His cardiac rhythm just changed to V Tach."

V Tach, what's V Tach? I wondered as if watching the entire scene as a detached observer. I heard people screaming, "Epinephrine, one milligram, IV push. Amiodorone, three hundred milligrams, quick. Crank up the defib to two hundred joules, no, three. Clear!" The last thing I heard before I crashed was Raquel's voice.

"C'mon, Frank. Stay with us. Stay with us. Don't give up now." But the blackness overcame me once and for all, and, for the second time in a few days, the world dimmed to nothingness.

CHAPTER
7

LAW OFFICES OF SHIPWRIGHT AND CHANDLER
DALLAS, TEXAS
TUESDAY, APRIL 29, 2008

I limp-tap-limped my way into the offices of Shipwright and Chandler using the gnarled walking stick I'd carved from a tree limb years before. The good wishes of a few low-level employees greeted me on my way in, but no one of any rank dropped by my office. I felt like old Josue Fuentes, sickly and disregarded, but I think Josue might've been in better shape.

There was surprisingly little on my desk considering my three-month hiatus. Chandler had locked my computer's access to the Forestglen account, and he'd not replaced it with much else. In my absence, my remaining casework had been distributed to other attorneys.

I twiddled my thumbs in my office and answered inane questions from well-meaning coworkers about the accident and my medical condition. I felt more and more the outcast, another useless fixture usurping valuable space. Was this how a large corporation isolated an employee prior to the final guillotining?

Plus, I still suffered considerable pain. The Vicodin tablets Dr. Mookerjee had provided seemed to last for shorter and shorter periods of time. When he wouldn't refill the prescription sooner than recommended, Dr. Anderson would. When he declined, I even persuaded Raquel to supply me a couple of times. Between them, I managed to obtain enough medication to tolerate things fairly well. Still, when the drugs wore off, I became sweaty and agitated, my guts seized with nausea, and I recognized the need for another dose.

I hated being dependent on those damn pills. It frightened me to think I might become a drug addict; addicts always seemed so pathetic to me, responsible for their own situation, yet making no effort to change it. Now I knew things weren't that simple. Either I took the medication or I couldn't function, period, so I kept getting refills. I despaired of ever healing to the point of not requiring the stuff again.

The doctors assured me that my bones were knitting properly, the lungs were fine, and the bladder functioned nicely. Best of all, my heart and brain showed no lasting damage. Then why wouldn't the pain subside? I determined to ask Raquel next time we spoke. She'd already saved my life twice; she'd just have to do it again.

At least Sheila didn't ignore my presence. She fussed over me and found busy work for me to do. "I'm telling you, Sheila," I said that afternoon, after inviting her into my office, "hard as it is to believe, I don't remember much about the entire first week. I remember waking up for a few hours after about four days, then nothing again for three more days. They say I was in an insulin coma."

"Why did they give you insulin? You're not diabetic."

"Ah, Sheila. You've asked the $64,000 question. No one knows. Maybe one of the nurses gave me the wrong medicine by mistake; I was receiving a lot by IV. Or maybe someone gave it to me on purpose."

"Who'd want to do that? It could've killed you, couldn't it?"

"It sure could've, and I don't have a clue why anyone would want me dead, but I intend to find out." My suspicion of Chandler lingered, but it still felt so ridiculous that I wasn't about to share it with Sheila. "I don't go anywhere without a gun anymore, but keep that under your hat, would you? Guns aren't supposed to be carried into the building."

"Tell the truth, I don't go anywhere without my Ruger .32 either. I've got the license, and I don't feel safe without it." She canted her head to the side, peering at me. "They say your heart had to be zapped with those paddles. Didn't you feel that?"

"At the time I didn't, but I sure felt it later. When I finally woke up, I still felt spacey, like I got lost in the twilight zone. I felt like I'd been run over again, had my chest branded, then tossed onto a gurney in some torture chamber and left for dead. At least this time I assumed they were trying to *save* me. Only the thought of Danny kept me going."

"That boy doesn't know what a wonderful father he's got. You're a courageous man."

"Thanks, Sheila. Courage and five bucks gets me a grande latte at Starbucks. Besides, courageousness hurts too damn much."

Sheila's intercom rang. She answered from the phone on my desk. I heard Donald Chandler's distinctive gravelly voice, none too pleasant either.

"Yes sir," she replied. "I'll tell him as soon as he arrives. Thank you, sir." She hung up and turned to me. "Have you arrived yet?

I'm sure you recognized Mr. Chandler's sweet voice on the other end."

"Indeed I did. What did he want?"

"Let's just say he desires your presence in his office the moment you turn up. I told a little white lie to give you some time to get organized."

"I'd give you a raise if it were up to me."

"That's not necessary, Mr. McNamara, but please keep a job open for me if you ever change law firms."

"Is that a polite way of saying you think my days at Shipwright and Chandler are numbered?"

"Let's hope not. But rumor has it that Mr. Chandler has a burr under his saddle for you, so be careful."

"Sheila, wherever I go, you'll be right there with me. As always, thanks for the heads up."

So I limp-tap-limped my way to Donald Chandler's private office. A sensation of foreboding undermined any confidence I might've otherwise possessed.

Ms. Battleaxe hove into view through the etched glass door. Chandler's gatekeeper still looked resplendently drab in her dour dowdiness, hair tucked into a bun at the nape of her ungainly neck. She seemed about as approachable as the Beefeater guard at the Tower of London, standing at attention with pike and blade.

"Why Mr. McNamara, so good to see you up and about again. We've all heard the story of your terrible ordeal." Her attempt at empathy sounded rehearsed.

"Thanks for your good wishes, Barbara. I'm fit again and ready to resume work. Did Mr. Chandler ask for me?"

"He sure did." She buzzed Chandler, nodded, and then bade me enter.

This time his office appeared positively tomblike. With lights dimmed and heavy drapery blocking out most of the sunlight, only a green-shaded lamp lit the desk where Chandler sat. It spotlighted his boiled-egg head and the spidery fingers attached to his spindly arms. He sat hunched over a thick file, staring at me.

From the dark shadows in a corner of the room came an authoritative voice. "Do sit down, Mr. McNamara."

"Mr. Chandler, how did you say that without moving your lips?"

"Your sarcasm is not appreciated, Mr. McNamara." He dwelt on the word "Mister" as if to emphasize my insignificance. The voice grated like steel dragged through gravel. "No, I'm not Chandler; I'm your real boss, Randall Cannon. I'm even Donald's boss—isn't that so, Donald?"

"Quite so, Mr. Cannon, quite so," Chandler replied in his most obsequious tone. I admit to being intrigued at the sight of Donald Chandler playing toady to anyone.

"A pleasure to meet you, Mr. Cannon." I began to rise to shake his hand.

"That won't be necessary; you may remain seated." Cannon left the shadows and moved to Chandler's side. Even then, all I could see was a short, brutish body clad in an expensive suit and stylish tie. I could make out diamond-encrusted cufflinks, but the lamplight afforded no view of the face at all.

Without warning, he twisted the lamp around to shine directly into my eyes. I shrank back into my chair, momentarily blinded. Squinting, I blocked the brightness with my hand as the hairs on the back of my neck stood up. Maybe I'd become paranoid, but the gun in my back pocket reassured me considerably.

"What's this all about, Mr. Cannon? I'm an attorney, *your* attorney, and this is supposed to be a respected law firm, not a CIA interrogation center."

He refocused the light onto Chandler's desk. As starbursts punctuated my vision, the disembodied voice said, "Sorry, McNamara, didn't mean to startle you."

"The room's dark as a morgue, and I can't see who I'm talking to. Is there a reason for all this?" I started to rise again.

The voice turned harsh. "Yes, there is. Sit back down if you know what's good for you…and Danny."

"What's Danny got to do with anything?" My anger surged even as I felt more vulnerable. "Leave him out of the discussion, please."

"Of course. I'm sure Danny's safe and sound, and I sincerely pray he'll stay that way. Apparently we've gotten off on the wrong foot." He sounded conciliatory again, but there was no missing the implied threat. "Let's start over."

The erratic changes in tone disoriented me. "That would be nice, Mr. Cannon. You could start by explaining the purpose of this meeting. Why all the darkness?"

"I asked Donald to darken the room because I've just come back from my eye doctor and he dilated my eyes."

I didn't believe that for a minute, but I wouldn't give him the snarky retort he deserved. I still hoped somehow to save my job.

"We've asked you here to analyze your work on Forestglen. Please review for me what you told Donald just before your unfortunate accident."

"I would have told you without all the theatrics. After all, as the client, you've got a right to know."

The ghostly voice replied, "Correct, Mr. McNamara. Don't ever forget that or your ethical duty to reveal nothing to anyone, at any time, arising from your representation of me or Forestglen. If you value your law license and career, that is."

"The first thing I undertook was a simple title search. That's how I discovered the three mechanics liens that had been filed against the Regency Office Tower property and the delinquent taxes as well."

Chandler sat mute and motionless while Cannon took charge. Cannon said, "Those issues have already been dealt with. I've got friends in high places."

"Apparently." I then summed up for Cannon what I knew about the property's transfers over the years through the Cannon family and investment firms. I added, "No taxes were ever paid on any of the transactions as far as I can tell."

"Maybe the tax returns were kept confidential."

"It's possible. I might have missed them, or they might have been excluded from the closing documents, but that would be very unusual. Lenders in financings of this size typically want to see tax returns for the previous two or three years. They need to assure themselves that their investment won't be superseded by an IRS claim against the building and that borrowers have the financial clout to meet their obligations. I searched high and low for the tax returns and found nothing."

"Dear old granddad. I owe him a lot for creating the family fortune. Wonder why Dad didn't pay his taxes, though? He's in a retirement home with advanced Alzheimer's, so I can't ask him. An interesting dilemma for Auntie Jane though, isn't it?" He asked it with relish, making me think there was no love lost between Randall and Jane Margolin.

"In any case," I said, "Caribbean Investments is incorporated in the Cayman Islands, a well-known tax haven, and I found no 'Foreign Investment Real Property Tax' filings on their sale to Dial/Douglas. You're an officer of Dial/Douglas, aren't you? I hope that doesn't create a problem for you with the IRS. Maybe taxes were actually paid, and I just didn't discover the returns."

He ignored that, but his voice finally registered a bit of anxiety. Apparently he wouldn't mind if Jane or his father tangled with the IRS, but he wanted no part of it himself. "Besides an alleged failure to pay capital gains taxes or silly FIRPTA filings, Mr. McNamara, what other problems did you turn up?"

Here goes, I thought. "Since you ask, there seem to be irregularities in the acquisition of the property where the office complex was originally built."

"What sort of 'irregularities'?"

"For starters, the Kilgore family might have been coaxed into selling its land at an inflated price and then bribed to convince their neighbors into selling cheaply. After all the required land was purchased, the developers may have bribed city zoning commissioners into rezoning the parcel from 'Single Family Residential' to 'Industrial 2,' which made it exponentially more valuable than before." Something about the situation and the expression on Cannon's face kept me from sharing what I'd discovered about the murders. It was still conjecture, anyway, and first I wanted to hear Cannon's response.

Except there wasn't one. He merely grunted and began to pace the room. During one pass, he paused behind my chair, and I could feel the hostility. It prickled the hairs at the back of my neck again, but apart from the sound of his footsteps, there was utter silence.

Finally he resumed his place in the cone of light behind Chandler's desk, his face still in shadows. He growled, "Is that it? Did you find nothing else?"

"Mr. Chandler asked me to cease working on the Forestglen account after I gave him this same report, so I did."

"You didn't do any other work on Forestglen after hours or at home? It'll go badly for you if you're not completely truthful."

"No, of course not." I lied, but how could he possibly be aware of the research I'd done privately?

"All right, McNamara, I appreciate your efforts on behalf of Forestglen. But I want to reiterate what Mr. Chandler has already instructed. Make no effort to investigate the matter further, and hand over any related materials to him immediately. That will be all. We'll no longer require your services."

"What exactly does that mean, 'no longer require my services'?" I rose to my feet, feeling very stiff. Neither of them budged.

Chandler finally chimed in. "It means you're fired, Frank."

"Just like that, after ten years of loyal service and an unblemished record?"

"I'm afraid so. You can pick up your severance package from Ms. Sweeney on your way out. It's most generous and comes with an excellent reference."

A reference wouldn't do much for a washed-up, forty-year-old attorney. I gritted my teeth and made my way to the door and into the Battleaxe's antechamber.

Her voice was rich with phony-pleasant irony. "How'd it go in there? Those two can be a difficult tag team. Don't worry. You'll find another job. Almost everyone survives." She looked so amused I thought she might elbow me in my tender ribs, but she just handed me a large manila envelope. "Everything you'll need is inside. Could you hand me your keys, please?"

"Here they are, and thanks for your good wishes." It was all I could do to be civil. I was furious—at myself as much as Cannon and Chandler. Why could I not leave this alone? I tried to make as quick an exit as possible, but she caught me as I reached for the door.

"I hope this won't spoil your enjoyment of the Autism Charity Benefit next week. Mr. Chandler's expecting you. The ticket is good for you and a guest."

"Gee, that's good to know. Wouldn't miss it for all the tea in China." I wasn't feeling very charitable. But the $500 was already a sunk cost. I didn't think I'd be such good company, and I couldn't think of a guest to bring either. Danny was a bit young for this type of affair. Would Raquel consider going? My debilitated body couldn't shuffle me out of the Battleaxe's lobby fast enough.

Back at my office, Sheila's appearance made me suspect something was terribly wrong. Had she heard already? She looked ashen, and when I addressed her, she could manage only a mumbled greeting and a flood of tears. She gestured toward my office door, which lay wide open.

Inside, the place was in shambles. I felt close to tears myself at the sight of my precious possessions vandalized. Bookcases had been emptied, books strewn all over the floor. The desk drawers were askew, and the lamp knocked over. My filing cabinet lay on its side, its shelves trashed. What distressed me most, however, was that my computer had been stolen.

When Sheila recovered her wits, she told me that two men in suits had burst into the office over her strenuous objection and ransacked the place. When I asked if she recognized them, she said no although she recalled that one of the men had a large, black mole on his cheek.

I sat down, shaking, and I suddenly felt the strain of the past few months, the anxiety I'd tried hard to conceal. My pain became intense; I throbbed from neck to toe. I needed a Vicodin, quickly. I fumbled for the pill bottle and swallowed one dry.

I thought I could discover the truth about the past and still retain my job. Then I had simply hoped to return to work after my stay in the hospital. Now, not only would I never make partner, but I had been disgracefully fired. I promised Sheila a job if I ever again had one to offer though we both knew that at this point in my career, the chances were slim. I gathered my personal belongings in a cardboard box, said a heartfelt good-bye to Sheila, and limped toward the exit.

Though they must have heard the ruckus, none of my co-workers had attempted to assist Sheila in any way. As I hobbled down the corridor for the last time, they averted their gaze. My former colleagues, whom I had thought were my friends, feigned total immersion in their work, ignoring my very existence.

With one last glance back, I left the offices of Shipwright and Chandler for good.

CHAPTER
8

FRANK MCNAMARA'S HOUSE
DALLAS, TEXAS
TUESDAY, APRIL 29, 2008

Chandler's hooligans had ransacked my office and stolen the computer with all its backup files, at least the ones they knew about. But they hadn't reckoned on the flash drive I kept as a backup at home. It contained every scrap of information I'd discovered about Forestglen. Cannon had overplayed his hand; after being threatened like that, I would *never* stop searching. He had to be hiding something big.

I should've kept the flash drive with me, I suppose, or somewhere less obvious than in a safe. I found the front door of my house ajar, and nausea struck my gut. The hallway had been trashed, my precious grandfather clock upended and smashed. I retrieved my Keltec .380 from the Beemer and entered the house via the garage.

The main floor was in chaos. Still not certain I was alone, I stumbled downstairs to the basement, leading with the gun.

Vicodin had erased my pain, but it made my brain foggy, and the entire experience felt surreal.

Chairs and a workbench were toppled over. Tucked away in a corner, inside a closet built to house it, I kept a large gun safe full of assorted handguns, rifles, cash, and other valuables. It was bolted to the floor, and it was so heavy that it required four men utilizing construction equipment to position it when I'd first moved into the house. The closet door had been pried open, and they'd found the safe inside but hadn't been able to move or open it. Gouges scarred the heavy door where they had tried. I spun the dial to the appropriate combination, and the massive door creaked open. My mouth was dry. I held my breath.

There were the rifles, including my prized AR-15 semi-automatic, the piled boxes of ammunition, and my sixteen handgun cases in orderly rows. The envelope of cash stashed behind them was still there too, and next to it, the vital flash drive. I swiftly pocketed it and the cash and then re-locked the safe.

After gathering my thoughts, I raced back upstairs to my study. "Raced" is a relative term, in this case, for a man leaning on a cane, limping, and woozy on Vicodin. My study had been ransacked as badly as the office, and the desktop computer was missing.

Frantic, I searched my closet for the laptop. Hidden behind some old newspapers, it had survived the destruction. Hands trembling, I managed to insert the drive and open the file; it was undamaged.

I called my in-laws in Plano to tell them about the break-in. Danny had just arrived uneventfully home from school. Without giving them all the details, I asked them to keep a more watchful eye on him than usual. Maybe the neighbors hadn't reported the break-in because they'd all been at work or picking up the kids from school. I would report the crime to the police the next day; nothing could be done now.

After copying the information onto four more flash drives I'd "borrowed" from the office, I addressed one envelope to Josue Fuentes, another to Raquel Jennings, and a third to my in-laws. A cover letter asked them to hold onto the drives for safekeeping and open them only if I were dead or disabled. The fourth drive I would use at my computer, and the original I'd place back into the safe.

I struggled back downstairs, replaced the original flash drive into its hiding place, and decided to check the contents of my gun cases. All present and accounted for: three .45s, two .40s, three .38 Specials, three 9 millimeters, one .357 Magnum, and a few assorted rifles. The lightweight .380 Keltec semi-automatic remained my favorite for concealed carry purposes, and I slipped it into my back pocket.

I stored about 250 rounds of ammunition for each caliber, originally intended for Danny and me to shoot on weekends. But in view of my altered circumstances, I was glad I'd stashed them away. I removed the H&K .45 and a box of .45 ammo, more .380 hollow-point bullets for the Keltec, and a 12-gauge shotgun. I placed all the weaponry inside a large duffle bag and labored back up the stairs.

A stiff Scotch helped wash down another Vicodin. Then I eased my aching carcass into the recliner and set the bag beside me. I had long been fascinated with guns. Target practice with Danny or friends provided companionship, and I found the technical aspect of using a gun irresistible too, especially stripping, cleaning, and reassembling the weapon. My time as an Army Ranger sealed the deal. I fell in love with anything capable of making a deadly bang, and not just guns, but grenades, bombs, plastique, and anything else explosive. I'd become an ordnance nut, but a law-abiding, sensible ordnance nut. Whenever Washington attempted to restrict gun ownership rights, I bought more of them because they said I shouldn't. Most of all, I was glad to have a firearm for my family's personal protection, particularly when someone was trying to kill me.

The second floor of the house hadn't been spared either. If anything, my bedroom had been given a more thorough going over than the downstairs. The task of cleaning up this mess would require some time, more than I could endure at that moment. I felt physically and mentally whipped.

Hunger led me to the kitchen downstairs. At least the bastards left me some cold, soggy leftovers. In my study, I ate the tasteless feast inside my cordon of alcohol and guns. With another Scotch in hand, I relaxed into an armchair, propping up my legs on the desk. Between the alcohol and the Vicodin, the pain demons remained at bay. I couldn't comprehend what terrible sins I'd committed to incur the wrath of the gods like this, but I'd be damned before I'd succumb to them so easily.

A gentle rain began to drum against the window panes. Lightning lit up the front lawn in flickering white. I patted the Keltec .380 in my back pocket for reassurance and placed the H&K .45 on the desk within easy reach. The Winchester Defender 12-gauge shotgun rested comfortably across my lap. Let 'em come, I thought, whoever they are.

I crashed in that recliner all night and imagined that I was whole again, cocooned against unknown adversaries, pursuing them instead of being hunted.

Overnight, raucous thunder and lightning rent the heavens, deluging Dallas in one of its typical spring torrents. Hellacious winds bent the trees and slanting rain fell all across town, hammering my windows. Yet in my narcotic oblivion I heard none of it.

When morning finally injected daggers of sunlight through the window shutters, I blinked awake to the sight of amputated tree limbs lying buckled in my front yard. Puddles filled hollows in the sidewalks and landscaping.

Intending to inspect the damage, I sat bolt upright, but something had gone terribly wrong. My legs and head seemed detached from my spine, and my whole body was suffused with agonizing pain.

Lancinating thunderbolts shot down my back and through my pelvis, culminating in a clutch of nausea. Explosions throbbed inside my skull. Desert sand had somehow invaded my throat in the night and cold, clammy sweat trickled down my face and neck. This was the exquisite anguish of a Scotch and Vicodin hangover, and it settled around my head like a vise.

I groped for my weapons but then realized I wasn't under attack, at least not externally. I tried to rise again, this time more gingerly, and succeeded in standing upright. My discomfort was reduced from excruciating to merely agonizing.

After hobbling to the kitchen, I gobbled down some aspirin and vitamins and another Vicodin, chased by leftover orange juice. Two cups of coffee later, after a shave, shower, and change of clothes, I'd regained some semblance of physical functionality. But inside me was another matter; inside I burned for revenge.

The ribs didn't trouble me much anymore. The lungs had healed, and I could breathe normally again. Nevertheless, every step became a new adventure in misery, and at times, another pill seemed the only way to survive it. But I didn't want to end up drug dependent either, desperate for another fix.

Quit wallowing in self-pity, I thought. *I'll start weaning myself off the drug today.* Or *sometime later on for sure.* Really I would.

CHAPTER
9

Grandma Kate's House
Dallas, Texas
Wednesday, April 30, 2008

My grandmother, Kathleen Kilgore McNamara, was Henry Kilgore's third child and only daughter. In 1948, when she was eighteen years old, she must have been a first-hand witness to the acquisition of her father's land. She was the only living person who might still be able to shed some light on it without trying to kill me. Her recollection, at least the story she'd always related to me, seemed poles apart from what Raquel heard from her Uncle Alfredo. Time to visit Grandma Kate for a little heart to heart.

She lived in a two story, English Tudor mansion in Preston Hollow, one of Dallas' most prestigious neighborhoods. She and my grandfather had purchased the house in 1973 with the proceeds of the sale of their ranch in far North Dallas. That much of her story I knew to be true, having researched the deed transfers at the Dallas County land titles office kept at City Hall. But how did they pay for the purchase of the original ranch?

The house nestled within an ivy-covered wall built of costly Austin stone. I entered the proper code at the front gate of the circular driveway, and two ornate, patina-encrusted doors swung outward. I drove the Beemer through and followed tree-lined flagstones surrounding a fishpond complete with a statue of Neptune spouting a trifurcated stream of water. As a child growing up here, I delighted in feeding the hulking Japanese Koi in the pond. And on hot summer days, I jumped right in and enjoyed a cool shower from the mouth of the god himself. I stopped in front of the house.

Faye Rudolph, Grandma's trusted housekeeper/cook/companion of over forty years, answered the doorbell. Her Creole patois was thick today though the accent typically came and went according to her mood. Despite that, I understood her just fine. "Why, Mister Frank. You don't come visit your old Miss Faye and Grandma near enough. I reckon we just too old to care about."

"Miss Faye, that isn't so and you know it. I've been laid up in the hospital these past three months. I sure did appreciate your visits and the fried chicken you brought, though."

"Thanks, Mister Frank. Praise be to God you all right. 'Cept for that little limp, you looking good. C'mon in and make yourself comfortable. I'll fetch your Grandma and a nice cold beer."

It was only 11:00 a.m., slightly early for beer, but she offered this to everyone, so I could hardly refuse. Besides, Faye had practically raised me. I waited in an overstuffed chair in the living room, where a gas fireplace offered welcoming warmth from the chill spring air outside. Familiar book-lined shelves flanked the fireplace, crammed with classic English and American literature and poetry, most of which I'd read growing up. Nowhere on earth felt more like home to me.

Grandma trundled into the living room, assisted by her cus-
tom-made walker. Squeaky wheels announced her like a cow in an
Alpine pasture tinkling its bell. The walker itself was a four-legged
work of ingenuity. Its two front legs were wheeled, of course, and
the back two were fitted with tennis balls. She'd affixed a newspaper
stand on the railing, a rear-view mirror, and an air horn in case of
emergency. A basket held her purse and other essential items, like
wadded up Kleenex and a brown-speckled banana. For the coup
de grâce, a wooden panel hinged downward to convert the whole
contraption into a padded seat.

Grandma stooped over the front of the device, her warped
spine so kyphotic that her nose barely cleared the railing. I rose to
greet her. After I kissed her proffered cheek, she proudly refused
the sofas and armchairs in favor of the cushioned seat of her walker
cum chair.

"Grandma, I've rarely seen you looking so healthy. How *do*
you do it?"

"You really are full of the blarney, aren't you, lad? You come
by it honestly, at least. A Kilgore family trait." She spoke with a
forceful Irish brogue she could never quite rid herself of. "I look a
damn sight better than you, though, don't I now?"

"Now you've hurt my feelings," I chided. "Thanks for making
the effort to visit me in the hospital. I know it wasn't easy for you.
Do you know how I got hurt?"

"Course I do, love. You didn't look both ways when you
crossed the road, like I told you a thousand times when you was
a boy, and you got run over. Damn fool, you coulda been killed."

"Nearly was, Grandma, twice." And then I told her everything: the car plowing into me, perhaps intentionally, Raquel's
part in saving my life, and even that someone purposely injected

a huge dose of insulin into my IV bag in an effort to finish me off.

"Why would anyone want you dead? What did you ever do to them?"

"I wish I knew; that's partly why I'm here, Grandma, besides wanting to see you. The only connection I can figure concerns the very last case I worked on before the accident." I described Forestglen's plans to acquire the old Regency Tower, how I'd seen her father's name on several documents relating to the original land, and about discovering the bribes and killings surrounding the acquisition of the property. "Shortly after I told my boss what I'd discovered, my troubles began."

"I wouldn't know about all that, Frankie. All I know is Pa got lucky and sold his store for some good money. Only a couple years after we moved, he and my brother William was killed when their tractor hit a downed electrical wire. Me and my Ma inherited the ranch. You know the rest."

"That's not exactly true, is it Grandma?" I spoke gently, but firmly. "Henry owned a tavern, not a store, didn't he? And he and William were found murdered at the bottom of the Trinity River, not killed in some 'tractor accident.' I know the truth, Grandma. Because I stuck my nose where other people thought it shouldn't be, I got hurt. Maybe if I'd been aware of the facts, I'd have been more careful. Please tell me what really happened."

"Oh, Frankie. If I'd known any harm would come to you, I'd a'told you long ago. I only tried to protect you." Her gruff demeanor dissolved in a flood of tears, and she dabbed her eyes with a Kleenex from her basket. She stooped even further so that her face was barely visible behind a mushroom cloud of snow-white hair. I rose to catch her as she teetered above the edge of the stool.

But she summoned a reserve of will and righted herself, nearly ramrod straight. Surprised, I resumed my seat. She started haltingly. "'Twas in 1948, I think. Lost me whole family over that stupid land." Her voice trailed off as the memories seemed to surge back. I thought how old she was back then, only a few years older than Danny.

"Best I can recall," she said after a moment, "a bloke named Teddy O'Boyle, one of Earl Cannon's boys, came to see me Pa sometime in March. It was around Saint Patty's Day. Said they was about to build a sewage treatment plant right next to our neighborhood and the land wouldn't be worth a tinker's dam after that. He offered Pa thirty times market price if he would take the money quick-like, move out, and encourage our neighbors to do the same. Only he wasn't to say nothin' about the fancy price; they wouldn't be getting anything like us.

"But me Pa never was one to keep his trap shut. Some of the neighbors heard him bragging about the money he got. Two of them from the Cortez family next door went into the tavern one night, picked a fight with me brothers, William and Michael, and ended up dead. Those Cortez folks was real nice too, before the troubles anyways. Me brothers was tried for murder, but they claimed it was self-defense and they got off."

"That's right. A criminal trial resulted in their acquittal."

"If you say so, don't know much about that legal stuff. Anyways, that's when things really got heated up. The next day, Mikey ended up shot dead right near our house. William thought Ricky Cortez done it, so he killed him back. By then we was living in a state of siege.

"A couple years later, once we'd moved up to the ranch and we thought we could start breathing again, Pa and William disappeared. I think they was murdered to shut 'em up 'cause Pa couldn't keep his big trap shut."

"I read about it. Pretty grisly, the way they died."

"Ma was a basket case over it; never spoke another word the rest of her life, living in a kinda trance. So I had to run the family by meself at only eighteen. Had to grow up fast, I tell you. Figured I better not breathe a word of this to no one, never, 'cause everyone involved seemed to end up dead. That's why I never told you. Thought I was keeping you safe." She blubbered, "Did I do wrong, Frankie, did I do wrong?"

"No, Grandma. Can't blame a woman for protecting her family, and there are plenty of others to shoulder the blame. I'd have done the same." Grandma had lived nearly her entire life off the wages of sin, and so had I for that matter. But would anyone else have done things differently? "What about my parents?"

"That part of the story's the Gospel truth, Frankie. Me son, Sean, your sweet father, and your Mum, Claire, was killed in a car wreck back in 1971. Wiped clean out by a drunk driver who survived with nary a scratch, wouldn't you know? When they died, I finally cracked too. I took it as a sign from God that the ranch was evil gained and would always be cursed, so I sold it, fast as I could. Wouldn't you know, I ended up with more money than ever before. More *evil* money, Frankie, but no happiness and no family except for you and Danny. My destiny was writ when me Pa took that blood money.

"And then your Sam died too. I tell you it's all my fault and greedy Henry Kilgore's fault. I'm cursed, Frankie," she wailed. "The Kilgore Curse, that's what it is." Tears streamed down her cheeks, staining her peach-colored shirt. "And that curse still lives inside me wretched body. That's why I want to die, Frankie, to end the curse. If there's anything I can do to make up for what Pa done, tell me and I'll do it."

I stood and wrapped my arms around the spindly old woman, who besides Danny was the only family I had left in this world. How could I be angry with her? "Now, Grandma, buck up, you tough old bird. Maybe we can help each other after all. I'm working on a plan."

"Just ask for whatever you need, boy. And take good care of yourself, hear?"

"I will, Grandma, don't you worry."

I left the homestead that held so many fond memories, troubled once more to realize how it had been purchased. I'd been raised in the bosom of plenty, using money rightly belonging to others. Had Raquel's uncle been justified in spitting on my family's graves? Did I come from a line of crooks, or worse, murderers? What had really happened that night in the tavern? I was beginning to feel I would never know, or if I did, the cost would be higher than I was willing to pay. The entire situation depressed me so much that I decided to take a small Vicodin pick-me-up, just one. I'd work on weaning off them later. I seriously would.

CHAPTER
10

THE GENTLEMEN'S CIGAR LOUNGE, DALLAS COUNTRY CLUB
DALLAS, TEXAS
TUESDAY, JUNE 27, 1950

Those fuckers said what?" Earl Cannon addressed this comment to his son, Grant, and his trusted associate, Teddy O'Boyle. They sat in a private room of the oak-paneled cigar lounge at the Dallas Country Club. Earl didn't much like golf, but he recognized that being a member of this bastion of white male privilege offered him unparalleled access to most of the wealthy businessmen of the city.

"Don't get your arse in an uproar," said O'Boyle. "Me and the boys'll take care of them, soon as you give us the word."

Earl smiled wryly at his longtime friend. "Don't 'uproar your arse' me, Teddy. Just be a good lad and tell me exactly what the motherfuckers said, word for word, without any of your usual Irish bullshit."

Earl and Teddy had grown up as boys in their native County Clare around the turn of the last century, united by hunger and hardship. In 1912, aged seventeen, they waved indifferent farewells to Ireland from the steerage section of a tramp steamer leaving the port of Kinsale, neither one sad to be leaving their impoverished families.

Neither wished to see his abusive father ever again. But for the fire that burned within their empty bellies, neither one possessed more than the meager belongings on his back and a willingness to work. The bleak poverty and lack of opportunity in Ireland propelled them to leave like so many others to seek their fortunes in America. Despite all that, they kept in their heads a memory of their homeland, a love of its religion and language, and a fierce pride in Ireland and all its ancient warrior heroes and saints.

Earl was the flamboyant dealmaker, and Teddy was his reliable henchman. They were closer even than family. Earl entrusted Teddy with the task of handling any mischief occurring on his many properties. In teaching the nuances of the business to his son Grant, Teddy also proved invaluable.

Two men as different in appearance and temperament could hardly be found this side of Dublin. Even at fifty, Earl Cannon was razor thin. His jaw tapered to a boney chin, and his ferret eyes had all the warmth of an iceberg in winter. His voice affected the accent of New York's Upper East Side, but that attempt at culture hardly camouflaged the cold-hearted individual inside.

Teddy O'Boyle, on the other hand, was short, balding, and affable. He had big hands and broad shoulders. He was the sort of sociable bloke you'd enjoy having a beer with, but all of that served only to accentuate a viciousness barely concealed under his calm facade. When angered, he displayed yellowed teeth, and the scars on his raw-beef slab of a face turned livid and hideous. Others obeyed him immediately; he never asked twice. He was the perfect enforcer.

"OK, your Earlness." Usually Earl laughed and ignored this jibe, but sometimes he became angry. Either way, Teddy got a reaction.

"Cut the crap, Teddy, or I'll kick your fat, Mick arse from here to the Trinity River. Now, tell me exactly what the man said, damn your eyes." He was no longer smiling.

"OK, OK." Teddy knew exactly how far he could push Earl. "About two years ago you chose Henry Kilgore and his sons to shill for us 'cause you thought they'd be trustworthy, on account of them being Irish and not spics. Well, it turns out they ain't so trustworthy after all."

"Why the hell not?"

"Just yesterday, Kilgore had the gall to ask me for more money. Said he'd blow the whistle if we didn't sweeten the pot. Don't know if he spent the money on women and whiskey or if he just got greedy. Could be he found out what we're planning for that land and thinks he can blackmail us."

If Earl looked angry before, he was furious now. "The cheeky son of a bitch! Is that the thanks we get for getting him a better price than anyone else in his shithole neighborhood? That's how he rewards us for paying the best attorney in town to defend his boys on that murder charge, eh? Cost me an arm and a leg to pay that shyster Buckler, but it was worth it to keep that fool Kilgore's trap shut, 'til now." His eyes narrowed to slits, and he spat into a cup. He touched his groin to emphasize how important this matter of honor was to him.

"He says he knows them spics got lots less for their properties than he got, and he's grateful for that. He thanks you for hiring

Buckler too. But he thinks we couldn't have done the deal without his help. Says the spics never would've sold. He says he's going to the papers or the cops, maybe both, if we don't give him more money."

Grant said, "It's true, Pa, every word. He gave you a deadline, 'til tomorrow at midnight."

At that, Earl exploded into fury. "A deadline, is it? What a shithead! I ought to chop off his dick and shove it up his bleeding arse while I fuck him where he breathes." He appeared to choke over the thick wad of spittle in his throat. His face purpled, and the veins at his temples bulged. It took a few moments for him to regain control.

"Teddy," he said at length, "do you remember when we decided to leave Ireland together? We swore a blood oath that we'd take care of each other, no matter what."

"Aye, Earl. That we did."

They stood by it too. On the tramp steamer they shared scraps of food left over by the paying customers while one stood lookout for the other. When they got to New York, they holed up in a fleabag hotel and shared meals until they could gain decent jobs working on the railroad. And when roughnecks were needed to work the oil wells in Texas, they had done it together and saved every penny so they could start a business of their own. They had gotten good jobs in Dallas and bought their first piece of land, a little motel down on Motor Street. Then they bought more properties, and bigger ones, as the years passed.

"We took care of each other back then, didn't we, Teddy? We made money and built a successful business together, all based on trust. Our word was our bond, wasn't it? When I told me Ma I'd send money to look after her and the other kids, I did it, and you did too. Did we ever have cause to distrust each other? No. If I told you something or vicey-versa, we could bank on it, couldn't we?"

"That we could, Earl, that we could. Never did need them legal-flegal documents to make it proper. Our word was our bond."

"Now we eat fine food, we wear fine clothes, and we can afford memberships at the country club, where they don't allow niggers and spics and Jews. And we're about to embark on the biggest deal of our lives, maybe the biggest real estate transaction in Dallas history. It's all come about because we trusted each other, right, Teddy?"

"Absolutely, Earl."

"Then tell me, Teddy, what the fuck is wrong with the world today when you can't even trust your own countrymen? Didn't we promise that bastard Kilgore we'd make him rich if he'd only keep his trap shut and do what we told him? And didn't we live up to our side of the bargain?"

"We did."

"And what the fuck did he do instead? Got greedy and tried to blackmail us for more money, that's what. I'm sick at heart over it, Teddy, sick to fuckin' death I am."

"So, what do we do about it?"

"Do? I'll tell you what we do. Take a few of the boys and grab that cocksucker, Henry and his son, William. Take them up to the lake house and teach them some manners. Find out all they know about our deal and what they already blabbed to the spics. And when you're finished with the lessons, dump 'em in the Trinity as a warning to anyone else who might want to cross Cannon and O'Boyle. Make sure it's done real quiet-like. Ain't the other son, Michael, already dead?"

"Yeah. Some spics beat us to the punch. Saved us a pack of trouble."

"Good. Let's finish up with that godforsaken family once and for all. It would've looked too suspicious during the trial, but now we can wipe out the Kilgore line for good. Take young Grant here with you. It's time he learned how we Cannons handle certain business transactions."

Teddy smiled his yellow-toothed, shrunken-gummed smile. "Yes sir, Your Earlness, Sir. Consider it done." Kidnapping, torture, and murder—Teddy's favorite pastimes. All things considered, it would be a good day.

CHAPTER

11

DALLAS COUNTRY CLUB, AUTISM BALL
DALLAS, TEXAS
SATURDAY, MAY 17, 2008

A sickle-curved sliver of new moon and a sky full of twinkling stars brightened the night, but they could hardly compete with the glitzy array of torches, searchlights, and limousine headlights that illuminated the luxurious Dallas Country Club. My poor ride appeared decrepit in the company of Bentleys and Mercedes, Ferraris and Jaguars.

It would've been easy to refuse to attend Donald Chandler's favorite charity ball—after all, I no longer worked for the man—but in truth, I enjoyed the opportunity to visit the exclusive Dallas Country Club, where I'd otherwise never be welcome. And I'd already made the $500 donation, which went to a worthy cause. Plus, my walking had improved so much I'd been able to discard my cane for the occasion. More importantly, Raquel had agreed to accompany me, so instead of grouchy, I felt elated. Finally I'd have an opportunity to take my mind off the events that had dogged me since I first met her at the cemetery.

In the circular driveway, I accepted a receipt from the valet and then hurried around the car to assist Raquel out. I stood dumbstruck in front of her, still sitting in the passenger seat with her arm outstretched for me. She was dressed in four-inch heels and a full length, emerald gown that draped off one shoulder, accentuating her ample bosom. Her straight black hair was swept back, and diamond earrings matched the sparkle of her smile. My God, she looked gorgeous.

"McNamara, are you still with us?" She laughed and snapped her fingers in front of my face.

"Of course, Dr. Jennings, please allow me to assist you." I finally took her hand. "We've arrived at the renowned Dallas Country Club, playground of the rich and famous."

We strolled together, arm in arm, down an elegant red carpet to the entrance of the building. Or rather, she strolled and I floated, suddenly feeling no pain at all in my damaged leg. Upon entering the grand ballroom, we audibly gasped; the decorations were extravagant. A huge chandelier sparkled over the center of the room, and willowy beige ribbons were swagged to wall sconce chandeliers between the four entrances. Flowers draped over the ribbons and framed the entryways. Tables for at least four hundred people encircled a generous dance floor, and sideboards laden with a vast array of foods lined each wall, attended by liveried wait staff.

Raquel nudged me. "Can you tear your eyes away from the food long enough to buy a girl a drink?"

"Sorry, ma'am, got a bit distracted. Let's head to the bar. I guess as long as I don't drink more than my doctor, right?"

"Oh Frank, you're sooo clever. I've never heard that one before."

We made our way through the throng of thirsty partiers to one of the astonishing bars in each corner of the ballroom. The one we chose was made entirely of ice. Yes, ice. The countertop was an unbroken sheet of frozen water, and an intricate ice sculpture on top delivered a steady stream of iced vodka via a carved serpent's mouth. A trough underneath siphoned off the water as the bar itself melted, slowly but surely.

We looked at each other and smiled. "Guess I'll have vodka," she said.

We toasted each other's good health, mine especially, and wandered to the appetizer table for some caviar. "Vodka and caviar," I said. "Wouldn't it be nice to be rich and have this stuff all the time?"

"You'd just get fat and slovenly like most of the high society types here. I wouldn't want you to do *that*."

"What if I had one of those frozen bars at my house? Would you come over for a drink?"

"Only if your flood insurance was paid up."

We found table number forty-two near the back of the hall. You'd have to donate much more than $500, I supposed, to rate a table in front with the bigwigs. That was where all the socialites sat; you could guess the size of their donations from their table locations.

"Any idea how much of the money raised tonight actually gets to the American Autism Association?" Raquel asked. "Bet it's not that much."

"How cynical you are, doctor. Don't you trust anyone?"

"Nope. Even my patients lie to me all the time about all sorts of things."

"What's this world coming to? Bet you're right, though. By the time you rent the country club and pay for the band, the food, and the staff, there can't be much left over for charity. Maybe ten percent?"

"You think? That's disappointing."

"These affairs are mostly organized by wealthy people to assuage their consciences over the outrageous lifestyles they lead. This way they get a big fat tax deduction, they get to hang out with all their rich friends, and tomorrow, the ladies can critique each other's photos in the society pages of the *Dallas Morning News*. Best of all, other people pay the tab."

"Surely some of the effort benefits charity."

"If these folks really wanted to help out, why not just write a big check to their favorite organization anonymously and let their reward be the betterment of our society and the knowledge that they'd done some good? No, I think personal recognition and self-aggrandizement is the biggest part of these benefits."

"Enough, Frank. You're usually a much more positive guy. Take me out there; let's dance and try to enjoy the evening." She dragged me onto the dance floor where people gawked at the goddess and her gimpy escort.

"But I *am* having a good time."

"Oh, shut up and dance, Frank. Or just stand there and gyrate; I'll lead."

I shut up and danced the best I could. Now, I'm naturally stiff legged, and the limp didn't help much. But as self-conscious as that made me feel, she infused me with confidence, gliding elegantly across the floor. Somehow she managed to maneuver me yet make me feel as though I was leading her. She smiled the entire time even though I occasionally stepped on a toe or two.

Finally the band played my kind of music, a Texas two-step. I shuffled her around the floor forward and backward with all manner of spins in between. I felt no pain at all, but that two-step saddened me all the same; I'd learned it during dance lessons with Sam, years ago.

We returned to our table to find our vodkas had been snatched by an overly attentive waiter, so I volunteered for bar duty while she sat. On my way to the Ice Bar, I noticed none other than my former boss, Donald Chandler, across the ballroom floor chatting to a short, pugnacious looking man. Guess I'd have to face him sooner or later. Maybe after one more drink. I limped to the end of the line.

This time, an unusually aggressive queue caused me to slip on the slick floor, wrenching my fragile back. I twisted to catch myself, radiating an electric shock of pain down my left leg. I managed to maintain my balance, but for a moment I could hardly breathe from the intensity of it. When I finally received my drinks, I surreptitiously gulped down another Vicodin.

I returned to the table and set one of the vodkas in front of Raquel. "Thanks, Frank. You're such a gentleman. How's the back?"

"It's fine. Why do you ask? Am I limping that badly?"

"I saw you at the bar trying to keep your spot in line. I noticed you slipped and winced. You OK?"

"I still get these spasms now and then, that's all. I'm fine."

"That's a relief. 'Cause it looked like you were hurting pretty bad there for a moment."

"You're talking to tough ol' Frank McNamara, remember? No slip-up is going to spoil the party for me."

She leaned close and whispered, "You sure it had nothing to do with the pill I saw you popping with that vodka chaser?"

"How'd you see that from way over here?"

"Frank, I'm a doctor for God's sake. I've been trained to notice every little quirk in my patients, especially someone who'll be driving me home in a couple of hours. Vicodin and alcohol don't mix; I know you know that."

I let out a slow breath. "I'm embarrassed you caught me, but I'm also glad. I've been depending on Vicodin for too long. In the beginning I couldn't get by without it, but lately it's become a crutch. Those little pills numb me to the reality of my problems."

"I know how it is. Vicodin works so well that it's not at all difficult to become addicted. I've had two patients actually forge prescriptions on my pads. I held a 'Come to Jesus' meeting with them and helped them gradually wean themselves off the drug, and I'll do the same for you too, if you'll let me."

"How would you do it?"

"First you'll have to stop seeing that 'pain specialist' you've been seeing. He means well, but like most of them, all they seem to accomplish is to get the patient more dependent on narcotics or other addictive drugs. You start out with a legitimate need for analgesia, but the pain specialists never stop prescribing and increasing the dose whenever you ask."

"The pain doctor says I'm progressing nicely."

"Yeah, progressing nicely right down the pathway to drug addiction. After a while, it's usually time to taper the narcotics; only a rare patient needs them long term. The body can deal with most pain by itself if you allow it. I wish these guys cared a bit more about the entire patient and didn't just focus on pain control. Now we've got to undo the damage he's causing. How many Vicodin do you take per day?"

"Ten, more or less."

"More, or less?"

"OK, twelve."

"Excessive but not that unusual. We'll set up a schedule where you start with eleven a day for the next week, then ten, and so on 'til you're off them entirely. There might be times when you feel you've just *got* to have an extra one, but don't do it, or you'll set yourself back. You might feel some pain as you wean off the drug, but you'll be able to tolerate it, I promise."

"I'll do my best. Thanks for caring."

"I'm warning you, I'll give you enough pills for one week at a time, and that's all. If you run out too soon, tough luck. No amount of begging will change my mind. If you need help at a weak moment, you can call any time."

Before I could say, "Thank you. You are the most caring physician I've ever met," trouble loomed in the personage of Donald Chandler and his odd-looking companion. They made their tipsy way toward us, seated at our table near the back of the ballroom. We were trapped; too late to avoid them now. Trying my best to be proactive, I stood manfully to greet them.

"Why Donald Chandler, fancy meeting you here." I felt no need to show much respect to my obdurate ex-boss. "Sorry I had to leave the firm on such short notice. I don't think I've met your friend?"

Chandler scowled. "Oh, I believe you have, Frank. The three of us enjoyed quite an interesting meeting shortly before you left."

The man's round face, accented by a scruffy red beard, seemed to be jammed directly onto his torso. His short trunk was about the same width as its height, with a couple of stout legs stuck onto the bottom as an afterthought. Most incongruous of all, a mismatched hairpiece topped his bowling ball of a head.

He stood in front of me, grinning and staring with coal-black eyes. He offered a plump hand. "Hello again, Frank. Good to see you fully recovered. I trust you're feeling shipshape and working at another law firm by now."

There was no mistaking that gravelly voice. I finally shook his extended hand, my own engulfed in his meaty paw. I had to squeeze hard in return to avoid being crushed.

"You must be Randall Cannon, my former 'ultimate boss.' Nice to finally see you in daylight. I thought you were nothing more than a voice from a loudspeaker, kind of like the Wizard of Oz."

"Last time we met you were quieter and more respectful as I recall."

"Last time we met you were even more disrespectful. You interrogated me like some sort of terrorist suspect, not a professional working in your behalf. I don't owe you a thing, Cannon."

"If you think I've lost even one wink of sleep worrying about your bruised feelings, McNamara, think again. When you work for Randall Cannon, you do what you're told. Ain't that right, Donald?"

"Right as rain, Mr. Cannon," Chandler said.

"Donald, please don't grovel; it's a bit much."

"Whatever you say, Mr. Cannon."

Cannon renewed his assault on me. "But you, McNamara, you don't know when to stop, do you? You stuck your nose in places it didn't belong."

"And I'm not finished, either. There were plenty of shenanigans involved in building the original Regency Office Tower years ago that haven't yet seen the light of day."

"If you were a wise man, you'd drop the subject now before things escalate any further." He paused. "Anyone who gets in my way usually ends up getting run over. What's that? You actually *did* get run over." He laughed at his brilliant joke.

"You wouldn't know who was behind that accident, would you, Cannon?"

"Of course not, dear boy. And if I did, do I look stupid enough to tell you about it? Enough said. The subject's closed." He switched gears effortlessly. "McNamara, you're not only insufferable, but you've no manners either. You failed to introduce me to the fine looking lady next to you."

I'd unintentionally ignored her. We all turned to Raquel, still seated and looking radiant but aghast at Cannon's crudeness.

"Sorry, I didn't think you cared much about anyone but yourself, Cannon. This is Raquel Jennings. Raquel, meet my former employers Randall Cannon and Donald Chandler, if you hadn't already guessed."

Cannon's raspy voice became silky smooth. "Pleased to meet you, Ms. Jennings. What's a beautiful lady like you doing with a loser like Frank McNamara?"

"I must say, you truly are obnoxious, Mr. Cannon, even worse in person than what I'd heard. I'd much rather be seen with a kind, well-mannered gentleman like Frank McNamara than a boorish buffoon like you. By the way, the name's not *Ms.* Jennings; it's *Dr.* Jennings, and just so you know, there are some people whose loyalty cannot be bought."

"'Scuse me, *Dr.* Jennings, but I've found that most anything in life can be bought. It's just a question of price. I'd like to know what your price is."

"It'll be a cold day in hell before I'd ever sell out to a crude lout like you, at any price."

He turned conspiratorially to Chandler. "Here's a prime example of the problem with women today, Donald: too uppity and
outspoken. Daddy always maintained we never should've given
'em the vote, and it looks like he was right. The trouble with the
medical profession these days? Too many women and minorities
in it. You two ingrates deserve each other. Let's go, Donald."

He marched away with Chandler in tow, leaving chairs askew
and guests gawking in his wake. I collapsed into my seat, worn
out by the effort of dealing with him. I reached for the vodka, but
my hand trembled too violently. Raquel placed a hand over mine
to steady it. "You don't need it anyway, Frank. Vicodin and vodka
don't mix, remember? Was Cannon the guy in Chandler's office
that day you got ransacked?"

"Yeah. Doesn't seem like much of a coincidence any more,
does it? Thanks for your support with those two goons."

"I meant every word. In fact, I didn't go nearly far enough.
Words like 'obnoxious,' 'arrogant,' and 'conceited' come to mind.
I'm amazed you lasted as long as you did at that firm. You're better
off away from there even if you're understandably insecure being
unemployed at the moment. Getting fired will be a cloud with a
silver lining, you'll see."

"Quite a vocabulary for a dry, scientific type. You weren't an
English Lit major as an undergrad, were you?"

"Hardly. I buried my nose in Chemistry, Physics, Zoology,
and Calculus. And one or two other topics best left mysteriously
unexplained."

"Hmmm. I'd give a lot to discover the mystery."

"Maybe one day."

An intriguing couple approached our table and stopped to
introduce themselves. He was Caucasian, maybe fifty years old, tall

and physically fit, with a full head of gray, close-cropped hair top-ping an alert face. She was a striking, light-skinned black woman in a short black cocktail dress, cut low in the bust to accentuate her stunning figure.

She said, "Whew, talking to that guy looked like quite an ordeal. Hi. I'm Tracy Park, and this is my escort, Arthur Shapiro. We're sitting at the next table, but we couldn't help overhear. Is he always so hateful?"

"Pretty much, yes," I said. "The skinny one was my former boss at a law office; the fat one, Mr. Cannon, is the firm's biggest client. There's no love lost between us."

Raquel and I introduced ourselves and invited them to join us at the table. Shapiro seemed lost in thought, surveying the ballroom as if searching for someone. Tracy did the talking. "Why does Cannon behave like that? He looked ready to blow a gasket."

"He was just emphasizing something he wanted me to do," I said, "or rather, not do."

"Oh?" Shapiro finally spoke up. Despite his apparent inat-tention, he'd obviously heard every word. "What did he not want you to do?"

"Sorry. I can't discuss it, lawyer/client privilege and all that."

"I'm a lawyer too, Frank. When a client behaves that way, though, I would have thought the privilege no longer applied."

"Then you, of all people, should know that the privilege goes on forever, Arthur; you take your secrets to the grave."

Tracy smiled and caught my gaze. People in the vicinity turned to stare at us, or more probably, at her. You don't see beautiful black women dating white men every day in Dallas, especially not at the conservative Dallas Country Club. She said,

"Raquel, would you care to accompany me to the ladies' room? We ought to leave the boys alone to discuss these tedious legal niceties."

Raquel rose, and a moment later they were off, chatting about girl stuff as they left.

I chuckled. "Women always seem to need company when they go to the restroom, don't they? Tell me, what kind of law do you practice in DC?"

"Tax law, Frank, boring old tax law."

"I don't know how boring it is, but there never seems to be a lack of work for tax attorneys, even in a recession. I'm in real estate law, and I'm out of a job. You've still got one, so yours sounds pretty good to me."

"When the economy turns south, the first bill people don't pay is the IRS, which invariably causes tax problems. So we get busier than ever, and we get paid up front too. If you ever decide to move to DC, look me up. I might be able to find work for you."

"Thanks, I'll do that." We exchanged business cards. "What about Tracy? What does she do?"

"She works for me at the tax office."

"Tax office? I assumed you worked for a private law firm."

"Heavens no, we're with the IRS in the abusive offshore tax shelter unit."

"Then what are you doing in Dallas? We're hardly offshore."

He feathered his hair, removed his eyeglasses, cleaned them with a cloth he retrieved from his jacket pocket, and then replaced them, readjusting. "Like you, Frank, I'm under an obligation to maintain confidentiality. But, since you're involved, I *can* tell you a little about our investigation. I'm hoping to solicit your help in a serious tax fraud matter."

All I heard was "you're involved in a serious tax fraud matter," and my pulse began to quicken. The last thing I needed right now was a tax problem with the IRS. When those guys get their hooks into you, they never let go until they've extracted their pound of flesh. Yet I couldn't imagine my connection to any tax fraud. I always paid my taxes on time. "How am I involved?"

"As it turns out, we're investigating Randall Cannon. We think he's been hiding money in an offshore bank account in the Cayman Islands for years without paying any taxes. Owning an offshore account isn't illegal, but not reporting it and failing to pay taxes on income earned certainly is. We think your former boss, Donald Chandler, has been complicit in helping him do it. So far, we have no evidence against you personally. We'd like to meet with you to see if you can help us nail Cannon and Chandler. If you cooperate, we can offer you immunity from prosecution. Keep in mind that your ethical duty of confidentiality doesn't include staying silent about *ongoing* crimes. And believe me, this one's ongoing."

I thought back to a nasty experience with the IRS I'd had in law school on behalf of a client. I defended a legal Mexican immigrant as part of my Tax Clinic assignment. He had deducted $2,000 for supporting his parents, still living in Mexico. According to the Tax Code, it's a legitimate deduction, but the IRS auditors didn't see it that way. They hounded the man for over three years trying to recover $3,000 in taxes, penalties, and interest on his annual income of only $15,000. He eventually fled back to Mexico.

"What's holding you back, Frank? You're out of work, aren't you? Something more pressing on your calendar?"

As much as I wanted Chandler and Cannon to get what was coming to them, I was reluctant to partner with the IRS. But what choice did I have? The IRS can slap a lien on your bank accounts and garnish your wages if they so much as *suspect* tax evasion. They can even take your house for unpaid taxes. And the burden of proof is on the taxpayer to prove the IRS was wrong. "I assure you, Arthur, I have no knowledge of any offshore accounts. I'm just a real estate attorney. Since there's no love lost between me and Cannon, you'll find me most cooperative."

"I hope all that's true, Frank. I'd rather not take you down with those two. It would be a good idea for you to meet with us on Monday for a debriefing. I have to fly back to Washington tomorrow, so you'll be meeting with Tracy. She's my number one field agent and has my full confidence. If you're honest and forthright with her, I promise you'll have no trouble with the IRS. If not, well, let's just say you don't want to piss us off. For the time being, let's keep this conversation between the two of us and Tracy, shall we?"

"Arthur, you're not here tonight for charitable reasons, are you?"

"Not exactly, no."

I felt lightheaded. The two ladies returned, telling cheerful stories. Shapiro and I stood to greet them. Raquel whispered, "Frank, you OK? You look pale. Not another Vicodin?"

"No, Raquel. Must've eaten a bad oyster, that's all."

"Let's have another dance, then. I'm beginning to loosen up."

We danced some more. I tried not to slouch, or bob too much, or step on Raquel's toes. But above all, I tried to make it seem like *I* led *her.*

Despite our nasty confrontation with Cannon and Chandler and my nerve-racking conversation with Shapiro, we managed to make the best of the evening. By the end, we both could honestly say we'd had a delightful time. Somehow though, I couldn't tear my thoughts away from Cannon's threats, the IRS's investigation, the attempts on my life, and the feeling that they were all going to come crashing together.

I drove Raquel home in my trusty Beemer and walked her to the front door of her duplex. We stood on the porch, the sexual tension between us palpable. I wondered whether she'd invite me in; then I wondered what I'd do if she did.

"I loved tonight, Frank, thanks for everything. I enjoyed dancing with you and standing up to those thugs together. I meant what I said about you. And I meant what I said about the Vicodin too."

"I had a wonderful time too, Raquel, and I promise to wean myself off the Vicodin. It's beginning to interfere with my judgment, like enjoying myself too much in your company."

"Very smooth, you silver-tongued charmer. Can't believe I'm saying these things to an attorney. I don't usually have much fun around lawyers, too concerned about lawsuits."

"Don't worry, I'd defend you for free."

She leaned over and kissed me then, only a small peck on the lips, really. Yet the effect was euphoric. She entered her house, and the parted curtain in the adjacent duplex closed on Uncle Alfredo's surveillance.

I felt like a teenager who'd just stolen a kiss on a first date. But my joy was tempered by some trepidation over meeting Tracy Park on Monday about the investigations. What had I gotten myself involved in this time?

CHAPTER
12

WINCHESTER RIFLE RANGE
DALLAS, TEXAS
SUNDAY, MAY 25, 2008

I promised to give Raquel shooting lessons, so I picked her up for a visit to the gun range. I invited Danny along too; it would've been hard to explain why I'd left him out otherwise. As we drove through the concrete jungle of 'Little Mexico,' my mind drifted back to the meeting I'd had with Tracy Park this past Monday.

We met at an unremarkable office building in central Dallas. Though I was initially anxious, the meeting went off without a hitch. Tracy reassured me that the agency wasn't after me personally and only wanted my help in bringing Cannon and Chandler to justice. I reviewed the Texas Code of Professional Responsibility and convinced myself that the duty of confidentiality didn't include information related to *ongoing or future* criminal activity, and Tracy had little difficulty proving that Cannon and Chandler's illegal offshore activities were indeed ongoing. I admit I wasn't all that hard to convince.

She interviewed me about construction of the original tower and its pending sale, probing for details about capital gains taxes or any knowledge of offshore accounts. I agreed to check my files for the irregularities she laid out, and she agreed to give me written immunity from any prosecution as an unwitting accomplice.

Tracy claimed she already knew all about me and wanted me to know a little more about her if we were going to work together. She told me she'd been born and raised in New York City, and after a stint as a runway model, she caught on with the IRS and worked in the DC office. Shapiro then recruited her directly into his Offshore Tax Fraud Department, where she utilized her feminine wiles on highly-placed diplomats and presumptive tax cheats in order to entrap them and bust their tax avoidance schemes. Apparently she performed her job exceptionally well since she'd been promoted nearly every year, presently working directly for Shapiro, the head of the department.

Her silken voice seemed more suited to a romantic dinner engagement than a business meeting, but maybe that was part of how she duped the tax cheats and precisely why she was so good at her job. She conducted herself professionally the whole time, though, and when I left, I was glad I had agreed to meet her. The IRS didn't appear to be after me, only Cannon and Chandler.

Raquel lived in one side of a neat duplex while her aunt and uncle lived in the other. Though this part of Dallas encompassed one of the roughest parts of town, Alfredo wouldn't move and Raquel could never leave them, despite having ample funds to do so. I rarely ventured this far south of the Trinity River floodplain, but Raquel had been raised near here and apparently felt right at home.

The houses were interspersed with parched grass and a few withered live oaks. Beat up pickups sat in front of most of the homes, people lounged on their front porches after church, and kids played everywhere. No trash dotted the landscape, though, and there was nary a yard sale to be seen, definitely a step up the social ladder from Josue Fuentes' neighborhood.

I pulled into Raquel's driveway, and Danny waited while I got out to fetch her. The curtains parted again on Alfredo's side, and I wondered what he thought of my seeing his niece. The curtains snapped shut, and I thought I knew the answer. I rang her doorbell.

She stepped out, locked up, and guided me to the Beemer before I could say a word. "Let's get going before Alfredo begins the inquisition. He's worse than a father quizzing a teenage girl's first date, and I'm thirty-five years old."

"I thought I saw him spying on me."

"Oh, he's just keeping an eye out. If anyone wants to know what goes on in this neighborhood, just ask Alfredo."

"Like I said, spying."

Danny jumped out of the front seat and gallantly ushered Raquel in, then got into the back. "Nice to see you, Dr. Jennings."

"Great to see you too, Danny. But remember, unless we're in my medical office, please call me Raquel."

"Yes ma'am, Dr. Raquel."

"You've trained him too well, Frank."

"I'll take that as a compliment."

We drove up the freeway on a glorious Sunday afternoon. A few wispy clouds dotted the pale blue sky, and the temperature was neither too hot nor too cold, a rarity in Dallas. I was with two of my favorite people, driving to the gun range for target practice, one of my favorite pastimes. Best of all, my pain had diminished, and I could walk without limping. I'd also reduced my Vicodin intake to six pills per day well ahead of schedule and felt much more alert. I felt good—except, of course, that I had no job, was in the middle of a high-stakes investigation with the IRS, and had suffered two recent attempts on my life. I figured I needed the distraction.

At the Winchester Gun Range, we bumped along the pot-holed driveway past areas labeled 'Rifle,' 'Tactical,' 'Shotgun,' and 'Pistol,' with gunfire crackling from each of them; Raquel clasped her hands to her ears. The thunder of gun reports startles nearly every first-timer.

At the office we paid for targets and were issued yellow wrist bands; then we unpacked back at the pistol range and donned eye and ear protection. Once Raquel's headphones muted the gunfire, she relaxed a little, wiping her moist palms on her jeans.

A well muscled, off-duty police officer blew a whistle and bellowed, "Cease fire. Guns on the tables in front of you, locked open. Please step back off the line." When the other four shooters had obeyed, he motioned to us. "You can put up your targets now."

We swiftly pinned our targets to the cork boards about seven yards away, then retreated back to the benches. The officer hollered, "Eyes and ears back on; fire when ready!"

Danny loaded the Sig 9 millimeter and soon joined the thunderous fusillade from the other shooters, blasting away at targets bearing likenesses of the Ayatollah, Hitler, and Osama bin Laden. His bullets tore gaping holes in vital places. But before Raquel could join the fun, I had a few instructions for her.

"First we have to figure out if you're right-eyed or left," I yelled. Our ear protectors and the weapon reports made normal conversation difficult. "Which eye do you use for peering down a microscope?"

"We use binocular scopes," she yelled back.

"Then which eye do you use to line up a putt when you're playing golf?"

"Sorry, Frank, but I've never played golf."

"OK, try this. Extend your arm in front of you. Now stick up your thumb and position it over the target. Look at the target with both eyes open and then close the right eye. Did the target move?"

"Yes. It shifted to the right."

"Now close the left eye. Did it shift this time?"

"No. It stayed right where it was."

"That means you're right-eyed. So when you sight the gun, you'll close the left and focus with the right, OK?"

"Got it."

"Next lesson. Take this." I handed her a Smith and Wesson Airweight .38 Special, perfect for ladies to shoot for its ease of handling, light weight, and gentle recoil. I figured she'd end up buying something like the .38 if she ever decided to own a gun. In the office building, she had spotted a T-shirt depicting one with the caption, 'The Best in Feminine Protection.' She loved it.

"The cylinder opens like so. Load up the chambers. And never, ever, place anything you don't want to shoot in front of the barrel." She loaded the bullets and snapped the cylinder shut.

"Now you're ready to fire. You'll want to stand like this, with your left foot in front of the right, posture leaning slightly forward." As I reached around behind her to demonstrate the proper position, my arms enveloped hers. I couldn't help feeling aroused, and I convinced myself that she was enjoying it too. At least, she didn't flinch.

"Hold both arms straight out. Now line up the sights so that the little red dot on the front sight fits into the groove of the rear one."

No matter the amount of training involved, the first shot always takes novices by surprise. They're shocked at the noise, the power, and the recoil of a gun. They hear the loud racket of other guns discharging on the range and it's scary. So they anticipate their shot and the arms collapse, sending the bullet wild. Raquel was no exception. No telling where her shot ended up.

"That's OK, an excellent first shot." This time I held onto the gun overtop of her hands and showed her while I did most of the work. "Now pull the trigger back gently so that when the shot finally fires, it comes as a surprise."

I coached her through it, and fifteen or twenty shots later, she began to overcome her anxiety and gain confidence. Soon great gaps began to appear in the Ayatollah's head and chest, seven yards away. Even Danny nodded approvingly in between shots at his own target. I blasted a few shots with each of my guns at Osama bin Laden, leaving a nice tight pattern on his forehead.

We were surprised how tired we became from shooting. Maybe it was having to hold a certain body position or the adrenaline surge of shooting a deadly weapon and being continually concerned about safety. In less than two hours, we'd had enough.

After we removed the ear protection, we found ourselves still shouting. Not until we returned to the relative quiet of the Beemer could we tone down our voices. There's something exhilarating about sharing a frightening experience with another person and overcoming it together. We were higher than a cocaine junkie.

"Frank," she asked, "how did you become so proficient with your guns?"

"I grew up around guns on our ranch, and later I'd go hunting with family friends. Shooting just came naturally. Then I spent four years in the Army, right after high school. Eventually I became a Specialist First Class, expert at sniping and munitions."

"Were you ever involved in a war, overseas I mean?"

I winked at Danny. "Oh yeah. I did a tour in Iraq under the first President Bush for six months. Killed a lot of bad guys trying to blow up our troops or innocent civilians. My commander liked my work so well he offered me a promotion to Staff Sergeant and a big raise in pay all the way from $25,000 to $27,500 annually to stay on." I hoped I didn't sound too sarcastic. "But I'd grown tired of killing people by then and decided to return to school."

"Did the government at least pay your way through school on the GI Bill?"

"They would've, but Grandma Kate insisted the family had enough money to educate its own, so the government could use the money on some other deserving soul. Patriotic of old Grandma, wouldn't you say?"

"Yes, and darn unusual these days. Everybody seems to want all they can get from our government. Sort of, 'what can my country do for me,' not 'what can I do for my country.'"

"Yeah. Grandma's kind of old fashioned that way."

Raquel said, "Shooting those pistols was quite a rush. I'm pretty psyched up. Can we go to the gun store right now? I need to buy one before I lose my nerve."

Danny and I laughed at her eagerness. "Many people react just the way you did. You cringe at the first loud bang, but soon you can't stop shooting. Then you can hardly wait to own a gun of your own."

"Should I buy the revolver or the semi-automatic? Which one is better for home defense, which one for concealed carry? Do I need two?"

"That's it! You're not allowed to mention another word about guns 'til we get to Northwest Pawn and Gun. Then you and Keith Glenn, the owner and a *real* gun expert, can discuss anything you like, 'til Danny gets hungry that is. Danny, you hungry yet?"

"Just one more thing," she said. "Why do you measure some bullets in millimeters and others in inches? And how do I get a concealed carry permit? I could use it when I go to the hospital late at night, by myself, don't you think?"

"I thought you said *one* more thing." Danny and I glanced knowingly at each other. "All will be revealed in the fullness of time by the famous gun prophet, my good friend, Keith Glenn."

Considering its location near Bachman Lake's strip joints, the Northwest Pawn and Gun Store was a diamond in the rough. A large green sign announced its presence in an eclectic suburban shopping center, surrounded by a dentist advertising $99 root canals, a Vietnamese restaurant, and a check-cashing business. Three-foot cement posts stood at the edge of the sidewalk to prevent any vehicle from smashing through the plate glass windows into the store. I pressed the buzzer outside the front door.

When Keith saw me, his rosy-cheeked, Irish face widened into a broad grin. He was gruff and fiery, but his eyes twinkled. "Why, Frankie McNamara, how the hell are ya? And Danny, you look good, boy. Jan, come see what the wind blew in." He turned and bellowed that last command to his wife, who usually hid in a back office, counting money.

"Good to see you too, Keith. I've brought someone to meet you. She'll need your help choosing a gun. Dr. Raquel Jennings, meet Keith Glenn, the most knowledgeable purveyor of fine guns this side of the Pecos and the third largest gun dealer in the entire country."

"Pleased to meet you, Raquel. I hope you're not buying this gun to protect you from the likes of Frank McNamara?"

"No, nothing like that."

"What kind of gun did you have in mind?"

If ever a man were content with his avocation, that man would surely be Keith Glenn. He loved weaponry and made a splendid living from his passion. He was a short man with pudgy cheeks and Popeye-thick forearms, and he'd become quite well-off selling firearms.

Keith spent three years in Vietnam, where he fiercely protected his comrades-in-arms. He and Jan had no children; their family consisted of a wide circle of customers and buddies. For a friend, this man would give away nearly his entire store, but an enemy would never know peace. Keith would dog him to the gates of hell.

In about twenty seconds, Keith monopolized Raquel's attention. With a gentle, bear-like arm around her shoulders, he guided her from one end of the store to the other, showing off his wide selection of handguns and rifles.

As Danny wandered through the store, I chatted with Jan, who told us business was booming with all the Democrats in office. They made more money in the first year of any Democratic president's term than at any other time, and she asked us to pray for Obama to get elected and threaten a clamp-down on gun sales.

She asked, "How's Danny holding up?"

"He's still angry about his mom and doesn't understand why, but he's gradually coming around. It's hard to be both a father and mother, 'cause at this age, a kid needs both. I wish I could do a better job with him."

"Frank, there wasn't anything in this world you could've done to save Sam. You've got to get on with your life too. You can't help someone else if you're still grieving yourself. If me and Keith can help in any way, I'd be upset if you didn't ask us."

We heard Raquel and Keith returning after their tour of the store. Keith sounded delighted with her. "So it sounds to me like the .38 would be the most practical gun for you, Raquel, especially if you ever obtain your Concealed Handgun License."

"It was my favorite to shoot, but what if I need more than five bullets?"

"In a self-defense situation, you're not trying to hold off a foreign army. You're calling for help, trying to delay your attackers, and hoping they'll leave you alone and search for an easier target. You could get the 9 millimeter, but you need more experience to use it properly."

"I guess I'll take the .38. Tell me about the different brands?"

He instructed her about brand and weight, and she made her choices. "I'm selling it to you at my cost, so don't worry about price. Now all you've got to decide is stainless or blued?"

"The blued one is really black, isn't it? The stainless is much prettier."

"Ain't that just like a woman, Frank? Chooses a gun on the basis of sex appeal."

Raquel replied, "No need to be chauvinistic, Keith. What's wrong with having a gun that looks good?"

I said, "Good thing Jan didn't choose you on that basis, Keith."

He laughed heartily, and Raquel said, "Can I take my gun to the range right away?"

Keith explained the waiting period with the paperwork and background check required. "After they've checked you out and found you to be the loyal, law-abiding citizen I'm certain you are, you must pick your gun up here at the store, in person, so I'll get the pleasure of your company at least once more."

"Keith, I'm sure it'll be much more often than that. Just look at Danny, he's mesmerized." She gestured at him, starry-eyed over a Remington .338 hunting rifle.

"Next time we can discuss getting your CHL. Since the Feds have to check you out in advance to obtain that, once you get it, you can purchase any gun you like and walk right out the door with it, no weeklong wait required. I recommend getting in a little practice with your .38 first. Come see me next week."

The ride back to Raquel's house was a boisterous affair. She jabbered on about firearms, and Danny tried his best to answer her questions. I listened wistfully, enjoying the camaraderie and the growing friendship between them.

When we reached her driveway, we watched her walk to the front door and shyly wave. Everything about her intrigued me— the casual way she propped her sunglasses on top of her head to search for the house key in her purse, even her earnest concentration when she squinted into the sun to look back at us. I found myself hoping I'd be able to spend more time with the fascinating Raquel Jennings.

Once she was inside, I turned to Danny. "What would you think if Raquel and I dated more seriously?"

"I figured you would, Dad. I'm not blind. I know you loved Mom, but it's been four years. If you've got to pick somebody, might as well be her." This was high praise indeed, coming from Danny. "Even I have a girlfriend," he added proudly.

I sputtered, "You what? Why have I missed out on this? Who is she?"

"You never asked, Dad. It's Taylor Godsoe. She's in the ninth grade too. We've been sort of going steady for a couple months. Don't worry. We're not going all the way."

Sort of been going steady? Not going 'all the way'? Apparently my young son wasn't so young after all. He'd grown up under my radar. He sounded so self-assured, but I knew it was mostly teen-age macho bluster. I definitely needed to have a man-to-man talk with him; the birds and the bees, and so forth. Or maybe he could teach me something? I wasn't sure which. Four years is a long time to be celibate.

Taylor Godsoe, eh? I liked the name; I hoped I liked the girl.

CHAPTER
13

DALLAS, TEXAS
TUESDAY, JUNE 3, 2008, 5:00 P.M.

A lone at home and still out of work, I occupied my time nurturing my obsession with the Forestglen case. I'd sent out numerous resumes to prospective employers but hadn't yet received any responses. Law firms weren't hiring much in this economic climate, especially not forty-year-old has-beens.

So I delved into my computer file, and gradually, the picture came into focus. I began to believe that both Raquel and Josue Fuentes might be right after all.

I had plenty of evidence against the people involved in the dirty dealings concerning the development of the Regency Tower. In 1948, Cannon/O'Boyle acquired the land to build Regency Tower lot by lot from unsuspecting Latinos. They actually accumulated too much property, so they sold some of it back to the city for the construction of Harry Hines Blvd, at an extra profit, of course. Building that massive thoroughfare tore the Hispanic district apart; the area became an island of urban blight, but Cannon/O'Boyle cared little about collateral damage.

That was long ago, and most of the participants were dead or demented. What did I have on Randall Cannon and Donald Chandler? Were they behind the attempt on my life? Were they somehow responsible for ransacking my office and my house? Why was Chandler so interested in having me drop the case? And if Chandler had a hand in it, could Cannon be far behind?

Cannon's father, Grant, lived in a nursing home with advanced Alzheimer's disease, but maybe Grant's daughter, Jane Margolin, would talk to me. She ought to know something about Earl and Grant and possibly Randall too. She'd be old now but hopefully still alert, and maybe she'd want to clear her conscience like Grandma Kate.

How could I use the information as leverage against whoever was trying to hinder my investigation? And who pulled the strings? And why did they bother at this late date? I had my suspicions, but suspicions are hardly evidence as any criminal attorney will eagerly explain. The answer to each question seemed only to sprout new questions. Maybe Tracy could help with resources available to the IRS I couldn't access.

I also had to face the fact that my relatives might have been complicit in Cannon/O'Boyle's acquisition of the land for the original development if they acted as shills to induce poor Hispanic families to sell their land cheaply. There never was a plan to build a garbage dump anywhere near those properties, and the false information panicked most residents into selling cheaply.

Some Hispanic families held out, though. You could still see a few dilapidated houses scattered in the wake of the Harry Hines corridor like flotsam jettisoned from a cruise ship. The offspring of those lonely souls still lived there, surrounded by a concrete jungle of stanchions and roadways, liquor stores, and junkyards, because they refused to be intimidated like the Cortezes back in 1948 or couldn't afford to move.

On the other hand, the McNamaras seemed to have profited handsomely at the expense of their neighbors. That's how Josue Fuentes saw things. I'd been raised on those profits, leaving me feeling discomfited because, though my family members might have been the victims of murder, they could have been murderers too.

Maybe Michael and William Kilgore did indeed kill the Cortez father and son in self-defense, but the other deaths seemed premeditated. That's what Alfredo Cortez and Grandma Kate believed anyway, and the newspaper articles seemed to bolster their argument. Who had bludgeoned William and Henry Kilgore and left them to drown in the Trinity River bottom? And why? I had no plan yet, but I was determined to find the explanation and make things right.

The doorbell chimed, interrupting my contemplation. I entertained very few visitors these days, and Danny was supposed to be at his grandparents' home in Plano by now. Through the picture window of my study, a Dallas Police squad car was visible at the curb. Two uniformed officers were at the door. When cops arrive unannounced, it's never good.

The sight of them triggered awful memories of two state troopers arriving at Grandma's house over thirty years ago to notify us that my parents had been killed in a car accident. Grandma's knees buckled; she was too stunned to believe what her ears clearly heard. The cops guided her to a chair while I stood there mute, just a young kid frightened as much by her reaction as by their words.

Now my heart leaped into my throat once again. I realized I hadn't received Danny's usual phone call after school. The terrifying thought struck me that these officers might be there because of him, and I felt the same viselike grip in my chest as before. Waves of nausea struck me as my mind imagined the worst possible scenarios. I promised God anything, any service He required, if only He'd agree to keep Danny safe. I trudged on leaden legs to the front door and ushered the two cops into the living room.

They stood fidgeting while I absently sought a chair. They told me, as gently as possible, about Danny. Their words were initially incomprehensible; they seemed to be speaking some foreign tongue. I asked them to repeat what they had said. The second explanation was no better. I kept thinking they must've made a serious error; they must be talking about someone else's kid.

Their information, they said, came from the eye witness reports of Lane Godsoe, mother of Danny's girlfriend Taylor, and from other parents and students at the scene. Apparently Danny and Taylor had been walking hand in hand from the Junior Varsity building of their school to the parking lot where Lane waited in the carpool line. She offered Danny a ride home, but he said he had to wait to be picked up.

Lane had scarcely opened the passenger door for her daughter when it was slammed back in her face by two men racing by. She recoiled from the attack, and her right hand nearly got caught between the door and the frame as it clicked shut. By the time she regained her wits, she looked through the passenger window to see no teenagers there at all.

She jumped out and ran around to the passenger side, frantic. Taylor lay in a crumpled heap almost underneath the car. She moaned, bruised and semi-conscious, with blood oozing from a gash on her forehead.

Lane screamed for help, for someone to call 911, while she scanned the school yard. She couldn't see Danny anywhere though he'd been right in front of her not a moment earlier. Students streamed out of Plano High School as usual, no commotion any-where. But when Lane glanced toward the far end of the parking lot, she spotted him.

Two burly men, clad identically in black T-shirts and blue jeans, had a tight grip on Danny's arms. They were dragging his inert body across the parking lot toward an olive green van with no windows except on the front doors.

Lane saw one of the men holding a cloth over Danny's face while the other ripped open the back doors. They heaved him in, jumping in behind. Even before the doors slammed shut, the van roared out of the parking lot and promptly lost itself in busy traffic. Mrs. Godsoe tried to memorize the license plate, but then she turned her attention to her daughter as other parents and students rushed over to help. The entire episode lasted less than a minute.

Taylor was examined at Plano General Hospital, stitched up, and admitted for observation. She would be all right, bruised and hysterical, but all right. Danny's whereabouts were still unknown. Later that day, Lane Godsoe finally had time to reflect on things.

She provided a more detailed description of the kids' attackers and of the van. She insisted that the license plate ended in 'VGN,' but she couldn't remember the three preceding numbers. She figured there must have been a minimum of three men involved: two to grab Danny and one more to drive the getaway van. Finally, she thought that one of the assailants who'd grabbed Danny, the one who also held the cloth over his face, had a large black mole on his right cheek.

Finally I understood.

One of the cops said, "I know you're upset, Mr. McNamara, but don't give up hope. We have an incredible hostage unit, and we'll find him. We'll probably hear from the kidnappers soon, demanding ransom. So, with your permission, the Special Abduction Squad will be here within the hour to tap into your telephone so we can monitor any conversations if they call. They might be able to track them down using our advanced GPS technology."

I ushered the cops to the door, distraught. They kept trying to reassure me; they seemed so optimistic. I felt a lot less sanguine about ever finding Danny alive. I knew that well over fifty percent of kidnappings ended in something less than a happy conclusion.

Despite my resolve to rid myself of the Vicodin addiction and despite my promise to Raquel, I felt such pain at that moment, both physical and mental, that I raced to the drug cabinet and rifled through it for the narcotic. I swallowed two of the tablets dry. I picked up the phone and dialed Danny's cell on the off chance that this episode had been nothing more than a juvenile prank gone terribly awry. The phone rang interminably before his voicemail came on. Three more frantic calls ended with the same result. I slammed my phone back onto its carrier in frustration.

The officer had begged me not to give up hope, so in the days following the policemen's visit, I complied with every police request without complaint. I cooperated as they set up a telephone monitoring station in my house and gave them access to the few of Danny's belongings they said would aid in the investigation. I answered all their questions and stayed out of the way.

A week after the kidnapping, I'd not heard a word concerning Danny's whereabouts. I'd spent my time listlessly wandering about the house, waiting by the phone, and fighting despair. A Detective Cromarty was assigned to lead the investigation. I harassed him every day for updates, but I knew my inquiries were a waste of time. After all, wouldn't Cromarty have called immediately if something came up, if only to head off my incessant calls?

Raquel was a lifeline after the kidnapping, calling regularly and attempting to lift my spirits. She insisted we go to dinner to get me out of the house for a while, and she continued to try to wean me off Vicodin. She dragged me to the gun range for some diversion, but my mind was elsewhere. My aim was terrible, and even her positive energy couldn't cheer me up. But our relationship matured over that week.

No one ever called asking for ransom. The police developed no good leads, and no one came forth with any helpful information. I'd allowed the police to handle the investigation until this point and wasn't any closer to locating Danny than I'd been a week before. Hope dissipated fast, replaced by discouragement. At least the vodka dulled my senses.

I decided I had nothing to lose, so I determined to become more personally involved. My Army experience had certainly provided the training to deal with terrorists. It was time to put all that knowledge to work, but I couldn't do it alone.

I called Raquel to discuss the situation. When I needed a friend the most, she'd been there for me. She suggested consulting Josue Fuentes again. He knew nearly everyone of consequence in the Hispanic community, and maybe he could make progress where the authorities might be restricted by legal niceties. She said he certainly owed me and Danny since we had saved his life. Why didn't I call in a favor?

I couldn't dispute her logic, so I made two more phone calls: one to Josue Fuentes, the other to my gun-loving arms dealer friend, Keith Glenn.

DUPLEX OF RAQUEL JENNINGS
DALLAS, TEXAS
TUESDAY, JUNE 10, 2008

A long time would pass before I learned exactly what happened to Raquel the night of June 10, but eventually she shared the entire horrific story. Even once I knew, though, it did little to help. I wasn't there for her when she needed me the most . . . .

Raquel lounged in nightclothes on her still-made bed. She'd just hung up the phone with Frank, and an internal debate resurfaced in her mind. *Where is this relationship going? The guy is a sweet man, a good father, and he's kind of sexy too. But do I want to get involved with someone who already has a teenage son? And do I even want a husband when my profession demands so much of my time?*

She had a busy day coming up and decided she'd better get some sleep. Yawning, she entered the master bathroom and began to brush her teeth when she heard a tinkling, like breaking glass, at the opposite end of her unit. She turned off the tap and listened again, the toothbrush suspended in midair and toothpaste dribbling down her chin.

She heard muffled voices; someone had entered the house. She rushed to the alarm panel only to find it disabled. All its flashing lights were dead. She pressed the panic button, but there was no special siren, no alarm. Nothing at all.

Raquel knew that her aunt and uncle took sleeping pills every night and would be out cold until morning. So she raced to the bedside table and grabbed her gun and cell phone, silently thanking all of her saints that she'd finally gotten around to picking up the .38 Special from Keith Glenn. A simple plan came to her. She pulled down the bedspread, then stuffed two pillows inside and pulled the covers up again, simulating a sleeping person. She doused all the lights and retreated to the closet where she hid behind some hanging dresses.

She dialed 911 and whispered, "This is an emergency; someone's breaking into my house." She reduced the speaker volume but left the phone open on a shelf so the operator could listen, and she briefly described what was occurring.

She curled up in a ball and clutched her revolver to her chest, heart thumping like a deranged sub-woofer and panic nearly choking her. A three-minute eternity elapsed in terrified silence, but nothing happened. The pounding in her chest subsided a bit; the nausea began to recede. Gaining confidence, she decided to crack open the door for a peek. She began to twist the knob. Just then she heard a distinct scratching sound in the bedroom outside her door.

She retreated into the farthest corner of the small closet once more, heart hammering in her chest again. Heightened senses registered 'every sound, but she could see nothing in the closet's darkness.

Two men had entered her bedroom. They scanned the room with a blue laser light, noting the person asleep in the bed. They tiptoed to opposite sides and signaled each other, then flung off the covers and grabbed at their expected victim. They came away with only stuffed feather pillows.

Cursing, they turned to search the room more thoroughly. Finding no one, the two men again signaled each other for silence and pointed to the closet door, the only hiding place remaining. Raquel attempted to withdraw farther into the closet, but she was already flat against the wall, trapped in her corner behind some clothing. She held her gun straight out like Frank taught her, shaky but ready. One of the men slipped toward her hideaway.

He gave a nod to his comrade, then yanked open the door. He'd expected an easy mark but instead was greeted by two powerful rounds from Raquel's .38 Special. He lurched backward as if sucked onto the bed by a giant vacuum, bleeding profusely from hollow-point gunshots to his chest and shoulder. He writhed there, mortally wounded.

The other intruder jumped aside where Raquel couldn't shoot at him, though she tried . . . but only once. She knew she had just two bullets left now. Her hiding place no longer secret, she gathered her courage and hollered pleadingly into her cell phone for the operator to hurry some help to her. She waited there in her closet, cowering in the corner, praying for Alfredo or Matilda to respond to the shots or for the police to arrive. If you make yourself a difficult victim, an assailant is supposed to run away, isn't he? Frank and Keith had said so, but this guy wasn't frightened, and he wasn't leaving.

In fact he appeared more determined than ever. He didn't seem to care that her gunshots might have alerted the neighbors. He threw one of the pillows into the open closet, startling Raquel. She fired off one more round and the taunting began.

"Shot all your bullets now, haven't you, bitch? Might as well come out. I promise I'll finish you quick." He laughed dementedly. "Don't make me come in after you. Then I'll kill you slow, slice off little parts of you one at a time."

Raquel stayed put, too terrified to breathe, let alone respond to the madman. She prayed the police would arrive in time.

The man kicked at the door once more and feinted charging inside. She fired off the last bullet, missing wildly, and the gun clicked empty when she tried again. At that point, he reached into the closet, grabbed a chunk of hair, and hauled her out. She screamed and tried to kick his legs. She scratched and clawed at his face, trying to gouge his eyes, but succeeded only in ripping off his ski mask.

Enraged now, he held her at arm's length as she flailed at him. He slapped her brutally across the face, drawing blood. Then he pistol whipped her on the head, which rendered her nearly unconscious. He slipped the gun back into his pocket and pulled out a switchblade knife, which he methodically clicked open in front of her dazed eyes.

"Don't scream any more, bitch, or I'll gut you from stem to stern like filleting a fish." Even in her groggy state she understood the threat.

He slit her nightgown down the middle and peeled it away from her now naked body, admiring the firm, high breasts and supple figure for a moment. Then he traced a hand down from her sculpted chin to her triangular pubic tuft. The sight and feel of it aroused him. With one hand, he jammed a calloused finger into her while with the other, he loosened his belt and pulled down his briefs. He grabbed her long black hair and made her kneel, forcing her head back and her mouth open.

"You'll have to compensate me for killing my buddy though I admit he wasn't worth much anyways." He pushed his engorged penis toward her mouth. "Suck it or die, you cunt."

She hesitated, revolted, so he prodded her neck with the point of the blade until it drew a trickle of blood. She knew he would kill her if she resisted further, so she complied, gagging, nauseated by the smell. He grunted in excitement and pulled his member out of her mouth before ejaculation but couldn't prevent a thick wad of fluid from splattering her hair.

He threw her onto the bed, face down, knocking his bloody accomplice to the floor. He forced her legs and buttocks apart, the sight of her anus and swollen vulva driving him into a frenzy. He spat onto a filthy finger and jammed it into her again, preparing to enter.

At that moment sirens wailed nearby. The man stood up, suddenly alert and still. He listened for an instant like a vigilant prairie dog and finally seemed to grasp his predicament. Then he straightened, viciously smacked her on the head once again to knock her unconscious, and hurried out of the room.

Raquel lay on the bed, naked and spread-eagled, fighting to regain consciousness. A couple of minutes passed before she dared move. She attempted to stand, only to topple over on top of her dead assailant. She lurched off him onto the floor and lay there groaning, semi-conscious, and bleeding.

As if in a fog, she heard policemen enter her apartment, hollering orders, clearing room after room as they advanced toward her. Eventually they made their way to the bedroom, guns at the ready. There they found Raquel still naked, humiliated, and sobbing on the floor beside the dead intruder.

"Raquel, thank God I finally found you." I'd rushed to her Intensive Care Unit room at Methodist Hospital just as soon as I got the news of the assault, but it took far too long. "In the ER they said since I wasn't a relative, they couldn't tell me anything because of HIPAA regulations. I had to search all over this damn hospital." Except for her head bandages, she looked well enough, but I knew that could be deceptive. "How do you feel?"

"All right I guess, Frank. Thanks for coming." She sounded groggy and remote. "I've got a thunderous headache and a lot of bruises, but I'm alive. I should be thankful, I suppose, but I really don't care much one way or the other."

"What do you mean?"

She fidgeted with the cropped hair on the left side of her head, where a specimen had presumably been taken. Her hand recoiled as from a poisonous snake when she realized I was staring.

"I feel unclean, Frank. Used. I'll have to live with this for the rest of my life."

"Raquel, there's not a thing in the world you could've done differently. None of this is your fault. I know you feel about as badly as any human being can feel right now, but you're going to make it, and I'll be with you every step of the way. Besides Danny, you're the most important person in the world to me. I owe you my life, and whoever did this to you will pay."

"Frank, you've got problems enough of your own; don't get involved in mine." She let out a sob and clutched my hand. "You saved my life too, don't forget."

"How do you figure that?" I savored her touch, even in her distraught condition.

"If you hadn't helped me buy a gun and taught me to use it, those guys would've killed me. You should've seen them, Frank; they were like crazed animals. I killed the smaller one, did you know that? But I ran out of bullets. The police say the only reason I'm alive is that I didn't panic and fought back. You taught me that. Otherwise I'd be dead; I know it."

"I sure as hell hope this didn't happen because you've been hanging around with me. Whoever 'they' are, they seem to be after me and anyone close to me. So I'm going to do whatever I can to make things right."

"Don't get yourself hurt. You're a lawyer, for God's sake, not a detective. Let the police handle it. Please."

"Don't worry about me. I only seem like a nice guy." I smiled. "Deep down, I'm a vicious beast."

That finally made her laugh. "Oh sure. You're a vicious beast, and I'm Jennifer Lopez. Hey, how'd you know I was in here anyway? In the hospital, I mean."

"You called me a few hours ago. Told me most of the gory details in fact. Don't you remember?"

"No, I don't. Maybe it's a good thing they're doing the MRI this morning. Any word on Danny?"

"No. The detectives have got little more to tell me than they had last week." My anger and frustration at the situation with Danny, never far from the surface, threatened to boil over at her mention of it, but I drew a steadying breath.

"Sorry." She sighed and briefly closed her eyes. "I'm getting tired, Frank. 'Fraid I'm not great company today."

"Get some rest. See you tomorrow if that's all right."

"I'll look forward to your visit."

I rose to leave. As I bent over to give her a peck on the cheek, she recoiled slightly and turned her face away. My heart sank. I turned for the door.

"Melanoma, that mole's gotta be melanoma," she mumbled as she dozed off.

I returned to her bedside. "What do you mean?"

"His face, that hideous face. I hope that big, black mole turns out to be a melanoma. It looked like one. Hope he dies a horrible death, with metastases in his lungs so he suffocates slowly. If I ever see him again, I know one thing—I won't run out of bullets next time."

"Are you saying the rapist had a big, black mole on his face?"

"Yes, on his right cheek, what of it?"

"My paralegal said the guy who busted up my office had a black mole on his right cheek. And the police report on Danny's abduction says one of the kidnappers had a black mole on his cheek too. Raquel?"

"Mmm, that so?"

She fell asleep, or the drugs got to her. It didn't matter. I wouldn't wake her. The man she'd just described must be the same one who took my son from me and trashed my office and probably my house too. Now he had raped Raquel. Maybe he was a hired killer. Hopefully we would be able to identify him from the DNA taken from Raquel during her exam. Whoever he was, I decided then and there that I would find him, and I would find out who sent him. When I did, I would kill them both. I didn't know how just yet, but I would do it somehow.

JOSUE FUENTES' HOUSE
SOUTH DALLAS, TEXAS
FRIDAY, JUNE 13, 2008

This time I made my way unerringly through the hovels of the Hispanic ghetto in South Dallas to Josue's house. His neighborhood seemed frozen in time except for the recently stripped remains of an abandoned car down the road. It looked like a big game carcass after the vultures picked it clean.

Josue had offered his help with the investigation into Danny's disappearance. A pang of regret assailed me when I remembered that my son had been with me on my last visit here. I avoided the pothole in Josue's driveway, near the spot where we resuscitated him, and walked up to his dilapidated porch. I rang the doorbell and heard the familiar tap-shuffle-tap of Josue's foot and cane as he approached the door.

"Good to see you again, Frank," he said, his voice subdued. "Sorry about the circumstances."

Little was different inside the house except the dim light bulb above his desk had been replaced by a brighter version. The books there were gone, replaced by a stack of old newspapers.

"You look in good health, Josue."

He rasped, "Do they teach that crap in 'Blarney School' or are you just full of it naturally? I guess I feel pretty good, considering. *You* don't look so good though I understand why. Awful what happened to Danny. And poor Raquel. "

"I feel like I'm drowning, Josue. My chest's so tight I can't take a deep breath. I've got no appetite, no motivation, no interest in life anymore. I can't sleep at night because of horrible nightmares, and I'm drowsy all day long. If it weren't for Raquel, I'd probably have seriously harmed myself by now. Look what happened to her for trying to help me."

"I know. The bastards are so chicken-shit they've got to come after women and children. No honor anymore."

"Raquel will heal in time, physically at least, but she's got deep emotional scars. Who knows if she'll ever be able to cope with those?"

"Do I sense more than just a professional interest?"

"Maybe. Right now we've both got more serious problems to deal with."

"I heard she killed one of her assailants with the gun you helped her buy. Good for her; that girl's a fighter."

"She is that. But if she hadn't met me, she'd probably never have been in that situation in the first place. Then there's Danny, just an innocent kid. I'm convinced he was kidnapped because I'm his father. I haven't heard any news in over a week, and I'm becoming desperate."

"Don't blame yourself for events you can't control. Do they have a suspect?"

"Maybe." I described how a man with a distinctive mole had been spotted in each circumstance. "The cops ran witness descriptions, reconstructive drawings, and a few random finger-prints through their database and came up with someone named Ricky Brunelli. It's possible the same guy ran me over in the parking lot too. I think these incidents are all somehow related and that Brunelli may be the perp. We'll know for sure once they finish processing the DNA they recovered from the man who raped Raquel."

"What makes you think the incidents are related?"

I described my investigation into the Regency Towers project and the corruption I'd uncovered, enough to make the City Council think twice about allowing the new Solar Towers redevelopment and enough to put several important people behind bars. "I think those developers know what I'm doing every step of the way and don't want anything dug up that could interfere with their plans. They're trying to send me a message. They're trying to shut me up."

"How could they possibly learn what you do on your own computer?"

"You're not a big technology buff, are you, Josue? Anything that goes on the internet these days can be exposed by a determined hacker. Criminals are hacking into credit card companies, medical records, and even the Pentagon nowadays. These guys have the money to buy talent like that. They might've bugged my house or hidden a device in my computer, but somehow they always seem to be one step ahead of me."

"They're trying to discourage you from pursuing your research or releasing your information to the public."

"Exactly. First they attacked me personally, and when that didn't work, Danny and Raquel became more convenient targets. By the way, this Ricky Brunelli goes by the alias of 'Psycho' and has a rap sheet as long as your arm. He may also have connections to the New York mafia. You can imagine how much comfort it is for me to know that a cold-blooded killer like that has my son."

"No es bueno, not good at all. I owe you and Danny for saving my life. What can I do to help?"

"Actually, Raquel said nothing of consequence really happens in Dallas that you couldn't find out. She said certain people make it their business to know what's going on, and you might be able to call in a favor or two and find out where Danny is."

"That's a tall order, Frank. Dangerous too. We'd be dealing with the Mexican Mafia, maybe even the Zetas. I know some of them for professional reasons, and you can't imagine how ruthless those gangsters can be."

"I wouldn't ask if there were any other way. So far I've played by the rules and got nowhere. All I know is that a psychotic Mafioso hit man has kidnapped my son. I'm crazy with worry. I'm ready to try anything."

"I still have a few connections in this town, at least with Latinos; some in high, some in low places. And many of them owe me. I'm not making any promises, Frank. The Dallas police are a damn good organization. If they haven't come up with anything, I'm not sure my sources will do any better. I'll put the word out, though, and let you know immediately if I hear anything."

"That's all I can ask. I don't know where else to turn."

"No problemo, mi amigo. I don't forget my friends."

"Thanks again." I turned to leave.

"Just a minute, Frank. Before you go, I'd like to show you something interesting. I've pulled out the report of the murder trial of Henry and William Kilgore, with Randall Buckler as the lead defense attorney. You recall they were acquitted by an all-white jury, hence my interest in the case?"

"Yes, I do. What's that have to do with Danny's abduction?"

"Bear with me. I tracked down old 'Swash' Buckler to a private nursing home in Abilene. He wasn't the least bit reluctant to discuss the Kilgore murder trial, even over the phone. He knew he ought not to talk about his clients' secrets, but he claimed he no longer cared much for the rules. Said the law didn't seem to be the answer anymore, that maybe too much law was the problem. I think he wanted to get something off his chest that had been gnawing at him, a kind of absolution."

"I'm not much of an observant Catholic," I said, excited now, "but I know all about absolution, administered on Sunday and broken by Monday. And I'm very familiar with so called 'legal ethics' that are usually adhered to with a wink and a nod. So what did he tell you?"

"So young and yet so cynical, Frank. Not everything about our church or our common profession is corrupt. Much good comes from both of them."

This wasn't the time for a debate on the merits of either. He had me captivated; I needed to know the answer. "Maybe. OK, OK, you're right. What did he say?"

"Brace yourself. He told me that your relatives, Henry and William Kilgore, were 'guilty as sin.' His words, not mine. He said the entire disagreement between them and the Cortezes could've been resolved amicably, but the Kilgores grasped the opportunity to rid themselves of a potential problem. Shot one of them while he lay on the floor, in fact, to make certain he died. And made damn sure everyone else in the bar was sworn to silence."

My heart sank. "I was hoping the Kilgores acted in self-defense. But we do know that the two Cortezes walked into the Kilgore Tavern and confronted the Kilgores over something, and it must have been plenty serious for them to have been so aggressive."

"Self-defense doesn't appear likely after my conversation with Mr. Buckler, but the all-white jury did see it that way. In any case, even more interesting is what he told me about his fee. Remember we wondered how a family as poor as the Kilgores could afford the services of a high-priced attorney like Buckler? He says he was paid in cash, a briefcase full of it, by the original developers of the Regency office tower, Cannon/O'Boyle. It was delivered by a man named Teddy O'Boyle, and it was the largest legal fee he'd ever earned to that point.

"And he said the same people posted the Kilgores' bail. They even paid for a psychologist to help Buckler choose a more favorable jury. Using trained professionals for a juror's psychological profile was almost unheard of in those days. Of interest to me personally, he also admitted that he manipulated the jury selection process to ensure that all Hispanics were excluded. It wasn't illegal then, but it is now, thanks to Pete Hernandez."

"And to you, Josue, especially to you. Whatever happened to Hernandez, by the way?"

"We got Hernandez a new trial all right, with lots of Hispanics on the jury this time. But they still found him guilty, which he was. I know 'cause he told me. They sentenced him to life in prison, where he eventually died in a brawl with some other inmates. You'll forgive me if I just violated certain legal ethics myself by telling you this, and I'll trust you to keep it confidential, but the man *is* dead."

"The wheels of justice do seem to work in mysterious ways, don't they?"

"That they do, Frank, that they do."

I rose to leave once more. "Josue, I want to thank you in advance for any information that might help locate Danny. I don't care where it comes from; in fact, it's probably better if I don't know. I'm determined to get him back, by any means necessary."

"One more thing, Frank. No need to rush off yet." I surmised that the lonely old man enjoyed my company and was loathe to see me go. "Wouldn't you like to know just how mysterious the ways of our justice system really are? If you've got a couple of minutes, take a look at those newspapers on my desk. I think you'll find them riveting."

"Careful, they're fragile," Josue warned me. The papers were brittle, and I handled them gingerly. Even so, the slightest touch kicked up a fine mist of dust. I found two of them folded open to pages concerning Canuto Cortez.

"Read the left-hand one first," he said. I did and was once again transported back in time to an expanding Dallas of the 1940s.

DALLAS MORNING NEWS, July 17, 1944
Brothers Slain, Two Charged With Murder in
Tavern Brawl

> *Charges of first degree murder were filed against two of the alleged participants in the Sunday evening knife and razor battle between the owners of two neighboring taverns in Little Mexico. Charged were former Golden Gloves Champion Canuto Cortez and his partner, Lupe Gamino, proprietors of the Gato Negro Taverna. Both men were also*

slashed in the battle, treated at Parkland Hospital and later released. The charges, filed by City Detective E. L. Gaddy, were accepted and docketed in Justice of the Peace W. L. Sterrett's court.

The two victims of the attack were brothers Jesse and Lee Orozco, owners of the Cantina Nueva, located just three doors away from the Gato Negro at 1315 McKinney near Field. The quarrel and knifings occurred about 1:00 a.m. Tuesday night in the Cantina. The fight apparently started after the Orozco brothers ejected Cortez and Gamino from their tavern. The two are said to have returned a short time later, brandishing knives. The Orozcos then produced their own weapons, and the fight was on.

By the time Patrolman E. B. Howard arrived, all four belligerents were laid out on the sidewalk in front of the Cantina. Jesse Orozco was pronounced dead at the scene, and Lee died on his way to Parkland Hospital. Cortez and Gamino were released from custody after posting bonds of $2,500 each.

"So Little Canuto wasn't such an angel after all, was he?" I muttered. "Looks like he provoked the Orozcos just like he provoked the Kilgores. Too bad he didn't receive a longer sentence. He might still have been in prison by 1948 and never been in a position to get himself and his son killed. But you can't change history, can you?"

"No, you can't, though it's fun to imagine," Josue replied. I must've been muttering louder than I thought. "Makes no difference anyway. It is what it is. God has his own designs for us, and man is not privy to His deliberations."

"So true. But surely we've got to try doing the right things?"

"Course we do. As the prophet Obadiah once said, 'Do justice, love goodness, seek no surfeit of gold, and walk modestly with God.'"

"I'm no biblical scholar for sure, and I've never heard of Obadiah. What he said sounds like good advice though why bother if the course of our lives is pre-ordained anyway?"

"That's a difficult theological question, Frank, and I certainly don't have all the answers. Canuto Cortez surely couldn't escape *his* fate, could he? You were wondering why he didn't serve a longer sentence for the murders. In fact, he didn't serve any time at all. He and Gamino were no-billed by a Dallas County Grand Jury and set free. White Grand Juries didn't seem to care much if crazy Mexicans killed each other in those days. Was he lucky or unlucky?"

"Both, I guess; lucky to get off the murder charge, unlucky he was in the Kilgores' bar at the wrong time. All in all, was he a good person or bad?"

"Both again," he answered. "Like most of us, you can't define him in black or white. The real world is done in many shades of gray. He seems to have been a strong family man, concerned about justice, his neighborhood, and his daughter's honor. Ultimately he became a victim himself. Yet he flirted with the wrong side of the law and killed two people unnecessarily. If you feel ambivalent about his life to this point, wait 'til you get a load of the second article."

"Before I do that, tell me about the judge in the case, W. L. Sterrett. Is he the same Lou Sterrett the jail in downtown Dallas is named after?"

"One and the same. Sterrett was a renowned jurist in those days. I knew him well, a fair minded man."

I turned my attention back to the newspapers and began the right-hand article. This paper was considerably older and, if possible, even more like parchment. I read without touching it. I didn't even breathe on it.

DALLAS MORNING NEWS, September 19, 1932
He Broke the Law, But It Was an Honorable Act, So He's Freed

They called Dan Cupid as an expert witness Thursday, in the Federal trial of Golden Gloves Champion Canuto Cortez, for harboring the woman he loved. The case was brought before Judge T. Whitfield Davidson. Cupid testified to the age-old axiom that love laughs at locksmiths and immigration laws. It was love and love alone that prompted Cortez to bring a woman into the United States from Mexico, his attorney told the Court, and for that he was due consideration.

Cortez bought the Gato Negro Taverna in Little Mexico a while back. Among the waitresses working there was a beautiful dark-eyed señorita named Mari Ortiz, with whom Cortez fell deeply in love. The love was returned, but suddenly the lovers were torn from each other's arms when she was arrested by immigration officers. Cortez poured out his heart to the officers, but they told him to forget the woman, that she was probably unworthy of his love, and they deported her.

She wrote her lover that she was with child. Cortez consulted an attorney who advised him to bring the girl back for the birth of their child, making it an American like its father and probably avoiding her deportation.

Three times Cortez tried to cross the International Bridge over the Rio Grande with her, and three times immigration officers headed him off. Finally Cortez paid another Mexican man a $15 fee to wade through the river with her in the middle of the night. Cortez waited on the American side for the woman he loved and brought her back to Dallas.

A baby girl was born. Then came the immigration officers again, along with the charges against Cortez. Last week she walked into the Gato Negro crying bitterly and threw beer in Cortez's face, proving the immigration officer's assertion that she was unworthy of such love.

"This man has broken the law," said Judge Davidson after hearing the evidence. "But in breaking it he has done an honorable thing. I will fine him $5 for the violation, but for his honor I will set him free. Unfortunately, Miss Ortiz is still an illegal alien, and I order her deported once again. Her trespass cannot go unpunished. The baby is an American, however."

Cortez paid the fine.

I sat back down across from Josue. "What a story." I laughed at the travails of Canuto Cortez, flummoxed like so many other men by a woman's love. "You couldn't make this stuff up. Truth sure is stranger than fiction. I love the linguistic turn of phrase the reporters used back then."

"Quaint, wasn't it? What do you think of Canuto now? Saint or sinner?"

"Both, I suppose. Basically well intentioned, but he treats the law as a contrivance to be observed only when it's convenient.

I know this: I'm gaining a lot of sympathy for the little man. I also know that he's given me the first good laugh I've had in a month. Do you know what happened to Mari Ortiz and her baby?"

"As a matter of fact, I do. Mari was eventually deported to Mexico again and never returned to the US. Her daughter was named Carmen. She grew up right next door to your Kilgore relatives with her three brothers Ramón, Enrique, and of course, Alfredo. Those three boys, incidentally, were sired by Canuto with various, unidentified mothers. Quite a Lothario, wasn't he?"

"Damn, but he did get around. How'd you discover all this? It wasn't in any newspaper I saw, and I looked, believe me."

"Like you said, I've got connections. Lots of people remembered Canuto Cortez and the feud that wiped out nearly his entire family."

"Tell me, besides entertaining me for a while, is all of this business about Canuto relevant to Danny's kidnapping?"

"Maybe. You already know how the three sons turned out. Did you ever wonder what became of the little girl, Carmen?"

"You're going to tell me, I'm sure."

"You haven't figured it out already?"

"No, but don't keep me in suspense."

"She grew into a beautiful, dark-eyed senorita, just like her mother, but with her father's passion. Unfortunately, she fell in love with a scoundrel, got herself pregnant at the young age of sixteen, and died giving birth to a baby girl in 1948. Care to guess who that child grew up to be? I'll spare you this time. She was Raquel's mother."

I nearly fell off the chair. Of course, it had to be. I'd been so involved with Danny's disappearance I just couldn't see it. If Carmen was Raquel's grandmother, who the devil could the grandfather have been? And how did all this figure into the Regency Tower development?

CHAPTER
16

DALLAS PISTOL ACADEMY
DALLAS, TEXAS
WEDNESDAY, JUNE 25, 2008

The summer sun smothered the city like a woolen blanket, the air so oppressive with heat and smog that people shuffled on leaden legs as if drugged. A noxious, brown haze hovered overhead like the Angel of Death, requiring yet another ozone alert. And unwholesome air created by 100-degree temperatures, combined with the exhaust of a hundred thousand automobiles, choked anyone outdoors.

Raquel and I braved the blast furnace to reach the Dallas Pistol Academy, where we practiced our marksmanship on adjoining shooting lanes in air-conditioned comfort. I had a Concealed Handgun License and carried a .380 Kel-Tec with me at all times, and because of her own particular tragedy, Raquel became determined to obtain her CHL also. The Academy offered twenty lanes for pistol shooting and another three for rifles. It also offered CHL handgun training.

Raquel's twinkling eyes had become piercing. Her strong face stared stolidly ahead, full of fury. She looked sad and more disheveled than before but still striking. Much practice made her deadly accurate with the new Sig Sauer 9 millimeter pistol she'd purchased from Keith. She blasted away at her homemade target, a drawing of a vicious-looking thug with a large black mole on his right cheek. I noticed most of her shots were to his head or groin. When she'd finished with that one, she continued tearing up two more targets she'd purchased at the range.

Last week she had taken the eight-hour instructional course for the license and passed the shooting portion of the test without difficulty. She'd also been photographed and fingerprinted for the background check. Had to be sure she wasn't a felon in order to purchase her gun legally; the felons can get theirs illegally on the street easily enough.

We stepped outside the shooting area and removed our eye and ear protection. We could still hear the irregular thud of high-caliber weapons discharging inside. I hugged her in congratulation for her improved marksmanship. Her permit would arrive in a couple of weeks, but in the meantime she wasn't awaiting official approval; she went nowhere without her gun.

When I placed my arm around her shoulders, though, she stiffened and stood there tense, devoid of the exuberance she'd shown before. "Raquel, is something wrong? Is it me?"

"No, Frank, it's got nothing to do with you. It's just this giant elephant in the room, my obsession with Mole Man. It spoils my feelings toward all men. I see him everywhere I go, especially at night. I picture him barging into my bedroom to attack me. But I'm not afraid anymore; I'm prepared. I keep a loaded gun under my pillow. I've practiced killing him a thousand times, but I'd rather torture him first, make him suffer for what he did to me."

"I can understand that, but it's not fair to compare me to a psychopathic killer like Brunelli. I'm nothing like him; you know that."

"Of course I do, objectively anyway. I just can't seem to control my emotions. What did you call him? Ricky Brunelli? 'Psycho' Brunelli? He'll always be the 'Mole Man' to me."

"Might as well be Mole Man as anything else. The cops have identified him as a career criminal—murder, extortion, burglary, and rape. I know this'll sound crazy, but you were actually lucky. You could've been killed by that maniac but for your quick thinking and your gun. He's raped and killed many others in the past."

"Some consolation. I don't feel lucky. I feel degraded and demeaned. I bathe and gargle several times a day, but that man's presence never leaves me. Sometimes I feel I'd be better off if he had killed me."

"Don't talk like that. I'm no doctor, but I'm familiar enough with cases like this to know you will get over it in time or at least learn to cope. What do the doctors call it? Post-Traumatic Stress Disorder?"

"Yeah. PTSD. Intellectually I know you're right, Frank, but psychologically I still have flashbacks and nightmares."

"Don't they have medication for that?"

"Yes, we do. I'm already taking Zoloft, an anti-depressant. You should consider it yourself. But I still see Mole Man nearly everywhere I go, and I'm still obsessed with revenge. I've got another appointment with my psychiatrist next week to try to work through this. Believe me; I'm trying hard but so far without much success."

"The best treatment for both of us would be to catch the bastard. You know very well I've got my own reasons to hate him.

It would be a great relief to see him judged guilty and punished in a court of law. I just pray there is a reason for him to keep Danny alive."

"I'm praying for him. Thanks for trying to make me feel better. Maybe you're right; it'll just take time. The thing is I don't really want to see the system punish Brunelli, Frank. You're missing what I'm saying. Retribution and vengeance, administered by me personally, that's what I want. I don't want to learn to live with this; I want to kill him with my own hands. I want him to suffer. Is that sick or what?"

"No, I understand it, Raquel, believe me I do. I'd like nothing better than to kill the deranged bastard myself. But the authorities frown upon vigilante justice in this country. They punish you for doing that, sometimes even more harshly than what they do to the original lawbreaker."

"Sadly, I know that too. Crazy system, huh? Sorry for being so self-absorbed, Frank. Here I am whining about my own problems while Danny's still missing. You've got your own personal hell."

"Yeah. I have nightmares all the time about what might be happening to him. Every time I close my eyes, I see that evil black mole, but I'll manage somehow 'til we find him."

"As you said, I'm sure the cops'll eventually catch Brunelli, and Danny will be safe. Why would Brunelli hurt him? He's just using your son for leverage against you, so it's in his interest to keep Danny healthy."

"Wish I were so confident. You never can tell with psychopaths like this guy. Their minds don't work logically."

She stared at me, eyes pleading. "OK, promise you'll keep me abreast of any leads from Josue Fuentes and I'll shut up. For the sake of my sanity, though, I need to be directly involved. I might even be able to help."

"Any help would be appreciated. And I'll keep you up to date."

She nodded. I tried to distract her by relating the news article I'd read concerning her great grandfather, Canuto. "What a story about him trying to smuggle his paramour back into the country after she'd been deported, eh? True love never runs smooth."

"Unbelievable. I knew my grandmother died in childbirth but not about her being the love child of Canuto and Mari Ortiz. I never realized that Canuto's four children were the offspring of four different mothers either. I almost wish you hadn't told me that part of the story; it has knocked Canuto off his pedestal, in my eyes at least."

Counter-intuitively, I found myself defending him. "Times were different then, different culture too. At least he was a good father to those kids. Just ask Alfredo; he's still grieving over Canuto's death more than fifty years later, isn't he?"

"He was a decent father, I suppose. He certainly kept the family together, but what did he teach them? He taught the boys to fight and steal and never forgive; he taught my grandmother it was OK to have unprotected sex; and he taught his family it was honorable to engage in a blood feud, which ended up killing them all. As far as Alfredo still grieving, I think retaining a bitter grudge is more like it. That's nearly all that keeps him alive these days, because physically, he claims nothing about his body works right."

I laughed. "Old people always say that kind of stuff. You should hear my Grandma Kate. Times change, but human emotions don't. For example, look who's holding grudges now? You and me, that's who."

She held my gaze earnestly. "But this situation's a bit different, isn't it? We're both looking for justice. This is no blood feud. We both agree Brunelli needs to be removed from society and punished; we might not agree on the type of punishment, that's all. You want due process. I just want him dead. Personally, I believe that if penalties were meted out publicly, without delay, there'd be fewer crimes and greater satisfaction with the system."

"Maybe so, but you're arguing the very principles of criminal punishment I learned in law school. I hesitate to even mention the one you left out. What about rehabilitation?"

"What a joke! As a physician, I used to believe in that garbage but not anymore. You can't rehabilitate a rabid dog; you can only exterminate him, but plenty of fools like to believe it's possible. No one could possibly rehabilitate a maniac like Ricky Brunelli. Let's just hope Josue can help us find him; then we can worry about obtaining justice or revenge or settling grudges or whatever else we choose to call it."

"I hope so too. Let's get back to target practice."

But I couldn't shoot any more that day; I'd had enough and felt out of sorts. Raquel was another story. With grim determination, she returned to the range to blast more holes in the mole-decorated paper replica of her assailant. I trudged around the lobby of the gun range inspecting different weapons and firearm paraphernalia, waiting for Raquel to finish.

A while later she emerged, grinning. "You were right; shooting is good therapy. I must've killed Mole Man a hundred times. But never in the chest or head, so he'd die a slow, excruciating death. He'll never have sex again, that's for sure."

"Careful, don't become obsessed."

"Obsessed, crazy, infuriated, call it what you like. I admit to all of it. But I'm not psychotic, and I'm still functional. And I will have my revenge."

"You're beginning to sound just like Canuto and Alfredo."

"Got the same bloodlines, don't I? Tell me you don't feel exactly the same."

I had no answer for that. On an emotional level, I did feel that way, but on a professional level, I just couldn't countenance meting out justice without the court's sanction.

We rode home mostly in silence. When we arrived back at Raquel's house, I leaned over to kiss her, but she turned her cheek and didn't invite me in.

I sat in front of her place for a long time afterwards. I thought I loved Raquel, but I harbored doubts. And her recent moodiness hadn't made things easier though she had good reason to be morose. When the curtains of Raquel's window opened and she peered out, I ignored her. She and Alfredo must share Peeping Tom genes in the bloodline too.

I don't know why I stayed in Raquel's driveway for so long. I squeezed my eyes closed, rubbed my temples, and tried to shut out the unfathomable: that Danny might never return. Then I looked up at the sky as a gentle, cooling rain spattered my car. Without Danny or Raquel to keep me company, or any legal work to accomplish, I felt lonely and insignificant.

Was Danny OK? Was he hurt, being fed? Was he even alive? How on earth would we ever locate him, let alone rescue him? It had been over three weeks since his abduction. Everyone knows that the trail goes cold with the passage of time, and we hadn't heard a word from either Danny or the kidnappers in all that time.

I wondered whether Raquel could ever be normal again. Her compulsion for revenge seemed amplified every time I spoke to her. A sort of wild-eyed intensity overcame her whenever she talked about the "Mole Man," which was most of the time, and the conversation invariably turned to the details of his future mutilation and death.

The jangle of my cell phone jolted me alert. I flipped it open.

"Mr. McNamara, this is Detective Cromarty, and I've got some news about Danny."

I'd met with Alex Cromarty on several occasions during the past weeks. He usually wore fashionably frayed jeans with an untucked dress shirt and a sport jacket. Despite the with-it image and a quirky smile, he seemed quick-witted and a dedicated professional. I believed Danny's fate was in competent hands.

I'd waited impatiently for this call, but now I wasn't sure I wanted to hear his report.

"Mr. McNamara? Are you there?"

"Sorry, Detective. I'm a little stunned to finally hear from you."

"I know. I'm sorry we couldn't have given you something earlier. This has been a devil of a case. We've been working day and night on it, I can assure you, and we've come up with very little until now. We think Danny is being held in a private home north of here, in Sachse."

It's difficult to express the emotions roiling inside me at that moment. Hope, yes, that above all, also fear, and then mostly relief. At last there would be some action.

"Where the hell is Sachse?"

"It's a suburb northeast of Dallas, just a small community. It's a country town up there; everyone knows everyone else. A citizen phoned in a report of suspicious activity at a neighbor's house. He knew the neighbor was supposed to be out of town. The Sachse police sent an officer to investigate. He inspected the grounds around the house first, and through one of the windows he noticed a young man with his hands bound in front of him walking in the kitchen. The policeman approached the front door and rang the bell, but no one responded."

"Rang the doorbell? Why didn't the officer back off and call headquarters for support? He might've already tipped them off."

"He should've. That's normal procedure, but he didn't. In any event, when the officer returned to the station house, he compared the description of the young man he had seen with reports and photographs of missing persons and unsolved kidnap cases. His description matched Danny to perfection. So the Sachse police called me as the detective in charge of the investigation."

I tried to control the anger in my voice. "He returned to the station house and left them without surveillance? How stupid can he be? Did you get someone back over there right away? They're probably long gone by now."

"The Sachse police returned to the location immediately, and we sent a Dallas team as well. Neither of them reported any suspicious activity. From the time the officer left the scene until the Sachse cops returned was only about an hour and a half. During that time, the neighbor noticed nothing unusual."

"So?"

"So we think Danny is still in the house."

"And?"

"We dispatched a SWAT team to extract Danny. As a matter of fact, they should be there by now. Don't worry, Mr. McNamara, these boys are specially trained for situations like this. I'll call you the minute I hear anything."

In only a matter of a few hours, Danny would be home again he said. But this wasn't a mere cop show on television where you knew the good guys would prevail in the end; this episode involved my son. Anything could happen in a kidnapping rescue, the good guys might even lose. I squealed out of Raquel's driveway, sped home, and kept the cell phone right beside me. My hands grasped the steering wheel until my knuckles whitened.

I whispered, "Please God, if you're up there, take good care of Danny. I know I could've been a more faithful Catholic, but that's not Danny's fault. He's a good kid. I'm begging you to return him to me safe and sound."

In a few hours more we'd be reunited. I just knew it.

CHAPTER
17

FRANK MCNAMARA'S HOUSE
DALLAS, TEXAS
THURSDAY, JUNE 26, 2008, 2:47 A.M.

Why hadn't Cromarty called yet? I watched my nightstand clock tick off the minutes and seconds. The house was silent. The natural rhythms of my heartbeat and deliberate breathing should have provided some comfort, but my mind whisked me back to gruesome battle scenes in Iraq. I heard the clangor of gunfire and shrieks of pain, and I obsessed about Danny. Had the cops been able to rescue him?

The telephone jangled in my ear, and I lunged for it. It was Detective Cromarty, finally calling with a report on the rescue. After a forced entry into the house by smashing through several windows and the front door, the SWAT team lobbed concussion grenades into the rooms to stun the opposition into submission. Then they charged through the openings, guns held at the ready. Sharpshooters were posted at every window to take out any remaining hostile threat, and no one was injured in the assault. Nevertheless, the news wasn't good at all.

No one was injured because no one was there! "I'm sorry, Mr. McNamara," Cromarty said. "The SWAT boys executed their attack perfectly. There just wasn't anybody home. They must've slipped away before my spotters got there." His voice alternately faded and surged as he no doubt tried to think of an excuse for his failure.

I could barely control myself. "Oh, they slipped away all right, Detective. They slipped away because that Sachse police officer wasn't smart enough to remain at the scene and call for backup. Now Danny's going to pay the price for his bungling. Who knows if I'll ever see Danny again after this screw-up?"

"I know you're upset, Mr. McNamara, and you've got reason to be. I'd feel the same if it were my son. But we never would've found Danny in the first place if it hadn't been for that patrolman."

"Damn right I'm upset. And it's easy for you to say you'd feel the same; it's not your son we're talking about, is it?"

"Because of this incident, we're working the case harder than ever. We're turning that house upside down, looking for clues. He'll turn up again, don't you worry."

"Incident? This isn't a mere incident, Detective; it's a fiasco. Danny is my life; without him, I have nothing. Do you understand me? Nothing! What if he turns up again but dead this time? You going to say you feel my pain? You sympathize?"

"Mr. McNamara, here's what I think. If they wanted to kill him, they would've done it already. Otherwise, why hang onto Danny for a month? No, they're keeping him alive for a reason. Maybe it's for ransom, even after all this time, or maybe it's to guarantee some kind of behavior. I don't know yet."

"Brilliant deduction, Detective. But we've had this conversation before. I've already told you that I believe Danny was kidnapped to keep me quiet about some old real estate dealings, and a related deal is in the works right now. When that deal closes in a few weeks, they won't need Danny anymore. What then, Detective?"

"We've looked into the alleged dealings you're referring to and come up with nothing illegal, nothing that seems like a motivation to kidnap Danny. We've checked out Chandler and Cannon as you asked. And every time we come across a lead, we get lawyers with court orders blocking our way. Without more than that, we can't keep harassing prominent citizens. To be honest, I'm getting pressure from the mayor and my chief to solve the case quickly without involving those two any further. So we're pursuing other avenues."

I almost hurled the phone across the room in disgust. "Fuck that Sachse cop and his stupidity, and fuck your bungling SWAT team, and fuck the mayor, and fuck your chief. And fuck you too, Cromarty, for that matter. You've had this case for nearly a month, and you've come up with exactly zip. And my son's still out there, suffering because of your incompetence. Thanks for nothing."

There was silence on the other end of the phone. I knew I'd struck a nerve, but I also knew I had to check my anger to keep Cromarty on my side, pursuing every possible lead. I believed his boss was pressuring him to shut down the investigation. So I said, "I know you're doing your best. Please bring Danny home safely."

"We will, Mr. McNamara. I understand your frustration. I'll keep you informed."

I hung up the phone. Though I still believed in Cromarty's good intentions, I now distrusted the motivations of the entire police department. The cops had bungled an incredible opportunity to rescue Danny, and now the most promising lead seemed to be the only one they weren't allowed to follow. While they chased their tails and discovered nothing but dead ends, the kidnappers had undoubtedly distanced themselves farther and farther from Dallas. With each passing hour, the chances of finding my son diminished fast. I despaired for Danny's safety.

I also had to make some major decisions about my finances. After this long without work, money was becoming scarce. I'd already exhausted my meager savings and cleaned out my small IRA account. Grandma Kate had money, but I hated to ask her for help though she would have offered it gladly. With those gloomy thoughts in mind, I decided to take a walk to clear my head.

When I opened the front door, I nearly tripped over a plain brown box sitting next to the morning paper. It was about one foot square by two inches thick and had been taped shut. Letters randomly clipped from a newspaper spelled the word "McNamara" on the front. I brought the box inside and placed it on the kitchen counter.

The box was very light. I shook it; nothing rattled and nothing ticked. Fear and curiosity got the better of me, so I slit the packing tape and ripped it open. At first, only crumpled, brown packing paper was visible. But inside I found a bulging, white envelope, smeared with dried blood, accompanied by a folded piece of paper.

On the paper, more clipped letters had been pasted to create a message: "**Don't try that again.**" Try what again?

Time passed in slow motion while I stared at the bloody envelope. I held it up to the light but saw nothing but a dark blob. I shook it and heard nothing. I slit it open.

A stiff, flesh-colored object had been stuffed inside, about the consistency of putty. My brain registered the hideous fact that it was an entire human ear. It had apparently been removed from its owner's head in one clean slice, the cut edge dried and clotted. Then I noticed it.

The lobe contained a small diamond stud exactly like the one Danny loved to wear. All at once, the realization whacked me like a hammer blow to the chest. *This ear belonged to Danny!* I gasped, feeling short of breath and light-headed. I had to grip an overhead cabinet door to remain upright. Then came the nausea.

I worked my way hand over hand to the kitchen sink and propped myself over it. I retched until my sour stomach had completely emptied, then collapsed to the floor, coughing and choking at the same time. I held my head in both hands, sobbing.

"What have I done to you, son?" I whispered harshly. "Danny, Danny, I am so sorry." I curled up on my side and tried to scream, but the vomit still in my throat prevented that. The only sound I managed to produce was a hoarse croak.

I knew now what I must do. I struggled up and dully walked to the bathroom where I cleaned up a bit, then to my study where I dialed the offices of Shipwright and Chandler. After asking for Donald Chandler's extension, Battleaxe Bobbie answered gruffly.

"Donald Chandler's office, Miss Sweeney speaking."

"Hello, Barbara. This is Frank McNamara. I'd like to speak to Mr. Chandler."

"Let me see if he's available. I hope everything is going well for you, Mr. McNamara," she replied, disinterestedly. I tried to collect my thoughts for what I intended to say, anticipating a lengthy wait on hold.

But the Battleaxe returned to the phone promptly. "He'll be with you in a moment." And then Chandler picked up.

"Frank, it's good to hear your voice. How've you been?"

"Not so good, actually. You heard about Danny?"

"I have. Most unfortunate." He sounded insincere. "Any communication from the kidnappers? Any demands or new leads?"

"Nothing at all. This is the strangest kidnapping I've ever heard about. There's been no contact. They haven't asked for ransom or made demands of any kind in over three weeks. Until today, that is."

"What happened today?"

"The police had information that a boy fitting Danny's description was being held in a house near Sachse, just north of Dallas. They sent over a SWAT team right away to rescue him, but the kidnappers escaped before their arrival."

"Are they sure it was Danny?" He didn't sound one bit surprised.

"We all assumed the boy was Danny because of the description, but the cops are working on matching some DNA found at the scene to hair and skin samples taken from his clothing and toothbrush. That'll take a couple of days, but something else happened today that convinced me it was him."

"What's that?"

"This morning I found a package on my doorstep. Inside I found a human ear with Danny's little ear stud in the lobe. The police are going to confirm that it's his ear with additional DNA testing, but I know it's his. I'm praying that the ear is only a warning, and a sign he's still alive."

"His ear?" This time the shock in his voice seemed genuine. He recovered quickly. "Those guys must mean business."

"I'm certain now they wouldn't hesitate to kill him, which is why I've come to a decision. As of this moment, I am officially off the Forestglen case. I think you know I've continued to investigate some irregularities to do with the purchase of the Regency Tower.

But from now on, I'll never again access any information about it, nor will I discuss it with anyone. I'm not sure if Forestglen has anything to do with Danny's kidnapping or not, but if there's even the remotest connection, it's not worth it to me. I'm going to do whatever it takes to get him back."

"Why are you telling me this, Frank? True, I wanted you off the account. But I can assure you that neither Mr. Cannon nor I had anything to do with Danny's disappearance. I would never countenance kidnapping or violence to anyone, least of all Danny. After all, I've known that boy a long time."

"Of course you wouldn't. I could never imagine that." It was my turn to lie. "I just wanted you to know that my interest in Forestglen is a thing of the past. I've destroyed my files on the subject. You can pass that along to Mr. Cannon."

"I'll do that. I'm sure he'll be pleased. And if you remember your duty to maintain lawyer/client confidentiality, I'm sure everything will work out fine. Let's hope Danny turns up soon, alive and well."

And with all his remaining body parts, I thought. "Thanks, Donald. There's no reason we can't still be friends even if I don't work at Shipwright and Chandler anymore, is there?" As if you could be friends with a snake.

"Absolutely not. Let's keep in touch. Incidentally, the Solar Towers sale to Forestglen is scheduled to close within the month."

That phone call convinced me that Donald Chandler was well aware of the kidnapping but maybe didn't know every detail. Was I unrealistic to expect him to give the word to release Danny? Probably, I decided, but anything was worth a try.

I worried that even if someone were holding Danny to ensure my silence, though they might let him go after the sale closed, they might just decide to kill him instead. In fact, they probably would kill him to eliminate any witnesses. Should I call Detective Cromarty? I didn't trust the cops any longer. There might even be someone on the take at the police department who warned the kidnappers.

Call Josue Fuentes? I couldn't bother him again with my problems. He was old and sickly and had already promised to spread the word about Danny. I trusted him to call if anything turned up. What about Raquel?

Now there was a riddle, wrapped in a mystery inside an enigma. I had strong feelings for her, but they didn't seem to be reciprocated. Since the rape, she'd become isolated and distant. All she seemed to care about was seeing her patients, shooting guns, and wreaking vengeance, not necessarily in that order. She had no time for anything else, certainly not for me.

I understood she'd suffered a horrific psychological trauma, but that knowledge didn't alleviate my frustration at being unable to communicate with her. It didn't help either that almost every time I thought about Raquel, her face morphed into an image of Sam. It was time to move on; everyone said so. But beautiful, flaxen-haired Sam still stared hauntingly at me, and her image brought with it feelings of guilt and loss, making focusing on Raquel that much more difficult.

Still, I needed someone to confide in, someone who understood my situation, and Raquel had been involved from the very beginning. I needed company, and a person with medical knowledge wouldn't hurt. So I picked up the phone and dialed her number.

After a moment, she picked up. "Hi, Frank, how are you?"

"At the moment I'm crying."

"You're not kidding, are you?" She could hear my snuffling over the phone. "Why?"

I told her about receiving the box with Danny's ear in it. "I can't believe this is happening, Raquel. It's surreal," I said at the end of my speech.

"Frank, may I come over?" She sounded much less remote.

"I wish you would. I need your advice, and your company right now wouldn't hurt either." I gave her the address; she'd never been to my house before.

"Place the ear in a bowl of tepid tap water, add a pinch of salt, and I'll be right there." Her professional manner comforted me.

I gladly ceded control of the ear situation to Raquel so I could think, but my thoughts were all malevolent and black. I needed to anesthetize my mind, so I surreptitiously downed a Vicodin with vodka and swallowed it quickly while she worked on the ear in the kitchen. Vicodin and vodka had become my new favorite combination, but I hated to hide it from her. She planned to transport the ear to Methodist Hospital to try to cryo-preserve it for replantation onto Danny's head at some future date. Providing, of course, we could locate the rest of Danny.

"Before I leave, let me take a swab from the inside of your mouth. I want to match your DNA to a specimen taken from the ear." She produced a large cotton swab on the end of a plastic stick and swabbed the inside of my cheek with it before I could even react. Then she placed it inside a test tube full of a clear liquid solution.

"You're no forensics expert. How do you know all this stuff?"

"Don't you watch any of the CSI shows on TV?"

"CSI?"

"Yes, for God's sake, Frank, don't be so obtuse. Crime Scene Investigation. OK, the truth is my pathologist colleague, Dr. Zwillman Levine, explained it to me right after you called."

"How does a DNA match work?"

"I'll explain later," she replied. "Zwilly says time is of the essence if we're going to preserve this ear. It'll take a couple of hours. Don't worry; I'll be back as soon as possible." And she flew out the door with the ear in a large saline-filled baggie and me sputtering in her wake.

I had lied to Donald Chandler. While I waited for Raquel to return, I went online and researched his personal life and those of the Cannon family as well, especially Randall. I was convinced that Danny's disappearance was a direct result of my perceived interference in the acquisition of the Regency Towers office building. No longer did I think of bringing these criminals to justice. Now I was motivated by revenge. I was so distraught and so unhinged at this point that I actually planned to kidnap some of the families' children in order to exchange them for Danny.

Randall Cannon had an ex-wife, three grown children, and six grandchildren. He and his second wife plus two younger kids now lived in a gated mansion located on St. John's Avenue in Highland Park, the most exclusive of all Dallas' neighborhoods. His children attended St. Mark's and Hockaday, the finest private schools in the city, always guarded by full-time security. He was a prominent member of the Highland Park Methodist Church.

The Cannons belonged to two country clubs. They also owned a ski chalet in Aspen, a penthouse apartment in New York City, and a house on Lake Cypress Springs in East Texas. I noticed that all of the real estate was owned personally, except the lake house. It was owned by Caribbean Investments, the present owners of the

Regency Towers building and had been held in one family entity or another for well over sixty years.

Donald Chandler, on the other hand, lived relatively unostentatiously. While he too resided in Highland Park, his "only" other home was in Palm Springs at the very private Bighorn Country Club, where he mingled with famous athletes and movie stars. He and his wife of forty years had two grown children and four grandchildren. The grandchildren also attended the same private schools in Dallas as Cannon's kids. Not surprisingly, they also belonged to the same church and country clubs.

Donald Chandler was the only living name partner of the firm, and he and Randall Cannon were connected at the hip, practically Siamese twins. Chandler was likely as deeply involved in any crooked real estate dealings as was Cannon and therefore possibly also with Danny's kidnapping.

The doorbell rang. Surprised, I looked up at the clock to see that it had been five hours since Raquel's departure; I opened it for her. "Sorry I'm so late, Frank. Besides learning about DNA matches and Cryonics from Zwilly, I also had to check on a few hospital patients."

"Does the ear belong to Danny? Does the doctor think it can be preserved? Will it be possible to re-implant it later if we find him?"

"The short answer is yes, yes, and yes. Pour me a drink, and I'll give you the details."

Her favorite drink, I knew, was Absolut pink grapefruit vodka with a splash of cranberry juice, club soda, and lots of lime. For want of a better name, she simply called it 'The Thing.' I mixed her the fastest 'Thing' in history and returned to her, perched with shoes off and legs tucked underneath her on the living room sofa.

She took a long swallow. "Thank you, just the way I like it. Now, as for the DNA, your genes match exactly half of those in the specimen we obtained from the ear. The other half would have come from the patient's mother, of course. So there's not much doubt the ear belongs to Danny."

"Is it still viable? There's no sense trying to preserve an ear that's too far gone, right?"

"Zwilly thinks it is. He believes the ear was removed about twelve hours ago, well within the twenty-four hour window for cryo-preservation. He'll cool it down to minus 196 degrees Centigrade with liquid nitrogen and keep it there, kind of like what they did with that baseball player, Babe Ruth."

I couldn't help laughing. "That would be Ted Williams, my sweet."

"Ruth, Williams, what's the difference? They're both just dead baseball players, aren't they? At least I got you laughing."

"Yeah, you did. Those two just happen to be the greatest ever to play the game. They say Williams is stored upside down in a vat somewhere."

"Exactly. The head is down to make sure the brain stays submerged in the liquid nitrogen."

"Sounds complicated."

"It is, but we're lucky; Zwilly's an international expert and one of the foremost practitioners of Cryonics in the country. He says that whole bodies are quite a challenge because you've got to preserve the entire brain and other organs properly. He's never done an ear before, but he said it should be a 'piece of cake compared to a brain.' Those were his exact words."

"Assuming we find Danny alive, how do you revive the frozen tissue and stick it back onto his head?"

Raquel explained the process of thawing the ear to body temperature in a saline bath, centrifuging it to remove the cryo-preservative, and then suturing it back onto the head. "It's a tricky operation; you've got to suture the blood vessels together using an operating microscope. But I know an excellent guy for the job."

"Good to know the right people, isn't it?"

"Yes indeed. You know what they say. It's not what you know; it's who you know."

"Now all we have to do is find Danny. Raquel, thanks for taking charge. Just having you around has kept me from obsessing too much about what Danny's going through. Do you have to leave?"

She said nothing, but she approached and hugged me. I took her in my arms and kissed her. Her presence that night kept me from going insane.

CHAPTER
18

FRANK MCNAMARA'S HOUSE
DALLAS, TEXAS
WEDNESDAY, JULY 2, 2008

Another week passed, and I awoke to yet another morning without any news of Danny. It had been a month since the abduction, a long time to keep up hope. I'd turn on the TV, full of tragedies, and they'd become my tragedies. I tried to sleep at night, but a horrible film clip filled with disasters would reel through my head. I dreamt of knives dangling over Danny's head and being powerless to intervene, so I drank bottles of vodka mixed with Vicodin and any other painkiller I could find to numb myself. Then I'd curl up in a fetal position, comatose for hours on my recliner.

There was no word from Detective Cromarty, Donald Chandler, or even Josue Fuentes. I shouldn't say no word at all. Cromarty did call occasionally but only to say that he had no new leads. He just wanted to keep me "up to speed."

Tracy had called as well with some information about the case against Cannon and Chandler. She told me what she wasn't really supposed to tell me, but at least it was a bit of good news for a change. Apparently the IRS had gathered enough evidence against Chandler and Cannon that Shapiro believed he could pursue a case against them with no more help from me; one less thing to worry about.

She said that the reason they weren't going to arrest those two for the time being, though, was that they wanted to try recovering whatever money had been stashed offshore before it disappeared into different accounts on different islands all over the world. So secrecy remained of the utmost importance until they were ready to pounce, and they trusted me to keep quiet. Imagine that—the IRS trusting me!

They thought the unreported proceeds they were tracking had gone to the International Bank of the Caribbean in the Cayman Islands, but they weren't sure. No record of the transfer had ever been found, and no proper tax returns were ever filed.

Those offshore islands are such a shelter for abusive tax schemes, she explained, because they have no tax treaties with the US. So the IRS can't seize the assets, and the islands don't tax income from sources outside their jurisdiction. They offer strict financial secrecy laws and won't divulge a client's information to anyone, ever. They also offer liability protection, meaning that US courts can't attach any property hidden there. Plus, the client can easily manage the money using sophisticated communications techniques and wire funds transfers. Best of all, the assets can be readily accessed by means of a credit card for use in the US, paid for by the offshore bank account.

"Couldn't be simpler," she said. "You can see why these tax havens would be irresistible to crooks like Cannon and Chandler. On deals of the magnitude they handle, they could probably save millions in taxes every year. If putting the squeeze on those two will help find Danny, maybe we'll have something for you real soon. Don't lose hope, Frank."

Great, I thought; even if she can take down Cannon and Chandler, will that bring Danny back?

Despite Tracy's assurances and Raquel's company, my despair deepened. I don't know much about clinical medicine, but I guess I had what they call a major depression. At least Raquel seemed to think so. She encouraged me to see a psychiatrist colleague of hers, but I denied needing any help. Just because I felt downhearted, felt like crying most of the time, and wondered if I'd be better off dead was no reason to diagnose "major depression," was it? Wouldn't anyone else feel the same?

She insisted, so I finally agreed to see her friend. The doctor declared that I suffered a "classic case" of major depressive disorder. Really? Not just ordinary but classic! He prescribed me an old reliable anti-depressant, Zoloft, to help get me through—same as he had done for Raquel. "You just can't live the rest of your life continually sad and surly," he said. And he recommended I cut way back on the Vicodin and Vodka; way back as in none at all. Apparently narcotics and alcohol plus anti-depressants don't mix real well. I vowed to do so, but I'd made that vow before, too many times.

At least Zwilly Levine had upbeat news. He was pretty sure Danny's ear would survive. He'd been able to cryo-preserve it before too much tissue deterioration occurred. And it could be kept in suspended animation for a long time if necessary. Now if we could only find Danny and attach it to him, I'd be a very happy man. Even if the ear graft didn't take, just find Danny. That figured to be the best tonic for my depression.

With the Forestglen deal scheduled to close in just a few weeks, time was of the essence. I had no work to do and too many worries to count, entirely too much time on my hands. The phone rang, and I answered diffidently. It was Josue Fuentes, and my ears suddenly pricked alert.

"Frank, you hangin' in there?" he started.

"I'm hangin' on by my fingernails, Josue, but I'm still hangin'. How's your health? Still doing your rehab?" It startled me to hear his voice over the phone. Even the slurred speech seemed to have improved; he sounded energized.

"I'm not much of a rehab guy, Frank, but I'm doing good, thanks. You know I'm not calling just to pass the time of day, don't you?"

"I figured, so why'd you call then? I know, you want to go back to El Taquito's for breakfast." But I could sense urgency in his voice.

"Since you ask, breakfast might be nice. But I'm calling because I just received information on a certain young acquaintance of ours that I can't discuss over the phone. How about you come over here and meet a friend of mine and take us both down to El Taquito's? Don't get your hopes up, Frank, but this person might possibly be the bearer of some good news."

"Be there soon as I can."

I grabbed my briefcase and flew out the door into the Beemer. The temperature had soared still further to a sweltering 105 degrees; sweat dampened my armpits and palms.

I weaved through the morning rush hour traffic down Central Expressway south toward Little Mexico. A pickup truck blocked my way, sporting a bumper sticker that read *American Infidels out of Afghanistan!* "Fucking idiot doesn't appreciate what a great country this is," I mumbled to no one in particular. "Get outta my way, Asshole!" So I honked and gave him the finger.

Road-rage madness had taken hold, but I had to find out what Josue knew about our "young acquaintance." All I could think about was Danny, only Danny, and a possible lead. But could this really be me, mild-mannered Frank McNamara? I arrived in Josue's neighborhood in record time, thankfully without incident, and found myself in front of Josue's familiar home, whose squalor no longer troubled me.

The same dilapidated wooden shacks surrounded his decrepit little house, and potholes still dotted the roadway. The neighbor across the street still hawked food, clothing, and assorted junk from his front yard. In my neighborhood, the homeowners would've been cited for all manner of code violations and fined. Or else bitter complaints to City Hall would've resulted in swift repairs, either by the homeowner himself or by the city. But not in this neighborhood; building code enforcers avoided the area if they could.

A jacked-up, black, F-250 extended cab Ford pickup truck with darkly tinted windows had preceded me through the muddy craters still pocking Josue's driveway and sat there, brooding, directly in front of my car. A locked tool chest sat in the truck bed with the name "Guzman" emblazoned in bold Gothic script on the back cab window. A typical laborer's truck, I guessed, until I noticed Louisiana license plates.

At the front door, a short, middle-aged Hispanic male with a round face and slicked, black hair greeted me. "You must be Señor Frank; my name Nestor Guzman. You can call me 'Nasty.' Nasty Nestor, get it?" He laughed. "Josue say you come inside."

Inside, a rejuvenated Josue sat behind a much more organized desk in front of much straighter, dusted bookshelves. "You look as good as I've ever seen you, Josue." I meant it this time. He stood without a cane, albeit shakily, and extended his good arm. He shook my hand firmly and held it a long time. A feeling of energy flowed from him, and he offered a beatific smile that made me understand the stories of extreme loyalty he engendered.

"I see you've already met Nasty Guzman," he said. "I represented him in a couple of legal matters some time ago. You can rely on him, Frank."

"He seems like a decent guy. We going for breakfast? Why do they call him 'Nasty'? Can he tell me about Danny?"

Josue conferred quietly in Spanish with Nasty for a moment, and then he continued. "He'll tell you about his nickname, and a few other things as long as you agree to represent him officially as his attorney. He insists I'm to be your co-counsel, so I can keep an eye on you. That way you'll have to keep whatever he tells you confidential."

I said, "Here we go again, lawyer/client privilege! He wants me to represent him so I'll have to keep quiet?"

"Nasty is as street-smart as they come. He won't talk unless you agree to represent him."

"I'd represent the Devil himself if it'd get me one step closer to finding Danny. Sure, I agree."

"Good. He also insists on paying you a retainer to make it official."

"For heaven's sake, Josue, I don't want his money. I'm now his attorney, his *abogado*. Anything he tells me will remain confidential."

"Nevertheless, he insists. 'Good and valuable consideration,' right?" Nasty handed over a ten-dollar bill, which I accepted reluctantly. "Now everything is legit. Go ahead, Nestor. Tell Mr.

McNamara, your new attorney, everything you just told me. Start at the beginning and don't leave anything out."

"OK, Señor Josue. Thanks for being *mi abogado*, Señor Frank. You help me; I help you. Wanna know why they call me Nasty?"

"Can't you tell me about Danny first?"

"It be better if you know how I find out about him, and to do this, you need to know 'bout me first."

So Nestor Guzman, my new client, proceeded to tell me an astonishing tale of gang related violence and drugs, torture, and murder. He'd grown up near Ciudad Juarez, Mexico, the ninth child of dirt-poor peasants; so impoverished, he said, that even the poor people in his village thought his family poor. Juarez's main product now, as then, is corpses; and the city is unusually proficient at producing them. Over two thousand people are executed in drug wars every year, making Juarez the murder capital of the entire world.

His parents couldn't support Nestor or his siblings on their meager income. They lived in the street or under bridges. He refused the generosity of the Catholic Church because he blamed it for their predicament. In his mind, too many children and no birth control only perpetuated the problem of poverty. He became anti-religion, loyal only to the *Sinaloa* drug cartel, the savior that took him in.

So young Nestor had been forced to join a drug gang at the ripe-old age of eight. The gang became his surrogate parents, feeding and educating him in the ways of the criminal life. After that, he never saw his family again.

Living in Juarez was just the crucible Nestor needed to become an expert at his trade. He acted first as a *burrero*, a drug running mule, moving shipments from the lower Gulf Coast to

the Texas border. Then he became a purveyor of cocaine and mari-
juana, and later on, because the war between the *Sinaloa* cartel and
the competing *Zetas* caused so many casualties, he was promoted
to the elite job of *sicario*, or hit man.

Apparently he was the consummate enforcer too. He'd as-
sassinated some twenty victims, he proudly told us. He claimed
to prefer the more personal combat of a knife fight to the relative
anonymity of a gun battle, but he'd kill or maim any way he had to,
and he executed his prey by whatever method the victim preferred.
Even to me however, his *abogado*, he refused to comment on any
role he might've had in the latest hangings of nine individuals
from a local highway overpass in Ciudad Juarez. Looking at his
earnest, wide face, I had trouble believing him capable of such
murder and mayhem, but I was beginning to understand the nasty
side of Nestor.

Most recently he'd been promoted again, to boss of a methamphetamine lab located in a nondescript log cabin a good hundred
miles east of Dallas, in the piney woods near Mt. Vernon, Texas.
A remote location, rarely visited by strangers, the place was perfect
for his business. There he supervised the manufacture of meth for
distribution to the voracious illegal drug market in Big D and the
Midwest.

As such, he kept a sharp eye out for any whiff of interest by
the authorities; not good for business or for Nestor. At $100 per
gram for the purest meth crystals the DEA had ever seen, business
was brisk.

Finally Nestor came around to the real point of the story.
While reconnoitering an area near his cabin for potential problems, Nestor discovered an upscale, isolated lake house about a
mile from his meth lab. Fronted by the lake on one side, it was

otherwise surrounded by dense woods and occupied by three men and a boy. He thought it strange, their living at the lake full time, when everyone else returned to Dallas on Sunday evening. But who was he to say what three men could or should do with a young boy, so long as they minded their own business and left him alone? Nevertheless, he kept a wary eye on the property.

Then Nestor heard via the grapevine that Josue Fuentes had an interest in a young gringo boy who'd been kidnapped. Nestor remembered his old friend, who had saved Nestor from going to prison on two separate occasions. Since Nestor's life revolved around a rigid code of honor and loyalty to his friends, he knew his duty, hence his appearance at Josue's house this morning.

Nestor hadn't been overly concerned about identifying kidnap victims, so his description of the boy didn't quite match Danny's, but it was close enough. Of course, I wanted a more positive ID, but I couldn't afford to ignore even the slimmest lead at this juncture. Then he said that one of the three men had a large, black mole on his cheek.

So I knew what I had to do. "Mr. Guzman, can you wait here at Josue's house for about two hours and then show me that lake house you discovered?"

"Sí, Señor Frank. I wait for you here. You are my new *abogado* now."

"Yes. And as your attorney, I advise you not to speak to anyone about what you've just told me, anyone except Mr. Fuentes, of course. Josue, I can't even imagine how to thank you. Maybe I'll come up with something fitting in the future, but for now my eternal gratitude will have to do."

"Nothing needed, Frank. Just rescue Danny; that'll be thanks enough for me. As far as breakfast is concerned, I'm afraid I got you here under false pretences. I know how much you love El Taquito, but trust me when I tell you that we three don't want to be seen together in public."

"Gentlemen, I didn't come all the way down here to miss out on El Taquito's." I threw Nestor's ten dollars on the table and added twenty to it. "Nestor, why don't you pick up something to go and bring it back here. I'll be back in a couple of hours. I've got a few arrangements to make." I raced out of Josue's house, accidentally slamming the screen door nearly off its hinges. I jammed my car into reverse and skidded out of the rutted driveway.

On the way home I made two calls: one to Keith Glenn, the other to Raquel. I anticipated needing assistance from both of them. The one person I avoided calling was Detective Cromarty. The cops had their chance to free my son and messed it up. This time, God willing, I'd take care of business myself, with a little help from my friends. And hopefully, after we'd rescued Danny, I'd be able to notify Cromarty about it when it was a *fait accompli*.

By the time I finished those calls, I arrived home and parked in the garage. I loaded up the trunk with all manner of supplies: dried food for a possible lengthy stay outdoors; extra clothing and a portable generator; my cell phone charger plus an extra battery; and guns, lots of guns, including several different calibers with plenty of ammunition. I tucked my prized AR-15 sniper's rifle, with four banana clips of .223 bullets, inside as well. None of the equipment could be seen from inside the passenger compartment of the car.

If Josue had seemed re-energized, I felt revved up to the nth degree. I recalled my Army Ranger survival training from years ago as vividly as if I'd practiced this situation every weekend. In fact, I did practice on the Dallas Police tactical gun range from time to time. After the forced inaction of the past weeks, I relished the idea of action to rescue Danny. Many possible scenarios ran through my head, but any firm plan would need to await a surveillance of the lake house location.

I hurried back to Josue's house. The entire interlude had taken only slightly longer than the two hours I'd promised. Josue's door stood open, and the two of them were chomping on taquitos and jabbering away in Spanish about the good old days I supposed.

With the anticipation of finding Danny, I began to jabber away in Spanglish too. I was so high on the excitement, I hadn't even needed any drugs or alcohol, and the gallons of hot coffee only served to heighten my high. My incomprehensible chatter served to launch Josue and Nestor into gales of laughter and light-hearted comments of "gringo loco" while pointing to their heads with spinning fingers.

My wristwatch told me it was then 11:30 a.m. It would take us another two hours to reach Nestor's cabin in the woods, so I said, "If we're going to find Danny today, we better get going."

"You right, Señor," Nestor said. "Adios, Josue. Hasta la vista." He rose from the table, bowed as if to the *capo di tutti capi* himself, pumped Josue's hand in grandiose fashion, and headed for the door. I rose too, hugged Josue, and thanked him profusely.

"Frank, before you go. Do you remember the prophet Obadiah from the Scriptures? We discussed some of his teachings last time you were here."

"As a matter of fact, I do. He's the one who preached words of wisdom for living the moral life?"

"Exactly, but he was no pacifist, I assure you. Here's what else he said: 'I say to him who would smite me down, I shall smite you first in rage and fury and drench you in blood. And I shall mete out such dreadful retribution that you and your seed shall be obliterated from the face of the earth, never to rise up again.'"

"The more I hear the teachings of the Prophet Obadiah, the more I appreciate him. Thanks again for everything, Josue."

"Vaya con Dios, amigo. Go with God."

CHAPTER
19

FRANKLIN COUNTY, EAST TEXAS
WEDNESDAY, JULY 2, 2008

We headed east on Interstate 30 toward Mt. Vernon, the proud birthplace of former Dallas Cowboys quarterback "Dandy" Don Meredith. I followed Nestor at a respectable distance, both of us at exactly the posted speed limit.

Twenty minutes later, we passed the turnoff for Sachse, then past the towns of Rockwall, Greenville, and Sulphur Springs. We reached Mt. Vernon in ninety minutes, where Nestor turned off the interstate into the local Dairy Queen.

Since I couldn't very well continue without him showing me the way, I followed. He said he needed a bathroom break and one of his favorite treats, a thick ice cream "Blizzard" made with Oreo cookies. I wanted to get going, but there was no hurrying Nestor when it came to his Blizzard, so I had one too. Damn, that thing was good. No DQs exist in Dallas any longer, having all been relegated to small towns.

Finally we got up to leave, but he didn't. He went directly to the ice cream cooler and dug out a dozen frozen Dilly Bars for his men. Apparently the chocolate-covered, vanilla ice cream delicacy was one of the main fuels that kept them producing profitable methamphetamine at his drug cabin in the woods. He said they'd "kill" him if he returned without them.

I sure didn't want them killing him, so I said, "We can't have that, can we? Get all the Dilly Bars you need, Nestor. In fact, let me pay for them, but let's get going before they melt." I tried to speed him up, but he didn't seem to share my urgency.

Finally outside, he plunged the Dilly Bars into an ice chest in his truck. From there, we traveled down a series of roads that grew successively smaller until we reached a dirt road leading to a forest of pine, birch, and sweetgum trees. Sweetgum leaves turn a brilliant reddish-orange in fall, reminiscent of northern maples.

Nestor threaded his truck up the rocky road, which tapered to one thin lane, with me right behind. His pickup was ideally suited for this type of driving; my low-slung Beemer, not so much. So I progressed more slowly and oh, so carefully, not wanting to destroy an axle in this remote place. I rocked along this way for two painful miles or so until Nestor glided his truck off the path into a concealed shelter. I pulled in beside him with plenty of room to spare. Unless you knew where to look, you'd never find this little hideaway, bounded as it was by tall, stout trees and roofed by an umbrella of wide branches thick with pine needles.

We stood together between our vehicles, and I flipped open my military combination GPS, topographical, backlit compass/chronometer. Though the stated time was only 2:11 p.m., it was nearly pitch black under the canopy of branches. Nestor placed a gnarled finger over his lips and whispered, "The lake house be just over this hill, Señor Frank. Come, I show you, but you must be very quiet."

He pointed to his left over a soft rise into the midst of the woods. I could see no opening between the thick tree cover whatsoever. Trusting that Nestor knew his business, I trudged behind him lugging a large pack of equipment, two pistols with extra magazines, and my AR-15 rifle. He was armed as well. Heavy trekking boots protected our legs from any poisonous vipers but caused far too much noise from the pine needles crackling underfoot though we trotted carefully. Prickly branches flayed our arms and faces and covered us with sap.

Meanwhile, woodpeckers hammered overhead, mockingbirds dive-bombed us, and blackbirds screeched their obnoxious 'caw-caw-caw.' Insects created a cacophonous buzzing while vampire mosquitoes had a glorious day siphoning my blood. In my haste to leave Dallas, I'd forgotten insect repellant. Why the insects left Nestor unmolested, I'll never understand. On the plus side, the forest symphony helped to disguise our clumsy, time-consuming progress through the trees.

We threaded a path through gaps between enormous tree trunks until, about a mile later, the forest abruptly ended, and I viewed Lake Cypress Springs, the most pristine lake I'd ever seen, at least in Texas. It was a spring-fed, natural lake, not merely a dammed-up river like most others in the state, and it was devoid of any boat traffic. Perched about one hundred feet from its bank sat an elegant lake house.

No other houses were visible for at least three miles, and those were on the far shore of the lake. Peninsulas jutting into the water guarded the house's privacy on both sides, the lake itself occupying the third side. Spacious lawns and footpaths led from the lake up to the residence. Only the forest side afforded us protected access, with about thirty feet of open space to traverse between the back porch and the forest's edge. Unfortunately, we had come out of those woods about fifty yards east of the place, much too far away. So we re-entered the forest and looped back around, eventually arriving directly athwart the back porch of the house.

I motioned Nestor to stop there while I retrieved a gooseneck fiber-optic viewing scope from my backpack. I needed to trust him now, more than ever before. While he covered me with the AR-15, I raced across the open ground, a .45 semi-automatic held at the ready, and flattened myself against the north wall, panting more from anxiety than actual exertion.

I tiptoed to the northwest corner of the building and peeked around it using the fiber-optic scope. A guard with a rifle in his lap sat on a picnic table not thirty feet away. I retreated, approached the nearest window, and cautiously redeployed the scope just above the ledge. Nothing would be visible from inside except its tip. Two more rough-looking characters watched television in a spacious living room, feet propped onto a divan.

I crawled across the porch, carefully underneath the window sill, and past a thick, bolted door toward the northeast window, then past that to the corner. Same scenario, only this guard patrolled between the house and the lake, rifle slung nonchalantly over a shoulder. I backed away, crouched low, and peered inside this second window with the flexible scope. Another man and an adolescent sat there at a kitchen table, playing cards.

Danny's legs were manacled with leg irons, but his hands were free. My son appeared gaunt and ashen. He coughed repeatedly, a racking fit that hardly ended before the next began. From my position, I couldn't see a damaged ear, but it was just as well. Misty eyes already blurred my vision.

The man across from Danny sat with his left side facing me; he looked vaguely familiar. He slowly turned his head to peer at the cards in his hand, revealing his right side. A large, black mole disfigured that cheek.

My search had finally ended. Now the rescue could begin. But it wouldn't be easy. First I'd have to neutralize five armed hoodlums and extract Danny from a fortified house without harming him. Plus, I wanted to capture the Mole Man alive to question him. Danny would almost certainly require medical attention, so I hoped Raquel would be able to join the crew. I retracted the scope and retreated as quickly as possible back to the safety of the woods where Nestor waited.

I began to perspire, and vertigo nearly overcame me. For the first time today, but not the last, I recognized the symptoms of uncontrollable fear. When I'd recovered wits enough to think clearly, I called Keith Glenn on my cell phone. "I expected maybe three of them, Keith, but there are at least five, including Mole Man. They're well armed, and they've got Danny in leg irons." I listed certain additional supplies he'd need to bring and gave him directions plus our GPS coordinates. "And don't forget the insect repellant," I hissed. "They're swarming and hungry."

"Bugs never bother me. Must taste funny. I'm packed and ready, but I'm thinking you might need a bit more manpower. How about Conrad Nevils? Connie's a bit long in the tooth, but he's a straight shootin' sumbitch—a Marine buddy of mine; very dependable in a pinch like this."

"I met him at your store a while ago, didn't I? You told me about his time in Vietnam. Loves explosives if I recall."

"Good memory, Frankie. He's usually keen for a gig like this, and I promise I won't let him bring any nitro along. Should I call Raquel?"

"Yes, we're going to need her. Pick her up at Methodist Hospital as we arranged. Tell her to bring as many medical supplies as she can muster on short notice. Danny doesn't look so good. And who knows what other injuries the rest of us might suffer."

"Not us, mate. It's better to give than receive, don't you think? This time we're not gonna worry about the legalities. No cops involved; they've got too many scruples and rules of engagement if you know what I mean. You'll have your boy back in no time."

"I like the way you talk, Keith. Can you get here before dusk? It's a hard place to find at night, even with GPS. I'll send Nestor Guzman to meet you at the carport, just off the dirt road. He's the guy I told you about; you'll never find us unless you've got a good guide."

"I'll make it by dusk if I can roust Connie and Raquel fast enough, and I'll find Nestor at the carport, don't worry. See you soon, Frank. Be careful 'til we get there."

"I will. Thanks for everything. And for God's sake, don't forget the insect repellant. They're eating me alive."

"Insect repellant, gotcha. See you in a few hours."

I hung up and returned to Nestor, who kept watch on the lake house. "Señor Frank, I must go to the house in the woods. I got some business to take care of. Better you stay here and watch this place."

"Fine, Nestor. I don't need to know what you're doing. In fact, it's better for everyone concerned if I don't know where that house is anyway. Will you be able to meet my friends Keith and Raquel at the carport about seven o'clock and bring them here? By the way, while I'm thanking people, I owe you a great big thank you too. You're a drug dealer with a conscience, amigo. Muchas gracias."

"No problemo, Señor. Hasta la vista."

Nestor left, and I retreated a little deeper into the forest to set up a mini headquarters. I placed a folding chair in an opening between two thick oaks with a good view of the lake house. I pitched a small pup tent, donned a mesh mosquito net and thin gloves, and sat down to wait for reinforcements and nightfall. From my vantage point, the entire back of the house, the driveway with its two sport utility vehicles, and a speedboat moored at the lake wall dock were all in sight. No one could enter or leave the place by water or land without my knowledge.

Time passed and the guards changed shifts every two hours, always two at a time. But Danny and Mole Man never ventured outside. This waiting before action is always a difficult proposition when you've nothing to do; luckily, I had plenty to occupy me. I busied myself checking my guns and their night scopes and laying out communications equipment, extra ammo, and explosives. The birds quieted, and the insect discordance softened to a dull buzz. Suddenly I heard something different, a human sound.

One of the guards swung his patrol around to the back of the house, directly across from my hideaway. He made a leisurely inspection of the tree line on his way, poking and prodding bushes with his rifle. I was almost certain he wouldn't see me, hidden twenty yards inside the forest, but I'd learned to be cautious and lined him up in my sights. I could've taken him out easily enough, but the blast would've alerted the other kidnappers. I knew I couldn't handle them all by myself, so I flattened my body behind a tree trunk, froze, and waited, barely breathing.

The man passed directly in front of me, with only a few trees between us for cover. But instead of continuing on, he swept his gun over the periphery of the forest and peered into the darkness. Satisfied, he unzipped his fly and urinated onto some bushes. He turned his back to me and surveyed the lake while he lit a cigarette, which took him a painfully long time to smoke. Finally he squished it under foot and, mumbling something about "wasting away out here in the boondocks," he continued on his rounds. The adrenaline rush subsided.

He tramped around the building toward the boat, where he stopped to chat with the other guard, then jumped into the inboard launch. After revving the engine, he cast off the mooring lines and eased the boat into the lake. He sped away to the southeast, leaving seaweed and a few dead fish in the unbroken arc of his wake. I let the guard go, one less adversary to deal with, and I couldn't afford to rouse the other kidnappers.

I waited and waited and waited some more. Time stretched out, slowed, crawled, ground to a halt. I began to wonder if nightfall would ever come. With nothing more to organize, no more arrangements to make, I had too much time on my hands again. I became agitated and reorganized everything in the backpack one more time then replaced the items into their original places. I rechecked my guns and ammo yet again. I knew that Keith wouldn't be arriving for another couple of hours at least, but that didn't help my impatience.

God knows, I wanted to get Danny out of there right away. A person shouldn't be alone at a time like this; you think crazy thoughts. You need a buddy to set your head right, someone more objective. But no one appeared except an impudent squirrel.

I couldn't stand the waiting any longer; it got so bad I craved the release of action, any kind of action. But I couldn't go off half-cocked by myself. So I started thinking while I munched on peanuts from my supply pack. I thought of making a Banzai attack on the stronghold, killing the Mole Man and all his henchmen in one dramatic assault, and making my escape with Danny. But I realized that my solo SWAT team would be badly outnumbered and that Danny might be harmed in the attack. I needed a better plan.

The squirrel rested on his haunches not five feet away, little paws curled in front of him like a tiny boxer, hoping for a mooch. I tossed him a few peanuts, which he devoured like tiny cobs of corn. I became punchy with the incongruity of the entire situation: me sitting in the middle of a forest feeding peanuts to a squirrel, like this was just a Sunday stroll in the park.

With nothing to do but wait, I watched the squirrel scamper up a tree, hop onto the roof of the house, pause for a moment, and continue across. My eyes were drawn up to the roof to follow him where I noticed two chimneys, each covered by a mesh chimney cap, and the rough outline of a viable plan came to me. I let the idea take wing and spin itself around in my head, a fragile sequence of possibilities.

My scheme was dangerous and required split-second timing, but it could be done. I'd certainly need reinforcements, though. I called Keith with a request for some extra gear. He hadn't left Dallas yet; Raquel still hadn't been able to arrange coverage for her medical practice.

The low growl of a marine engine sounded in the distance, then became louder and closer. The launch eventually pulled around the eastern peninsula and approached the dock. This time it contained two men. I stopped to stare and ponder; that made six of them. Nothing could be done about that now. The two gangsters jumped out of the boat, greeted the nearest guard, and made their way to the house.

The plan I devised had better work; my son's life depended on it.

The summer air was heavy with the fragrance of wild mint and juniper, and the sun pulsed warm in an aqua blue sky. As it began to plop over the western edge of the lake, I extended my hand and eyeballed two fingers of distance between the horizon and the sun. Since each finger represents ten minutes of time, as I'd learned in the military, I expected about twenty more minutes of daylight before sundown. Streaks of sunlight gradually dwindled, and the sky turned to slate at the far end of the lake. A wave of increasing darkness swept across the water's surface.

The landscape stilled as daylight folded into blackness, lit only by a few early stars. The moon hadn't yet risen, but no light could've penetrated such a dense forest anyway. After a while, I could hear only the occasional screech or howl of a prowling nocturnal beast. The birds and insects finally ceased their chatter, all but the dive bombing mosquitoes. Those damned mosquitoes descended upon me like a horde of flies to a pile of new dung. No amount of swatting could keep the pests at bay. But I told myself I could endure anything to save my son.

The forest at night creates fear. Alone under the canopy of swaying, groaning pines and oaks, the darkness magnified my insecurities, made me obsess about the possibility of failure. A suffocating sense of danger overwhelmed me. My mounting panic convinced me I would fall short, and Danny would die in this remote place.

I waited inside my small tent, peering out, trying to avoid the mosquito swarm and adjust to the forest's rhythm. Eventually I cocked my head at an unnatural sound. The soft crackle of pine needles underfoot grew louder. A flashlight beam zigzagged toward me from tree to tree, probing for a path. I grabbed my AR-15, crept out of the tent, and retreated behind an enormous oak trunk. I listened, motionless.

Once I thought I heard the faint crunching of twigs and needles, but when I froze, there was nothing. It happened again, accompanied by insistent whispering this time. Then a man eased warily into my small clearing, someone I couldn't immediately identify in the gloaming. I caught him in the green glare of my night scope and aimed my rifle at the man's heart.

When he saw the green dot appear on his chest, the man's voice penetrated the stillness more urgently. "Frank, Frank, don't shoot. It's me, Keith."

I recognized his voice and lowered my gun, relieved. "Right on schedule. You got here just in time to save me from going crazy."

"Glad to be of service, amigo. Nestor here led us right to you, like a regular homing pigeon."

One by one, my motley band entered the campsite. After Keith came Nestor, then Raquel, carrying a huge medical suitcase and backpack, and then a man I recognized from one or two chance encounters at Keith's store, Connie Nevils.

Keith had told me Connie was a crack platoon leader in Vietnam though the wiry little man didn't look that tough. He gave the impression that a breeze might knock him over. He looked so frail, in fact, that I had to remind myself he had earned the Bronze Star for bravery in 'Nam and that in every fight he'd been in the thick of the battle. When Keith vouched for him, that was good enough for me. Over one shoulder, Connie carried a long rifle case, which nearly engulfed him.

I shook Connie's hand. "Nice to meet you, and thanks for volunteering. Any trouble lugging that Barrett through the forest?"

"No sweat," he said with a slow Tennessee drawl. "A few trees got in the way, but I've seen much worse. You can thank me proper if you find something for me to blow up."

"You'll be the second one to know."

He puffed out his chest like a bantam rooster and said, "Thanks. My motto has always been 'smoke the bastards, smoke 'em some more, then smoke 'em again for good measure. Smoke 'em 'til they're breathing through a little, brown shithole in their underwear.'" He sounded like a modern day reincarnation of the prophet Obadiah, and I was swept up by the little man's infectious enthusiasm.

We gathered close together in the small campsite, and I thanked them all for coming to help, and then I turned to Nestor. "You don't know how much I appreciate you finding Danny and guiding everyone here. But this isn't your fight, and you've got your own situation."

"All the same to you, Señor, I like to help. It's boring making drugs day in an' day out, every day, same thing. No senoritas, no action; nothing happens out here in the woods. I have the need to kill someone."

"Good. We've got some vicious customers who need killing, and we can sure use your assistance." I took Keith aside and explained my idea for rescuing Danny.

"I like it. Intricate, but it'll work. How'd you figure it out?"

"Oh, just sitting here all day preparing, planning, and watching squirrels."

We settled down to wait for midnight. We needed everyone in the house to be sleepy for the plan to work. I removed the mosquito netting covering my head and arms and applied liberal doses of the insect repellant Keith produced. I whispered to Raquel, "I'm glad you're here too, but I heard you had trouble getting coverage for your patients."

"Yeah, but I managed. I just had to be here; I've got my own reasons."

"I understand, and that's why I'm worried. Please don't let emotions cloud your judgment. Stay back here, away from the shooting, 'til everything's secured."

"I appreciate your chivalry, Frank, but you don't have to worry about me. I can take care of myself. You taught me how, remember? But I would never allow anything to get in the way of rescuing Danny if that's what you're implying."

Through slats of tree trunks, we spotted a bulbous moon rising in the east, casting an eerie radiance across the lake like a giant flashlight beam. On any other night, I'd have called the panorama beautiful or romantic. On any other night I'd have lain back, relaxed, and enjoyed the spectacle, maybe even smoked a cigar.

But tonight wasn't like any other night. The dazzling lunar glow was just another implement in the arsenal of tricks I would utilize to rescue my son. It wouldn't be long now either. With my eclectic band of warriors there to sustain me, I was able to focus on the task at hand. Nothing would stop me now; I could not fail.

CHAPTER
20

Lake Cypress Springs
Franklin County, East Texas
Thursday, July 3, 2008

A little past 1:00 a.m., and the lights at the lake house had been doused for over an hour. Two sentries patrolled their respective sections of the property. These two had relieved the previous guards at midnight; it seemed that their shifts lasted two hours. Keith and I agreed to an assault just before the next shift change, around 1:50 to 1:55, when they were hopefully at their least vigilant.

We synchronized our headsets, checked our sniper rifles and ammunition once again, added more insect repellant, and cleaned the lenses on our night scopes. We had a final team meeting to review everyone's assignment and departed for our posts.

Keith silently worked his way east through the trees while I angled west. When we came to points directly across from our targets, we turned toward the border of the woods but stopped just before the edge, still under tree cover. At the same time, Connie, with four canisters of tear gas, moved to a spot opposite the back door to the lake house, followed by Nestor, carrying a lightweight aluminum ladder. Raquel remained at the base camp and turned the pup tent into a miniature field hospital.

I unsheathed the Barrett M82 A3 .50 caliber sniper rifle, which Keith and Connie had so lovingly transported from Dallas, and set it up on a short tripod. I peered through its night scope to locate my target. There he was, lit up nicely in a pretty emerald-green phosphorescence about two hundred yards away, well within the rifle's range. This Barrett was the same type I'd used in Iraq, with accuracy to a distance of two thousand yards. My target would soon be dead, eradicated with a single shot—hence its nickname, "The Beast."

The walking corpse of a kidnapper had no idea his time on this earth could be measured in scant seconds. He paced slowly along the seawall, pausing now and then to glance over his shoulder at some sound inaudible to me. I adjusted the Beast's sights for range and windage, "doping the scope." I wouldn't get a second shot before all hell broke loose, but I knew this routine. When I was ready, I alerted Keith through the headset.

At the east end of the lake house he'd performed the same maneuvers I had, except that he used the Colt AR-15 assault rifle, firing .223 caliber rounds. It was a damn good weapon, almost as accurate as the Beast. Since his target sat smoking a cigarette only seventy-five yards away, his shot promised to be easier than mine.

"It's time, Keith," I whispered through the ear buds. "I'm just waiting for a clear shot at my target; right now he's passing by some trees that are blocking my line of sight. As soon as you hear my gun, take out your man. Connie, you hear me?"

"Yes sir, Frank," came back his reply in his soft drawl. "I'll be ready to go when I hear that first shot."

"Good man."

I focused on the target exactly 209 yards away, but he wouldn't cooperate. He wound his way between some trees, rifle slung over a shoulder, for an inordinately long period of time. He stopped with only a bit of arm and leg visible, leaning against a tree and didn't move. One minute passed, then another, and another. I wondered if he'd decided to take a snooze standing up. Patience was one thing in Iraq, quite another with Danny trapped inside that lake house.

"Come on, you bastard, give me a shot, move," I whispered. "Easy, Frank. Wait for it. You've done this lots of times before." True, but this was personal.

At last the man moved away from the grove of trees into an opening, silhouetted perfectly by the shimmering lake and the moon behind him. But he was turned sideways to me. I'd have to take a head shot to be sure of the kill. I couldn't wait any longer, or he'd disappear into the trees again, so I lined him up in the ghostly green light of the night scope and steadied my weapon. I aligned the crosshairs directly over his left ear and squeezed the trigger—a slow, smooth pull.

The shot erupted from the barrel with a thunderous roar, but the weight of the gun prevented much recoil. A fraction of a second later the guard's head exploded like a ripe watermelon into a mass of brain and bone and bloody spray, tinged a luminescent green through the scope. One man down.

Almost immediately I heard the report from Keith's AR-15, then a mumbled "Shit!" through my earpiece. "Frank, he twitched when he heard your shot, and I only winged him. He ducked around the corner of the house, heading your way." I left the Barrett dangling on its tripod, grabbed my own AR-15, and dashed down the northwest side of the lake house, stopping at the far corner. I peered around it.

The wounded man hurtled toward me unaware. His rifle was raised, pain showing on his face. He fired several wild shots when he spotted me. I ducked behind the corner of the house as bullets whizzed past my head, thudding into the wooden logs of the cabin. I raised my rifle to shoulder height and poked it around the corner, pumping three shots in rapid succession, one-handed, without looking. His footfalls suddenly stopped. I peeked around cautiously. He lay on the porch, limbs askew, crumpled like a rag doll. Two down.

The anxiety I'd felt before my first shot had evaporated entirely. The battle calm had come to me and with it the clarity of what had to be done. I felt the same stillness I'd experienced during action in Iraq: a blessed peacefulness. It is as if life slows. I could see the enemy moving as if he were wading in quicksand, but I was kingfisher fast. I felt rage, but a controlled rage, and a certainty that death wasn't in store for me that day, only for my enemies.

"He's down, Keith. Do I always have to clean up your mess?"

"Sarcasm will get you nowhere, buddy. Heard from Connie?"

"Nothing yet. We ought to have stirred up a hornet's nest inside though."

I heard Nestor swinging our portable ladder into position against the north wall of the house. Connie scurried up like a monkey climbing a tree, hardly touching the rungs at all. I heard him run across the roof to one of the chimneys and snip off the chimney cap with tin snips. The mesh screeched as he peeled it away, then he dropped two canisters of teargas inside. He raced to the other end of the house and did the same with the second chimney. The wiry little man was back on the ground a few moments later.

"It's done, boys," Connie said. "Dropped those canisters down like shit through a goose. Just wait a minute or two."

Keith slid into position at the southeast corner of the house. The ominous silence changed into a clangor of shouts and hollering from inside. By now we'd obviously lost the element of surprise. I heard men grabbing weapons and clicking off safeties, all the while barking curses, choking, and stumbling against furniture and walls. My only regret was that Danny had to suffer along with them, but it couldn't be helped.

We didn't have long to wait. Two vicious-looking thugs tumbled out of the south door onto an expansive patio facing the lake. Tears streamed from their eyes; they hacked and coughed but didn't lower their weapons. I shouted, "Drop your guns and hit the floor, face down. Any other move will be your last." The two stopped, looked at each other, and turned toward me, trying to focus. For a moment, they stood there exposed, back to back, one facing Keith, and the other facing me.

Then the fools made a fatal mistake. They began shooting at us, wildly off target, and they died where they stood from our return fire. My biggest concern was for Keith; standing directly behind those two, I didn't want a stray bullet to hit him. But the wily veteran had taken cover behind the opposite corner of the house before he fired. Four down.

I spoke into my headset, "Connie, can you hear me?" There was no immediate answer. Then I heard the crash of two more gunshots from the vicinity of the back door of the house, near the woods. "I hear y'all fine, Frank. Got one a' them bastards trying to sneak out of the house by the back way. Like shooting ducks in a pond, bubba."

"Good work, Connie. Only one to go, and that's the Mole Man. He's got Danny, so I want to take him myself. Keep a sharp eye out. I'm going in through the porch door."

"Careful, Frank," Keith said. "We'll cover you."

I donned my gas mask and tested it; airtight, it worked perfectly. The door lay aslant, unhinged from a stray bullet during the melee. I stepped warily through the opening and hugged the wall, staying low. I crept around to the north side of the house, facing the woods, clearing two bedrooms as I did. I passed the kitchen and living room and crossed to the east side, which yielded another two bedrooms and a media room. I poked the tip of my rifle around the entrance to the first bedroom and swept the room. Nothing. Then, just inside the threshold to the media room, I found them.

Mole Man stood behind Danny, using him as a human shield. He tied a dampened washcloth over his own mouth and nose, and swimming goggles protected his eyes. He looked bizarre, but he could see and breathe fairly well. He held Danny upright, with his left arm around Danny's chest and the right extended, holding a pistol to Danny's temple. The bastard hadn't even cared enough to supply Danny with a wash cloth or goggles, so my unfortunate son choked and wheezed and cried in the Mole Man's grasp.

I pointed the gun at him. Could I risk a shot? "Let him go and drop your weapon and you've got a chance to live, Brunelli. All your men are dead, and mine have surrounded the house. They're covering every exit."

"I don't think so, McNamara. If you know my name, you also know I'm not afraid to blow Danny's head off right now and take my chances. Drop your weapon. Tell your men to back off and give me a passage to my truck or he dies right here in front of you—brains splattered all over the place. You'll have no one to blame but yourself. Don't fuck with me, asshole, drop it now!"

The most basic rule in any hostage situation is never to allow the kidnapper to leave the scene with his prisoner. The location where he takes the hostage next will invariably be much more secluded and dangerous than the present one. We're taught that if you ever get car-jacked, you drive into an obstruction like a pillar or a tree or another auto and hope for the best. If you're held at gunpoint, you run. Chances are the attacker will flee or at least not fire, and there's a good possibility he'll miss if he does.

So I couldn't let this deranged psychopath leave with Danny; at the same time, I knew the man was desperate and might just do what he threatened. I began to lower my weapon. "OK, OK, take it easy. We're going to resolve this without anyone getting hurt. I'll call off my men and tell them to give you safe passage to the truck. Then you let Danny go. I give you my personal guarantee you can leave unharmed."

"Not good enough, Mr. Lawyer. Everyone knows scumbag lawyers can't be trusted. First you drop your gun, then me and Danny go to the truck, and when I'm clean away, I'll drop him off somewhere and tell you where to find him."

Sure, I thought to myself, but will he still be breathing? I couldn't allow that to happen, not now, not when I was so close to rescuing my son. I raised my arms as if in surrender, the AR-15 still in my right hand, my finger still hovering over the trigger.

"You win, Brunelli. I'm putting it down." I spoke into my earpiece, "Boys, let him pass." I crouched as if to place the weapon on the floor and said, "Just don't hurt Danny. If any harm comes to him, I'll hunt you 'til my last breath on this earth." I hoped that last bit of bluster would lull him until I could get into position.

My opening for a shot was narrow. I'd succeeded before with less but never with another person's life at stake, much less my son. I kneeled and made as if to lay the gun down. Suddenly I rolled to the left, raised the rifle to firing position—left hand supporting the barrel, left elbow balanced on my knee—then sighted quickly and fired. The entire action took less than a second. The powerful .223 cartridge passed through Brunelli's right elbow and took the forearm clean off, the pistol still tightly gripped in the fingers of its amputated hand.

A grimace of shock registered briefly on his brutish face, and his left arm reflexively released Danny, who whirled away and flattened himself on the floor. Arterial blood began gushing from the ragged wound in Brunelli's elbow. I fired another round at the opposite shoulder, and he shuddered as that bullet tore into him. He wobbled but wouldn't go down. Incredulous at the man's strength of will, I fired a third round through his right kneecap. Brunelli collapsed, his face registering excruciating pain.

I raced out of the room to notify the others and nearly smashed into Keith, charging the other way at the sound of the gunfire. "Everything's under control. Danny's OK, Mole Man's down. Find Raquel and tell her to get in here. If we don't do something quick, that bastard'll bleed to death, and we'll never find out who hired him."

"Under control?" Keith replied when he saw Brunelli. "You call this mess 'under control'? Looks like you almost dismembered him." The chilling look on my face must've appeared savage. He spotted Danny on the floor struggling to breathe. "You take care of your son. I'll get Raquel."

Keith hurried to find Raquel while I helped Danny up and guided him onto the porch outside where the cool night air would eventually clear the gas from his lungs. He coughed and sputtered; his eyes streamed tears. He was sickly and would need plenty of medical attention, but at least he was alive. I had him back; the damaged ear counted for nothing. I held him tightly to my chest.

"Danny, I don't know if you will ever find it in your heart to forgive me, but I hope, in time, we'll be able to patch things up."

"Dad, I don't blame you for any of this. It wasn't your fault. I place the blame where it ought to be." He wheezed and erupted in a coughing fit.

"Don't try to talk, Danny. There'll be time enough to discuss things later when you're well. Raquel will be here in a minute to give you some treatment. We'll talk after that."

He struggled for control of his breathing and wiped his eyes with his sleeve. "No, Dad...I want you to know right now. I don't blame you at all. I blame Brunelli and whoever he works for. He hacked off my ear, Dad! He practically starved me. You've gotta find out who they are and get even."

"I will, Danny, I promise."

"Frank, Frank, you all right?" Raquel hurtled around the corner, carrying a large black medical bag, followed by Keith. They joined us on the porch. "Thank God." She hugged me hard, briefly, and then became all professional again. "Let me see Danny."

"OK, but make it quick." I pointed inside. "The Mole Man is in there, bleeding all over the place. He won't last long unless we do something."

"Danny's more important. Give me thirty seconds." She whipped a stethoscope from her medical bag, plugged it into her ears, and slapped it onto Danny's chest in various locations, asking him to breathe deeply each time. "He's got pneumonia and bron-chospasm, but his heart's strong. He's suffering with dehydration and malnutrition. He'll need some work, but he'll be all right. Can you guys take him back to the tent, give him some oxygen at five liters per minute and start an IV? I'll be there in a minute."

Keith said, "Yeah, Connie was once a Corpsman in the Marines. He'll know how to do that stuff. Where the hell is Connie, anyway?"

He had barely asked the question when a massive explosion blew the back door completely off its hinges. It hurtled across the kitchen counter and landed a good twenty feet inside the house in the middle of the living room. Outside, on the porch, we all ducked reflexively. Connie appeared in the doorway like a cari-cature out of a Rambo movie, a huge machine gun cradled easily in his left arm and a bandolier of bullets strapped across his chest. Nestor followed right behind.

"Smoked 'em good, didn't we, ladies and gentlemen?" Connie said, bowing. "I had this bit of plastique I just couldn't abide wastin'. Thought it would freshen the air in here a bit faster if we opened things up some."

"I knew you'd find an excuse to blow up something sooner or later," Keith said. "You really must get some therapy, Connie. Explosives Anonymous maybe?"

"Aw, don't get all huffy, Keith. It was only a little ol' door. Don't need no therapy; me and Nestor can take care of ourselves." The two of them seemed to have hit it off.

"Keith, can you and Connie take Danny back to the tent and get his treatment started?" I asked. "Nestor, if you'll join me and Raquel in the media room, we've got some unfinished business with the Mole Man. I may have need of your skills."

"Certainly, Señor, it will be my pleasure," he replied, also bowing low, emulating Connie.

"Omigod, now there's two of them," Keith said. "Nestor, you've been hanging around Connie too long."

Nestor and I escorted Raquel into the media room. The air had cleared somewhat, but we still couldn't believe our eyes. The Mole Man was wiggling grotesquely toward his amputated arm with the obvious intention of retrieving the pistol still clutched in its stiffening hand. He squirmed and slithered like a mad snake with his one good leg and his semi-useful left arm, inching ever closer to the gun.

"Brunelli, you sure don't quit easily, I'll give you that." I looked inside myself and saw a black heart. I leveled my rifle at him, motioning for him to stop, but he wouldn't. He was practically daring me to shoot again. I shot him one more time in his last functioning limb, which finally arrested his pitiful progress. He shuddered. Raquel then tightened tourniquets around his bleeding limbs.

"Finish me off," he rasped. "I'll never make it anyway. Have mercy, do it quick."

"Mercy?" Raquel answered for all of us. "Don't make me laugh. Were you merciful when you tried killing Frank? Or maybe when you kidnapped Danny and cut off his ear and starved him? Or how about when you made me suck your ugly, stinking cock?"

She continued, "You don't deserve mercy, you bastard. I've dreamt of this day for a long time, and I've prayed to see you suffer as we all did at your hands. Guess what? The Lord works in mysterious ways, and here you are. I'll give you some medicine to help you on your way, but you gotta help us first. Answer a few questions, and you get the medicine. Otherwise, we turn you over to Nestor."

He didn't need much persuasion. He admitted running me over and trying to kill me with an overdose of insulin; he admitted to raping Raquel all because she was connected to me; and he admitted kidnapping Danny, slicing off his ear, and sending it to me as a warning. He couldn't very well deny it any longer. But he didn't know the ultimate reason behind it all; he was only told what to do, not why. Who paid him? Who gave him his orders? He obstinately refused to answer those important questions.

"They'll kill me if I give you that information."

"I don't think you understand your predicament, Brunelli," I said. "I'll kill you now if you don't, and it will be slow and painful. Either way, you'll be dead; make it easy on yourself."

He still wouldn't talk, so Nestor provided some extra encouragement in the form of his boot heel grinding into the open shoulder wound. I watched friendly, agreeable Nestor morph into a positively evil man, and I realized why he'd been so useful to the cartel. He displayed utter emotional detachment.

"Sí, Señor, I can kill you now, or your boss, he kill you later. This lady, she is a trained doctor whose job it is to keep you alive so I can make you suffer. Or she can give you the medicina to take away the pain. Which you prefer?" Nestor applied more pressure to the shoulder, grinding his heel ever deeper into the gaping wound.

Brunelli uttered a wailing shriek so pathetic even I turned away. But Nestor was implacable, and Raquel was clearly mesmerized. The man grimaced and writhed and bled some more. Finally he spouted out that he reported to Donald Chandler, who forwarded instructions from whom he didn't know. He received payment at a post office box in Dallas in cash—all unmarked bills in an unmarked envelope. He gave us the address of the PO Box. In fact, he said, there should be a payment waiting for him at this very moment. A little more persuasion from Nestor convinced Brunelli to produce the key.

He knew nothing else, and I believed him. I stood in awe that a human being could withstand such abuse and that another could administer it so dispassionately. Nasty Nestor's nickname was well deserved. Brunelli groaned and pleaded for relief, so Raquel finally relented and gave him morphine—a dosage that seemed rather excessive to me. But then I'm a lawyer, what do I know about medication?

She left us to care for Danny. Keith and I began to clean the place up a bit. We didn't try to remove the blood or the bodies, of course. We wanted the police to find those. The house had suffered so much damage that a total cleanup would've required many days of intense labor. We only attempted to remove evidence of US military ordnance, anything that might tip off the authorities to Keith's role in providing most of the supplies for the mission.

We rummaged through the place searching for shell casings, especially the one from the Barrett, which we found at the edge of the woods. We removed all traces of tear gas and retrieved the canisters. And we cleaned up the temporary campsite of any evidence we'd been there.

Raquel administered intravenous fluids and antibiotics to Danny and oxygen by means of a face mask. A half hour later, she said he could safely be transported to her hospital in Dallas. She and Connie would drive Danny there in one of the vehicles while Keith and I finished the cleanup. We'd meet them in Dallas later. Nestor accepted our heartfelt thanks for his help and returned to his meth lab in the woods.

Raquel said, "Frank, before I leave, I need one last look inside the house to account for all of my medical equipment."

"You sure you want to see Brunelli again? Maybe it'd be better to go and leave the inspection to me and Keith. Besides, we gotta get going before the cops start snooping around. Someone might've heard the noise."

"I'll be fine; I just need a couple of minutes. We'll leave soon, I promise." She reentered the house, black bag in hand. I followed her.

Brunelli lay on the floor where we'd left him. With no functioning limbs, he no longer squirmed after his gun. He looked pale and used up and groaned quietly. Raquel went about removing all the bandages she could find and even removed the tourniquet from Brunelli's right arm. Arterial bleeding recommenced but much slower than before. She removed the IV syringe from his left elbow.

She opened her black bag to stuff all of that in and said, "Frank, give me a minute alone with him, would you?"

He was so feeble I couldn't see the harm in it, so I walked out the media room door. Moments later I heard a primeval scream and rushed back in. Raquel was on her hands and knees, stuffing Brunelli's severed penis into his mouth and hollering like a raving madwoman, "Suck on that, you bastard. Taste good? Here, have some more." As she shoved the disgusting thing down his gullet, Brunelli choked and gasped for air. "Just one itty-bitty little bite more."

I gently grasped her shoulders and tried to lift her to her feet. She shook me off.

"Don't touch me right now, Frank. I've got something to do, and you don't want to stop me. I've had nightmares about this repulsive son of a bitch for months. Each time I think I've exorcised the demon, his face pops up to haunt me some more. I'm going to make sure he never hurts me or anyone else. Never again! It's the only way I can get rid of him. Never again, never again, never again!" She chanted like a frenzied witch over her cauldron.

I thought if I intervened, she just might go over the edge completely. As things stood, she was nearly out of her mind already. And I would be a hypocrite to stop her when, as an attorney who should be first in line to uphold the law, I had taken the law into my own hands and then tortured a prisoner. I had justified it by the extenuating circumstances of our situation. Should different rules apply to Raquel?

I stood back. She returned the bloody scalpel she'd used to her bag, and from it she withdrew an object I recognized. In fact, I'd purchased it for her from Keith. It was the Kimber "Guardian Angel," a gun-shaped device with a trigger mechanism designed to fire a liquid jet of pepper spray up to thirteen feet at ninety miles per hour. On contact with an attacker, the cayenne pepper mist penetrates into eyes, pores, and membranes. It causes temporary blindness, gagging, and pain. If sprayed directly into a person's nose and mouth, it can cause the airway to swell shut, resulting in a choking, suffocating, excruciating death.

"You're not about to do what I think you're going to do, are you?"

"He wanted mercy, didn't he? I'm about to demonstrate my merciful side by euthanizing him. This'll be relatively quick, but don't watch if you can't take it."

Raquel yanked the severed penis from Brunelli's mouth and discharged both tubes of the noxious liquid directly into it from a distance of mere inches. Then she crammed the penis back in again, like a grotesque wine cork. Within seconds, he began to cough and sputter and choke.

The membranes inside his throat swelled until his windpipe closed over. His eyes bulged nearly out of his distorted head, and his facial color quickly transformed from pale white to a purplish-blue. In a couple of minutes, it was over. Brunelli lay still. I admit that I too felt an immense release wash over me at his death.

Could I disapprove of Raquel for breaking with her Hippocratic duty to help her patient at all costs, even forsaking herself in the process, when I'd done the same by violating my own oath? I intended to breach my ethical duties one more time tonight too. I'd have to deal with the consequences of my decision. I hoped she'd be strong enough to cope with hers as well. But I worried for her sake; having a conscience can sometimes be a great burden.

She sighed. "Maybe now I'll be able to sleep again."

"I could never have done that, but I understand why you did. Even so, I'm glad you came with us today."

"Thanks, Frank." She retrieved her medical bag and rose to leave. She paused for a moment and turned to look back at Brunelli over her shoulder. She parted her lips as if to speak, seemed to think better of it, and finally said to me, "I hate him now, even more than before, for making me break every professional oath I've ever sworn." She held back the tears. Only then would she allow me to escort her to the car. She left for Dallas with Connie and Danny.

Between Nestor, Raquel, and me, I'd witnessed a number of dark sides today.

CHAPTER
21

THE PINEY WOODS
FRANKLIN COUNTY, EAST TEXAS
THURSDAY, JULY 3, 2008

Keith heard all the commotion and entered what once passed for a media room in time to witness the pepper spray incident. The room now resembled more of a sadistic slaughterhouse than a place of entertainment. Blood streaked most of the walls; a partially dismembered torso and its various body parts were strewn about. The big-screen television had been shattered by a random bullet, glass was scattered underfoot, and the bookcase had toppled over.

"Quite a scene," Keith said. "In all my sixty-one years, I've never witnessed anything even remotely close. And I'm a gun dealer; I've seen the seedy side of life, believe me. You don't ever want to be on the wrong side of that woman, for sure."

After one last inspection to ensure that no trace of our presence remained, we retrieved the Beemer at the outdoor carport and loaded up our gear. Instead of driving back down the main road toward Dallas, however, I drove farther west, deeper into the forest. If Keith wondered where I was taking him, he didn't let on. About a mile down the ever narrowing dirt path, the road ended. I turned down a driveway leading to the right.

"Please keep what you saw in there under your hat," I said. "If word got out, it wouldn't be good for her career or reputation nor mine either. Not to mention the legal ramifications."

"You kidding? I can't wait to go blabbing about all this." He looked at me and smiled. "Don't worry, my lips are sealed."

"Don't you want to know where we're going?"

"I'm sure you'll tell me soon enough."

"Truth is I've got one more task to complete before we blow this county; this one's for the good of society. Hell, everything we've done today is for the ultimate good of society. You'll be benefiting mankind yet one more time, Keith."

"Wonderful, I'm a very altruistic guy. Something like a donation?"

"Yeah, something like that. Don't you always say it's better to give than to receive? I don't want to spoil the surprise, so just go with the flow."

The path segued into a pebbled driveway constructed through the forest to create a dense, tree-lined tunnel. A short distance later, with some difficulty, I backed the Beemer off the driveway into a small opening between two huge tree trunks. We gathered branches and finished the job of concealing the car. The remainder of the journey would be on foot.

"Grab your rifle and follow me," I whispered to Keith. I shouldered a backpack.

"This gets more interesting by the minute."

Keeping the driveway on our left, we trekked roughly parallel to it through the woods. The early dawn light began to crack through the treetops but never reached us on the forest floor. We utilized our hooded flashlights again and tried to walk softly. The birds in their perches high above us noticed the new day and began a quiet chatter. Keith said it reminded him of many a trek through the overgrown jungles of Vietnam.

About a half mile later, the trees thinned, and we approached a clearing just as the eastern sun began to bleach the sky yellow. In the middle of the clearing we saw a pleasant, two-story log cabin with a green shingle roof. Wisps of smoke wafted from a stone chimney, a neat stack of firewood stood piled to the right, and a short, covered porch led to the front door. The driveway ended at a carport where two pickup trucks were parked. I recognized one of them as Nestor's. So did Keith, and he smiled in recognition.

We crouched in the underbrush, roughly seventy yards from the house, weapons ready, though I hoped they wouldn't be necessary. But Nestor and his boys were a rough bunch; it wouldn't do to go unprepared. Hope for the best but plan for the worst, my commander in Iraq always preached. I pulled the cell phone from my pocket, praying we had decent phone reception in this remote area. I faced away from the house to muffle my voice as much as possible and dialed Nestor's number.

He answered sleepily on the fourth ring. "Sí?"

"Nestor, this is Frank. Remember when I said I would find a way to thank you for all your help? Well, I think I found it."

"Sí, Señor Frank, but nothing is necessary. Why you call so early?"

"Because this is an emergency; for you this time, not for me. This call could save your life, so listen carefully."

"What is it?" In an instant he became more alert.

"I've been listening to the chatter on my police band radio. The cops somehow got word of the fireworks at the lake house last night. They seem to think it's gang related, and they're sending some officers over to investigate."

"But this is far away from me, Señor, no?"

"Yes. But the worst part is that they also have a search warrant for your cabin; they think whoever lives there might've done it. I can't be sure, but it sounded like they're planning to raid the place in about an hour. There's no point in taking chances, Nestor. As your attorney, I advise you and your friends to get the hell outta there, now."

"Ay, Dios Mio! Muchas gracias, Señor Frank. Me, Nestor, owe you one."

"No you don't, Nestor; we're even now. How many men do you have in there?"

"Cuatro, including me."

"I think y'all can make it out if you hurry. Take off right away and don't look back."

"I'm glad I hire you as mi abogado, Señor Frank. You are a good man."

I began to feel embarrassed, guilty even, over the praise I knew I didn't deserve. Just one more incongruity I'd have to learn to reconcile. "Only looking out for my client, that's all. Now, don't waste any more time. You and your men get outta there fast. Go, go, go!"

Keith and I stayed low in the bushes, the day now bright enough to observe the scene through our camouflaged binoculars. Immediately after my call, lights flashed on in the cabin followed by the sounds of a ruckus inside. Not fifteen minutes later, three burly men and Nestor bolted out of the house and made for the two trucks. They tossed large duffle bags into the truck beds and peeled away down the driveway, spinning the tires and spewing pebbles in their wake.

I hoped they'd not dally long enough to discover the Beemer hidden halfway between the cabin and the main road. I also hoped they'd be far, far away by the time the shit hit the fan, which would happen in about twenty minutes.

We waited that long to be certain they'd gone. Then we made our way to opposite sides of the cabin. We smashed in the side windows with the butts of our rifles.

"On the count of three, Keith. This is for Danny and all the other high school kids in America. One, two, three!"

We both hurled incendiary grenades through the shattered windows and beat a hasty retreat back across the lawn to the woods. Before we reached safety, however, we heard the near simultaneous detonation of the two grenades. The concussion hurled us to the ground, dirty and disoriented but far enough away from the blasts to be unharmed. We jumped up, ran for the tree line, and dove behind some trees for cover.

We peered around to glimpse the conflagration. The original blasts had blown great gaps in the cabin walls. In rapid succession those were followed by at least five other explosions as the highly flammable liquids and equipment needed for the production of methamphetamine erupted. The entire cabin became engulfed in a mounting inferno, flames licking the sky as high as the tallest tree-tops. Keith and I raced down the driveway, no longer concerned about concealment.

We made it back to the Beemer in record time, removed the covering branches, jumped in, and tore away. Back down the driveway, left onto the dirt road and past the original carport we drove, slewing and skidding around curves as traction improved and the path steadily widened. When we were far enough past the turnoff to the Cannon lake house for safety, I used the cell phone I'd taken from Mole Man Brunelli to call 911.

I reported both the lake house and meth house events to an incredulous operator, posing as a concerned neighbor and feigning my best East Texas accent. She was dumbfounded. After all, this sort of behavior just didn't occur in sleepy Franklin County. Two emergencies, not one? You sure? I said there'd been multiple gunshots at the lake house location followed by an explosion and fire at Nestor's cabin though I didn't use any names of course, lawyer-client privilege being what it is. I insinuated that both crimes might be related.

There'd been rumors of a meth lab somewhere up in the woods around here, I told her. I said I hoped that emergency vehicles could extinguish the flames before any more of the forest was damaged, Mother Nature being so precious, and all. That part, at least, was true; I hated that so many trees might burn. I gave as my opinion that the shootings were in retaliation for the fire or vice-versa and just had to be by drug-related gangs. I gave no name or other information and clicked off.

"Now that was a beautiful moment. Old Connie will be pissed he wasn't here to see it," Keith said. "Thanks, Frank. I haven't had this much fun since 'Nam. And to think that we rescued Danny and performed a good deed by blowing up a meth lab all in one day. When we get back to Dallas, I'm buying you a drink."

"Thanks, I could use it." I then realized that I should be thanking him. "Keith, I'm glad you enjoyed yourself. For me, though, today was a matter of life and death, literally. I couldn't have made it without Danny. I owe you for that, and I can never repay you. By the way, I only hope I'm as spry as you when I get to be your age, you old bag of shit! You still get around pretty well."

"The pleasure's been all mine, son. Tell me, though, how'd you figure out the location of that meth lab? I'm sure Nestor wouldn't spill the beans."

"You're right, Nestor would never talk. In fact, I told him I didn't want to know, so as his attorney, I could claim to have plausible deniability. Call it an educated guess."

I wondered about that myself. It might have been something Nestor said, maybe the way he gestured up the road, combined with my own deduction. It might have been Fate or just dumb luck, I don't know. Whatever it was, I wasn't going to ask too many questions.

CHAPTER
22

METHODIST HOSPITAL
DALLAS, TEXAS
MONDAY, JULY 7, 2008

During his hospitalization, I lived in Danny's room at Methodist Hospital. In view of my experience as a patient, I was afraid to take my eyes off him for an instant. The room, the ward, the entire hospital, in fact, became eerily familiar. Usually I slept in a cot beside his bed, or if sleep wouldn't come, I'd pace the hallways late at night. I discovered that the sounds of silence are never so hushed nor the atmosphere quite as creepy as hospital corridors in the depths of the night. Every now and then, as I wandered, I could hear the groaning echoes of a grievously ill patient above the mind-numbing nothingness of what sometimes seemed like a morgue for the barely breathing.

Fortunately Danny had a cheery room on the pediatric ward with a pleasant view of a neighboring park. The atmosphere on his ward was upbeat; no one was supposed to die there. He enjoyed bantering with the bright young nurses caring for him. Yet he felt awkward with all the toddlers and young children he'd see in the hallway on his regular jaunts round the nurses' station, pushing his IV pole and wearing a hospital gown that opened all too easily at the back, revealing his underwear.

But sometimes rules are rules, and the rules specify that no "children" under the age of sixteen could be admitted to an adult medical ward. When Danny was sick, he didn't notice or care much about his surroundings. But as he began to improve, he felt uncomfortable among little kids, so he griped and begged to go home. Doctors apparently love to hear their patients talk that way, pestering them about being discharged. They say it's a sure sign of progress.

Raquel had handed over his care to a pediatric internist and a plastic surgeon, but she continued to keep a solicitous eye on Danny. She reviewed every aspect of the treatment program with his other doctors. They probably thought her an interfering pain in the rear, but she couldn't have cared less what the others thought. She personally supervised his care, and I loved her all the more for that.

Raquel conferred with the other doctors and then introduced me to Dr. Sally Renfro, the pulmonary specialist consulted to help treat Danny's pneumonia. The three of us chatted outside Danny's room. She was a rather matronly woman of about forty-five with wispy gray hair. A stethoscope dangled around her neck. "He's making excellent progress," Dr. Renfro told me. "The pneumonia is clearing rapidly."

"You'd expect that, wouldn't you, in a boy as fit as Danny?" I asked.

"Right. It's a good thing he was fit at the start because he wasn't in great shape when he arrived here, that's for sure. It's obvious that his captors didn't feed him well and didn't allow him much physical exercise; he was pretty run down. Besides the pneumonia, he's suffering with anemia and malnutrition. Despite everything, though, he's recovering fast and should be able to go home soon."

I wanted to say, "Those bastards. I'm glad they're all dead," but I held my tongue. Instead I said, "Thanks for your help, Dr. Renfro. And thanks for the good news."

Dr. Renfro said she had other patients to check on and left. When Raquel and I were alone again I said to her, "About Danny; if you're ever asked, you know nothing except what I've told you, nothing about his captivity. And all I told you was that I found him in the care of a Good Samaritan on a country road somewhere east of Dallas. I'll say that a rancher, driving along, noticed Danny wandering aimlessly, sounding delirious, and bundled him into his truck. The only thing Danny said that made any sense was a phone number he repeated over and over. So the rancher called the number, and it rang to my cell phone. That's how I found him, and that's all you need to know. Be as vague as possible.

"If the police need more details, tell them to talk to me. I'll give them a hazy description of a man that could match hundreds of East Texas adult males. I'll say he wanted to remain anonymous, so he wouldn't give me his name, and I was so preoccupied with my son's welfare I couldn't really describe his pickup truck, except that it was white. And, of course, I won't be able to recall the license number either."

"What about when they question Danny?"

"We had a lengthy discussion about that. He's smart enough to play dumb. When he initially gave a statement to the cops, he really was incoherent, and if they question him later, he'll claim he's developed amnesia. He'll say he recalls nothing at all after the kidnappers abducted him from the schoolyard until he woke up here at Methodist Hospital. I really don't think the police will be too persistent in questioning him or us anyway. After all, those six weren't exactly law-abiding citizens. Cops are human too; deep inside they might even feel like thanking whoever did their work for them. Or maybe they'll think the murders were payback for a certain meth lab that went up in flames, a pox on both their houses, so to speak. No one really cares much about criminals killing each other."

"What about Brunelli?"

"What you did to Brunelli makes it look all the more like a mob hit. They say mobsters like to stuff a man's penis down his throat while they're torturing him to show their disdain, sort of a calling card."

"Then are you still so sure we shouldn't go directly to the police and tell them the whole story? Wouldn't they understand rescuing your own son? I have a hard time lying, Frank, always have. Isn't it better to tell the truth?"

"Only if you feel like undergoing endless interrogations, hiring criminal defense attorneys at outrageous prices, and losing untold time away from your medical practice and your patients. If they ever do connect us to the six dead bodies in that lake house, they might even charge you with murder and me with who knows what sort of heinous crimes. I don't know about you, but I don't relish the idea of spending the rest of my life in prison for actions I still believe were right."

I could still see the doubt in her face, so I continued. "Look at it this way; it's not really lying; it's only bending the truth in the interests of justice. Plus, Keith and Connie don't deserve to be placed in jeopardy, do they? All they did was give us their unconditional help when we needed it. Believe me, things are much better left unsaid in some circumstances, and I think this is one of those times."

"I guess you're right, I'll keep it to myself. Hey, I got so distracted I almost forgot the most important thing. Danny's ready to go home in the morning."

I performed a little jig and hugged her. "That's wonderful news. Thanks to you and the rest of his doctors. We owe a huge debt of gratitude to this hospital and its physicians for saving both of our lives."

"No one expects anything more than what your insurance will cover; don't worry about any other costs."

"You are truly amazing. Just one more question. What about Danny's ear? Will his hearing be affected?"

"No, his hearing is perfect; the external ear, it's called the 'pinna,' has nothing to do with hearing. So there's no urgency about re-attachment; it's purely cosmetic. It can stay in deep freeze a lot longer if necessary."

"Cosmetic to you, maybe, but it's still what Danny and I think of as an ear."

"I know. Most people do. When he's fully recovered, Zwilly Levine will thaw out the pinna and prepare it for reattachment by a plastic surgeon. I know an excellent guy for that job too."

"Who's that?"

"Mahmoud Hamza, without question."

"Arabic?"

"Lebanese Christian. He's one of the most skillful reconstructive surgeons in town. He's even done a bit of work on me."

"Has he now? Where?"

"That's for me to know and you to find out, Frank."

"And here I thought you were a natural beauty; no wonder you look so perfect."

"Glad to see you've regained your sense of humor. Thanks for the compliment. There's nothing wrong with a little 'enhancement' now and then, is there?"

"Guess not. I suppose it's not important who the doctor is as long as he's really good at re-attaching ears. He can be Martian for all I care as long as Danny's ear finds its way back onto his head in the right place. How will Dr. Hamza do it?"

"Danny will need some anesthetic, of course. 'Mammy,' that's his nickname, will remove any dead tissue and join the edges from the ear to the scalp using an operating microscope. He'll painstakingly identify as many blood vessels as possible on both scalp and ear and suture them together. Finally he'll close the skin over that. It's exceptionally delicate work, believe me."

"I didn't hear you mention any nerve reattachment. Won't the ear feel numb if you don't do that?"

"The auditory nerve is intact, and the sensory nerves in the skin are too small to suture, so we leave them alone. Amazingly, they'll find a way to regenerate, and about a year from now Danny's ear will probably have normal sensation. Except for the scar, which will fade in time, he'll never know the ear had been lopped off in the first place if all goes according to plan."

"Let's hope it works. You're sure his hearing will be OK?"

"It already is, we've done an audiogram, and it's normal."

"That's great news. Dr. Mammy Hamza, huh? I'll Google him."

"I knew you would."

"Speaking of Zwilly Levine, is he the person to thank for identifying the fingerprints on the brown envelope we found in that Mt. Vernon post office box?"

"He is. I think I already mentioned he's a forensic pathologist, didn't I? He does a lot of work for the Dallas Police Department and occasionally for private investigators. As a favor to me, he didn't charge anything for his services."

"A useful man to have around, isn't he?"

My first concern was to get Danny home again and well enough to return to school at summer's end. We needed to get the ear reattached, within the month if "Mammy" could arrange it. Basketball could come later.

Baby steps, I thought. I'd be able to take Danny home in the morning. That alone would make it a great day, a new beginning. After I got him re-situated, there'd be time enough later on to deal with Donald Chandler.

CHAPTER
23

LAW OFFICES OF SHIPWRIGHT AND CHANDLER
DALLAS, TEXAS
TUESDAY, JULY 29, 2008, 8:00 A.M.

I stepped off the elevator onto the sixtieth floor of the gaudy Petroleum Building in downtown Dallas one last time. The oil derrick still perched arrogantly on its roof. The same attractive receptionist waved at me from her desk in the sumptuous lobby of Shipwright and Chandlers' law offices, which still occupied the entire floor. She managed to juggle two telephone conversations on her headset, file her fingernails, and yet greet me warmly, all at the same time.

"Why Mr. McNamara, what a joy to see you. I thought you'd left town for good. You look much better than you did the last time we met. Here for business or pleasure?"

"You continue to radiate sunshine, Janet. I see you're handling things with your usual cool aplomb this morning."

She flushed with pride. "Just another day at the office, Mr. McNamara."

I leaned over her desk and whispered conspiratorially, "I'm actually here on a social call with my dear friend, Mr. Chandler. I'm going to wait in his office, if you don't mind. When he arrives, please don't let on that I'm there. Wouldn't want to spoil the surprise. By the way, do you know where Sheila Redfern is working these days?"

"She's Mr. Botwin's paralegal now, fifth door on the left. She's doing medical malpractice litigation. I don't think she much cares for it though."

"I can well imagine; nasty business, that. Please don't tell her I'm here either. I'm going to surprise her later. Good to see you again, Janet." I began walking nonchalantly down the corridor toward Chandler's office.

"Good to see you too, Mr. McNamara," her words trailed off as she returned to her fingernails and the various telephone conversations.

I arrived at Chandler's private office before his guard dog, Battleaxe Bobbie, got there. Thankfully I'd not have to deal with her, at least not yet. The door was locked, but I let myself in with a not-so-secret key hanging beneath the Battleaxe's desk. The two of them thought they'd kept it hidden, but the location of that key was known to many at the law firm. After replacing the key, I entered the darkened cavern of his inner sanctum, re-locked the door, and took a seat on a corner sofa, out of view of the doorway. I left the lights off and the drapes drawn, just as they'd been, and settled in to await the Great One's arrival.

At nine o'clock, both Chandler and the Battleaxe arrived on the scene together. She assumed her post outside his door; I could hear them chatting quietly. Something about those two, together all the time, made me wonder if there might be more to their relationship than what appeared at first glance. Couldn't quite put my finger on it.

A key turned in the lock, and the door swung open. Donald Chandler stood silhouetted for a moment, his bald head reflecting light from the hallway. He surveyed his gloomy domain but couldn't see me in my darkened corner. He flipped on a few dim lights and opened the drapes a little, leaving the place still mostly shrouded in darkness.

I began to enjoy the secret power I held over him, watching him putter about his desk, blow his nose, and even lift one buttock to fart. All the mundane actions of a man unaware he wasn't alone. Finally I could wait no longer. I made my voice as deeply resonant and fearsome as possible. "Hello, Donald. Thanks for arriving so promptly."

He jumped visibly away from the sound, plainly taken aback. "Who the hell are you? Where are you? And what are you doing in my private office?"

"Don't you recognize your old associate? I thought you'd know my voice right away. It's me, Frank McNamara. I've come to rekindle our professional relationship, chat about old times, as it were."

"Frank, is that really you? How'd you get in here?"

"You look like you've just seen a ghost, Donald. Thought you'd seen the last of me, didn't you?"

He recovered his wits somewhat. "Come into the light where I can see you."

"What light, Donald? I always considered this office about the dreariest place I could imagine. I thought you liked it this way. The last time I sat in this office, you kept me in the dark, remember? Our friend, Grant Cannon, was here too. Turnabout is fair play, don't you think?"

"I can maintain my personal office any way I like it, can I not?" he replied huffily, inching his right arm from the stuffed chair to the underside portion of the desk.

"Please move your hand away from the desk, Donald. We wouldn't want you to press that alarm button by accident, would we?"

"You don't give the orders here, Frank, I do. You're no longer welcome. And you're guilty of trespassing and breaking and entering. Tell me why I shouldn't call security to have you arrested immediately."

"Go ahead if you must. Press the button, call security, call the police if you like. I won't stop you, but I thought I'd give you the opportunity to make amends before things blow up in your face, before they haul you off to prison. For the sake of you and your family, you might want to hear what I have to say first. Then if you want to have me thrown out, I promise I'll go quietly."

"Why would anyone put me in prison? Have you taken leave of your senses? You haven't planted a bomb in here, have you?"

"No, Donald, I've never been more sane, and there's no bomb. I simply caught up with a lovely fellow named Ricky 'Mole Man' Brunelli. You might have heard of him. After a bit of shall we say, 'enhanced interrogation,' he told me a lot of interesting things concerning you."

Chandler fidgeted in his chair, seeming to shrink into its bulk for protection. His hand slid slowly away from the desk.

"Smart move, Donald." I tried to keep my voice composed, non-confrontational, which was no easy task, as I related the details he needed to hear. "Because of my candid discussion with the late Mr. Brunelli, I know that you are the person to blame for my accident and injuries. And to think how you welcomed me back to work, knowing the truth, both saddens and sickens me.

"Not only that, but it seems that the ultimate blame for Raquel Jennings's rape can be laid at your feet as well. And worst of all, you were the one who ordered Danny's abduction, weren't you? How could you have done that after watching him grow up all these years? How could you have had the gall to commiserate with me over the loss of Danny's ear? Even if you didn't actually order the amputation, you know as well as I do that you're still accountable for any injury resulting from the original felony. You did order the kidnapping, didn't you, and that's still a felony last time I checked. What kind of a monster are you, Chandler?" I strained for control.

He sat there aghast, trying to shrink further into the chair's protective embrace. I think he'd have been happy to have disappeared at that moment. Then he began to plead. "Frank, look at me. As you say, I've known you and Danny for over ten years. How could you possibly believe I'd ever be capable of those accusations? I've always been a law abiding man, a pillar of the legal community, for God's sake. You've got no evidence of any kind, only the word of a convicted felon, and you say he's dead. It'd never stand up in a court of law and you know it."

I couldn't imagine the man still had the nerve to deny it, but I could see he was teetering. "How'd you know he's a convicted felon, Donald, if you had nothing to do with this? I'm not too concerned with evidence in a court of law right now anyway; this is just you and me talking. But if you want hard evidence, I'll give you hard evidence. Remember how you paid Mr. Brunelli to do your dirty work? You placed money in a brown, unmarked envelope in a PO Box at the Mt. Vernon post office once a month. Guess what,

Donald? When I asked real politely, Brunelli told me all about it and even gave me the key. Very agreeable of him, wasn't it?

"Know what I found when I looked in that envelope? Fifty thousand dollars in hundred-dollar bills, that's what. I guess I should thank you for the money; it's come in handy lately for 'expenses,' you understand, since I seem to be unemployed at the moment. And I found your fingerprints all over the envelope and the bills. I'd have thought a man with your knowledge of the law would've been more circumspect. That means I don't need Brunelli's testimony any more. I've got you dead to rights.

"So don't give me any more sanctimonious crap about being an 'upstanding guardian of the law' or 'how could you possibly have done what I'm asserting,' or I'll puke right here on your expensive Persian carpet, and then I'll go straight to the cops."

I entertained the notion that the thought of me vomiting on his precious Persian rug might bother him even more than my threat to go to the police. In truth, involving the cops was the last thing I wanted to do, but he needn't know that.

His resolve finally crumbled. I wondered if he might break down in tears, and for a moment, I felt something near sympathy for the man. He sniffed, "What do you want from me?"

"I want justice, that's what I want. And I want you to accept public responsibility for what you've done. I will accept nothing less, considering the damage you've caused the three of us, not to mention the numerous people you swindled out of their property."

Everything in life is negotiable, and he knew it. "If you wanted my public humiliation, you'd have gone to the cops or the newspapers in the first place. No, you don't want that at all, do you? There's something else. Tell me what you really want."

I decided to come to the point. It's always a wise strategy to give a trapped quarry a possible escape hatch. "Maybe there *is* another way, Donald." I studied my fingernails, allowing his anxiety to twist his knotted stomach even tighter.

"Tell me, Frank. I'll apologize to everyone and compensate them. I'll do almost anything to make things right, just no public disgrace, please."

I turned away and strolled idly behind him, around the desk toward the window. I peered between the folds of the drapes to the street far below. I saw the area bustling with traffic and people, all of them unaware of the drama being played out high above. A more honorable man might have grasped the opportunity to hurl himself out that window and end things properly, but Donald Chandler was not an honorable man. The windows were sealed in any case. He began to squirm.

At length I said, "I'm going to need two things from you, Donald. Neither one will be painless, but both are essential if you're to be spared the humiliation of prison confinement. First I need money, lots of money. And then I'll need information."

"How much money are we talking about?" The old negotiator in him was rising to the challenge, preparing to barter.

I'd set the hook now, so I reached for the moon. "Five million dollars. I know it's a lot, but that's what it'll take just to begin to make us whole again. You know as well as I do what plaintiffs' attorneys always say about compensatory damages. What price can you place on the physical and emotional injuries we've suffered? Since there's no accurate way to evaluate it, we do our best and say five million might begin to cover it."

He exhaled loudly through his long nose. "Five million! You know I don't have that kind of money."

"Don't bullshit me, Donald. You've still got that bank account in the Cayman Islands, don't you? Quite a tax haven they've got down there, and you've been squirreling money away for years. I know you've got the money, so don't try to pull that crap on me."

He opened his mouth, but before he could say a word, I interjected, "Don't bother to deny it. Remember I worked at this law firm a long time, underappreciated I might add. I know a lot of your dirty little secrets."

"And if I say no?"

"Would that really be in your best interests, Donald? I thought we weighed that option already." As if instructing a simpleton, I continued, "Let me be more explicit. I've got the Mole Man's statements admitting his crimes against me, Dr. Jennings, and Danny; and I've got witnesses to prove his veracity. I've got your fingerprints on the payroll envelope and on the money used to pay him, all of which connects you to murder, kidnapping, and rape. The sentences for those crimes alone will put you behind bars for the rest of your life.

"Need more? All I have to do is pick up the phone and call the IRS to report the tax evasion you've been doing these last twenty years. That ought to be enough to get you another life sentence. And you don't have that many lives left. You'll be screwed, blued, and tattooed in prison, Donald; hope they have enough lubricant for you. I hear the other prisoners really enjoy raping lawyers, kind of like turning the tables on their tormentors. Or maybe you'll score a cushy job in the laundry room and only have to give blow jobs to disgusting, smelly guys who come in to pick up their laundry." He shuddered.

"You'll lose your law license too, of course. Ironic, isn't it, upstanding guardian of the law that you are? Lots of public humiliation in that. Think of your family at least, if not yourself; they'll be shunned and penniless because of your crimes. I'm offering you another option, one that'll allow you to avoid prison. I'm throwing you a lifeline, Donald, even though you don't deserve it. Grab it before I take the offer off the table."

"OK, Frank, OK. But five million? It'll just about wipe me out. How about three?"

"Donald, the price just went up to six. I'm not going to negotiate this any further."

"Six? Are you crazy?"

"That's the second time you've called me crazy in the last few minutes. Now it's seven. One more word out of your mouth other than 'yes,' and it'll be eight."

"Eight? But I'll be broke."

"We both know that's not true, you sniveling little weasel. You must have close to fifty stashed away by now. You asked for it—eight million."

"Yes, yes, yes. I give up. I'll get you your filthy money."

"Filthy?" I screamed into his cowering face. "Talk about the pot calling the kettle black!" I regained my composure with great difficulty. "You've been so cooperative to this point, Donald; let's have coffee before discussing the next issue. Call Battleaxe and ask her to prepare some, please; cream, no sugar. A cinnamon roll would go nicely with that if it wouldn't be too much bother. I haven't had breakfast yet."

We sat across from each other in silence while the Battleaxe fetched the coffee and rolls. I felt perfectly comfortable in the gloomy stillness because I knew if he uttered one more self-serving statement, I could throttle the bastard. At last she placed the coffee on his desk and returned to her post outside the door.

"Now then, Donald, this next problem doesn't involve money at all, you'll be happy to know—just a bit of information. I know your 'legal ethics' might dictate otherwise, but the answers to these questions are an essential part of our deal. I want to know who else you worked with on this. I have my suspicions, but I need confirmation. Who gave you the money for Brunelli? I know you're too cheap to pay it yourself. Who gave the orders to shut me up and kidnap Danny? You don't have the balls for that. Who's the brain behind the operation? Who do you report to?"

At first he denied everything. He said no one else had been involved and muttered something about attorney-client privilege, how he was duty bound to keep silent about his client's secrets, even to the grave. Such an ethical man! Inevitably he revealed the real reason for his concern. He said that if he told me the man's name, he'd be as good as dead.

I reminded him that some things in life can be worse than death. His public humiliation would be one of those if I released what I knew to the newspapers and the IRS. So it might be the better part of valor to take his chances with his client. I argued that breaking confidentiality amounted to a tiny ethical breach compared to the horrific crimes he'd already committed.

I finally convinced him. Donald Chandler, pillar of the legal community, told me the name of his co-conspirator to be classified as top secret, of course. He admitted the man's part in the conspiracy and begged me again to keep his involvement confidential.

"Cannon," I exploded. "I thought as much, but I couldn't really believe it. The man has everything. Why does he need to be so greedy?"

"I'm sorry, Frank, so, so sorry. I didn't mean for things to get out of hand this way. You've got to believe me." He begged for my forgiveness. I lied and promised to keep things strictly between the two of us.

"Now, please pick up the phone and call your bank in the Caymans. Have them transfer the eight million dollars to this account immediately." I gave him a slip of paper with my account number written on it. "It's in a neighboring bank, to make the transfer simpler."

He paused with the telephone clutched in his left hand as if reconsidering. Then he inhaled deeply to gird himself and dialed. I opened up an application on my iPhone with a direct link to the bank account. I said, "As soon as I have confirmation of the transaction, I'll be out of your hair and out of this office."

Someone at the bank answered his call and registered the request, apparently without surprise. They must be used to dealing with the transfer of large sums of money at a moment's notice. When requested, Donald covered the mouthpiece with his free hand and mumbled an account number and a password into it. I waited a few more tense moments, half expecting some last minute glitch in my plan—nothing ever goes this smoothly. But for once it did. Less than a minute later, numbers rolled across my screen indicating the eight million dollar deposit had been completed.

"Thank you, Donald. It's been a pleasure doing business with you. Take care of yourself," I said on my way to the door. "I won't breathe a word of this conversation as long as you keep your end of the bargain."

"What guarantee do I have you'll keep your word?"

"You'll just have to trust me on that. Oh, one more thing; please ask Barbara to smile at me on my way out? That sour look of hers gives me the willies."

"Frank, while I'm getting things off my chest, you might want to have a word with Randall's father, Grant. Randall keeps him cooped up in a nursing home here in Dallas, but he's not at all demented. His mind's quite sharp, actually, and he's the man who started the offshore banking scheme to begin with."

Surprised, I replied, "Most cooperative of you, Donald." As I turned to go, I noticed his right arm sneak toward his desk drawer. Thinking he intended to press the alarm button underneath, I said, "No need for an alarm now, is there? The money's already been transferred. We're done here. I'm leaving."

He just nodded blankly. Instead of pressing an alarm button, he opened the drawer and extracted a revolver from it. Mesmerized, as if witnessing the coiled ballet of a cobra, I hesitated. Finally realizing my danger, I ducked low to my right, around the left side of his desk to avoid the shot I thought was surely coming my way. But he hadn't intended to shoot me at all. Methodically he placed the barrel of the gun to his right temple.

Oblivious to my presence, he stared straight ahead, gathering the courage to pull the trigger. I almost relished the idea of Chandler blowing his brains all over his precious Persian carpet; what a double tragedy that would have been. Maybe a glimmer of honor burned within him after all. Then I thought of the certain inquest afterward; I'd have too much to explain.

So I scrambled around the corner of the desk, launching myself upward, and drove my shoulder hard into his chest. I knocked the gun halfway across the room and landed sprawling on top of Chandler. The force toppled him and the chair over backward. The back of his skull hit the floor with a sickening thud. He looked stunned but still conscious, as if shaken awake from a nightmare. Then he began to groan and bleed all over his expensive carpet.

I rolled off him onto the floor and retrieved the revolver, which I pocketed. I tilted Chandler's chair back to an upright position, with him still in it, and grabbed the handkerchief from his breast pocket, using it to apply pressure to his scalp wound. I rearranged his limbs, his clothing, and even his wispy hair. When I punched the intercom button on the telephone, Battleaxe answered immediately. "Barbara, would you please come in? Mr. Chandler needs your immediate assistance."

A moment later, she entered the office, concern plainly visible on her wrinkled face. "What happened here? Donald, are you all right?"

He uttered nary a word, not even a groan. "Oh, he'll be fine," I said. "We were just reminiscing about the old days. He had his feet propped up on the desk, so relaxed he must've leaned too far back in his chair and it toppled over. He seems to have suffered a nasty bump on the back of his head though. If you wouldn't mind, an ice pack would probably do him a world of good."

"I don't believe you, McNamara. Donald's not silly enough to topple over backward and certainly not foolish enough to allow the likes of you into his private office. What've you done to him? How'd you get in? I'm calling security."

"Now, Barbara. I'm not sure how it happened, but he did fall over in his chair. Ask him yourself. I'd keep a close eye on him though; for some reason he seemed confused just before he fell. Maybe he suffered some sort of small stroke or a brain hemorrhage. Probably be wise to get him checked out. I'll be going now, so it won't be necessary to call security. Thanks for the coffee. A pleasure, as always."

The Battleaxe began fussing over Chandler and glowered at me as I passed her. Despite that, and despite Chandler's suicidal tendencies, I felt euphoric after the meeting with my former boss. My own depression and physical pain had completely disappeared even if his had only just begun. At that moment, I felt a large burden had been lifted from my shoulders.

I passed by Janet's desk again, waved casually, and headed down the left-hand corridor toward Sheila Redfern's work station. I stopped to share a few pleasantries with her, my ex-paralegal but still loyal friend.

She greeted me with tears in her eyes and hugged me. "God, I've missed you; you can't imagine what a tyrant Mr. Botwin is. Everything's an emergency that should've been completed yesterday. If I didn't need this job so badly I'd quit in a New York minute. Have you come to rescue me from my misery? Please say you've got a job for me. You did promise, you know."

"I remember, Sheila, don't you worry. In a sense, I have come to your rescue. No job just yet, but I may have the answer to your problems after all. Give me a few more days; I've got a plan."

I left Sheila, made my way to the elevators, and took one to the main floor of the high-rise office tower I'd grown to hate. I checked the micro recorder I had hidden in my breast pocket, thankful it hadn't been damaged during the melee and praying it had picked up the numbers Donald Chandler had spoken into his telephone.

CHAPTER
24

Memory Lane Nursing Home
Dallas, Texas
Friday, August 1, 2008

I timed my visit to the Memory Lane Nursing Home for three o'clock on a busy Friday afternoon, when the nurses change shifts. Raquel had instructed me there'd be more people milling about and more confusion than usual at that time; patients, visitors, and nurses all vying for attention. Reports had to be given, drug supplies accounted for, and paperwork completed so the three to eleven shift could begin with a seamless transition.

Because of its expensive appointments and dedicated staff, Memory Lane wasn't the hellhole of a human waste bin I'd been expecting. I exited the elevator on the fourth floor. Despite the place being immaculately well-scrubbed, however, the pungent odor of stale urine and fecal gasses still permeated the hallways.

I strode down the corridor past helpless victims slumped in their wheelchairs listing to one side and the open door to a room containing a shrouded corpse. Only the occasional shriek of a demented patient disturbed the tranquility of Grant Cannon's premature tomb in room 422 at the far end of the ward. His place looked more like a fancy Las Vegas hotel suite than a room in a nursing home. They must've knocked out a wall and converted two ordinary rooms into one huge suite for the old man.

I hid my recording device in my jacket pocket and turned it on before I entered. From it, a microphone on a wire was taped to my skin, just below my left collarbone. "Hi, Grant. You remember me, don't you? Your old friend, Teddy O'Boyle." The air smelled considerably fresher inside his room.

"Teddy, is it really you? It's been such a long time." Good, his mind seemed just befuddled enough to mistake me for Teddy but not enough to be completely irrational. "What happened to that Irish brogue of yours?"

I'd need to be careful with the old codger who, I knew, was pushing eighty-two and suffered with some sort of neurological disease though he seemed too alert for Alzheimer's. His face was lined and drooped to the right, but his blue eyes twinkled brightly, and he had nearly a full head of closely cropped gray hair. Though he hadn't held a position of authority in many years, in his bearing and demeanor, he remained every bit the chief executive he'd once been. He seemed much less demented than I'd been led to believe. Chandler had been correct.

I tried to recall the accents of my Irish relatives whom I'd heard telling fanciful stories of the old country around the dinner table many years ago. "Took American English lessons I did, Grant. Always tryin' to better meself, I am."

"That's the old Teddy I remember."

"Course 'ya do. It's really me, in the flesh." I knew that O'Boyle would be well over one hundred if he were alive today, but he died a violent death back in 1973. I hoped Grant's unreliable memory would overlook that inconvenient fact but not their entire history together. I wanted to encourage selective recall.

"Teddy, I haven't seen a friendly face in years, and that's including my son, Randall. But you sure do look different than I remember. You seemed shorter and plumper back then—stronger too."

"I did lose a bit o' weight all right; me doctor said 'twas either that or I'd have a stroke."

"Ach! I know all about strokes. Had one myself a while back; paralyzed my right side. See?" He lifted up his right arm with his left and then let gravity suck its dead weight back onto the bed. "At least the legs still work, sort of; I can get about with my walker to lean on. Guess it affected my memory a bit too, not what it used to be. But it ain't Alzheimer's like they say, and it ain't bad enough to need locking me up in this old folks' home like a prisoner."

"What did 'ya mean, 'including' me son, Randall?"

"You didn't hear, did you? Randall managed to stack the Board of Directors of Forestglen and had me declared incompetent. They removed me as CEO. Then he stashed me away in this nursing home and made sure they kept me drugged up 'til I couldn't see straight. I'm held captive here, Teddy, and can't do a damn thing about it because of the stroke. And then the ingrate took over Forestglen, the company my father founded and willed to me. Me, not Randall." He teared up at the thought of that and coughed up a thick wad of phlegm into a bedside cup.

"I knew your Da', Earl, and I loved 'im like a brother, I did. A finer man never left the blessed shores of Kinsale for America. Didja know we come over on the same boat?"

"I did. Da' used to tell me stories about you two in the old days. He said there was no better man than you, Teddy. He trusted you more than anyone he ever knew."

"I know. I felt the same. What about this stroke, Grant? 'Ya looks fit to me. Is there nothing can be done to get 'ya outta here?"

"Can't move my right arm or leg; otherwise, I'd march right out. But there's nothing wrong with my brain like Randall says there is. He almost never comes here, and when he does, it's just to get me to sign papers. Don't know where I went wrong with that boy; gave him everything he ever wanted, too much maybe. How could he turn on his own father like this?"

"Can't figure it, Grant. Things ain't like they was in the old days; there just ain't no respect anymore."

"True. I'd almost rather anyone but Randall was running the company." From somewhere deep inside Grant, a gleam of curiosity flickered within his damaged brain. He asked, "What brings you here to visit me after all these years?"

"I've come to see 'ya on a delicate matter, Grant."

"How's that?"

"Remember the Kilgore clan, the ones what got greedy and tried to squeeze us for more money back in the fifties?"

"How could I forget? First time I ever killed a man."

I tried to control my excitement. "Right. 'Ya was a bit squeamish, but to your credit, 'ya got the job done."

"Bagged those knockers on their way back to their bar one morning, trussed them up good, and threw them in the back of your Cadillac as I remember. Then we drove them up to the lake house. Wonder if Randall still owns the place? He knew I loved it, so he probably sold it."

My hands trembled, and my fists clenched and unclenched involuntarily. I wanted to jam one of them into Grant's smug face. His horrific family used that lake house back in the fifties for the same purpose as today. They must've kidnapped and tortured my great grandfather and uncle the same way they mistreated Danny. At least he'd survived the ordeal; nobody had come to the Kilgores' rescue. I turned away and walked to the window, surveying several wheelchair-bound patients in the courtyard outside. I took in a few gulps of air to steady myself.

"You OK, Teddy? You look strange."

"Never better, Grant." I felt a murderous rage and knew I'd never be the same again. But that was an issue for another time and place. "Remember how those two ended up in the Trinity River? Looked like they'd been worked over pretty good."

"Don't blame me for that, Teddy. You taught me that if you don't beat the hell out of traitors the first time, they come back twice as strong the next. It ended in a bloody mess, but you got them to cough up the names of everybody they blabbed their fool mouths off to; there were six of 'em, remember? Then we finished off the ungrateful bastards." Sweat dampened my armpits, but I managed to maintain my composure.

"You did the first one and made me do the other," he continued. "Showed me how to strangle them proper. 'Learning on the job,' you liked to say. I've never seen a man who enjoyed his work as much as you. When their eyes bugged nearly out of their heads, it seemed to make you intoxicated. Remember the look on the faces of those bastards they blabbed to? You never had to lift another finger 'cause they were so scared of what you might do to them."

"We all have our failings, Grant. I'm older now, and I've got regrets. But I've made me peace with God."

"I'm glad for you, Teddy, I truly am, 'cause you sure were a disturbed individual in those days. But you knew your business, that's for sure. Showed me how to weight the bodies with chain and cement so they wouldn't float to the surface; and you wrapped 'em in carpet so they wouldn't stain the trunk of your nice new Cadillac."

"Yep. We drove back to Dallas with those two stiffs in the trunk and dumped 'em in the deepest part of the Trinity that very night."

"It went off without a hitch too, except for that State Trooper who pulled us over for speeding, near Greenville I think it was. He gave us a pretty good once over before he let us go. We nearly shit our pants. Remember that?"

"'Course I do." I hadn't known about that. "Seems like yesterday. Them was the good old days, eh?"

"They sure were; not so many rules back then. A man with ambition could do some deals and really get ahead. If you knew how to handle yourself, nobody stood in your way. I thank you and my Da' for teaching me that, Teddy."

He talked like a man at a college reunion discussing fraternity pranks and former professors, not ancient murders. I think I would've enjoyed meeting the real Teddy, so I could have shoved a red-hot poker right up his ass and watched him twist. It would be the least I could do for my Kilgore ancestors.

Still, facing me was Grant Cannon, one of the co-conspirators, and he'd just badly incriminated himself. It wouldn't have taken much convincing for me to finish him off right then and there. But I couldn't bring myself to do it; he seemed so helpless and vulnerable. Imprisoned in this nursing home, hated by his son. He seemed tormented far worse already. His final judgment could wait 'til later. I thought he had more to tell, and I wanted to hear it.

I stowed the sympathy, and then I had an inspiration. "The real purpose of my visit here today is to warn 'ya, Grant."

"Warn me?"

"Yeah, the cops've been snooping around. They opened up the old Kilgore case again. There ain't no Statute o' Limitations on the crime of murder, and they aims to find out who killed 'em. So I come to warn 'ya to keep quiet if they come 'round. If 'ya was daft, like Randall says, 'ya couldna tell them nothing anyways. But since 'ya be completely with it, I just had to warn 'ya personal. I know the secret's safe with you and me. Randall doesn't know about the Kilgores, does he?"

"Not on your life. I'd never trust him with that kind of information. I'll just pretend to the cops that I'm *non compos mentos*, like they say I am. I owe you one, Teddy. Thanks for coming." His tremulous voice cracked with emotion. "And let me tell you where to find the paperwork you'll need to stiff Randall."

Grant Cannon, real estate entrepreneur, multi-millionaire swindler, and cold-blooded killer actually had tears in his eyes after that speech. No one had demonstrated any kind of allegiance to him in a long time, especially not his own son. Who could tell what terrifying thoughts roved inside his befuddled skull? I now had indisputable proof of the guilty parties in my family's murders and of their motive. And he told me where to find certain deeds and contracts I would need.

"One more thing I don't want Randall to know," he said. "Don't tell him about a certain bank account in the Cayman Islands. Nobody but me knows about that; me and you, that is, 'cause I'm gonna tell you right now." I'd already learned far more than I had a right to expect, and now this? I hoped the wire was working properly.

He continued, "Somebody has to deal with all that money, and I don't want any of it sticking to Randall's greedy fingers. You could probably use it better, you and 'The Irish Orphans of America.' It's a charity me and my Da' founded many years ago to benefit poor Irish kids. Just don't give any of it to the Church, OK? They've got plenty already."

My interest peaked again, and I wanted him back on the topic. "'Ya have me sacred word on it. The Cayman Islands, 'ya say?" It seemed like everyone who was anyone in Dallas business circles had a secret bank account in the islands.

"On Grand Cayman Island there's a bank called the International Bank of the Caribbean. The manager's a man named Isaac Stanbury, an old friend of mine. He's the one to speak to if he's still alive. If he's not available, speak to his son, Quincy. It's a family-owned bank, just the way me and Da' liked it. You'll need to make this transaction in person; we never wanted any wire transfers. Too risky. Tell him Grant Cannon sent you and give him the account and code numbers."

"What're the numbers?" This was the same bank used by Donald Chandler. I was so excited I temporarily forgot my Irish Brogue. He didn't seem to notice.

"The account number is—let me think a moment. I made it simple so I could remember it and not have to write things down. Let's see. There's letters first, my initials GMC. Grant Michael Cannon."

"I got that part. What else?" I hoped I didn't sound too impatient.

"Numbers too. They have to do with my birthday, I think. No. My mother's birthday, may she rest in peace. Or maybe it was Pa's? No, I've got it now. It was my mother's Ma, my grandma's birthday, that's it! Then you'll need the pass code. It's another bunch of numbers."

"Whoa. When was your grandma's birthday?"

Without warning, the door to the room burst open. An officious-looking nurse carrying a small tray of medicines and needles bustled through the doorway. "Why Mr. Cannon, I didn't know you had visitors." There was venom in her voice. Turning to me she continued, "Sir, our policy is that all visitors must check in at the front desk, and I'd know about it if you had. I'm afraid I'll have to ask you to leave."

"But…"

"There are simply no buts about it, sir. Either leave now or I'll call security." She prepared an injection for Grant.

Strange how people seemed so eager to call security on me. What had I done to deserve such treatment? "Right 'ya are, nurse. I was just saying me farewells, weren't I, Grant? Did 'ya think of the code, by any chance?"

"Indeed I have, Teddy. It's…"

"I've got strict orders, no unauthorized visitors," the nurse interrupted. "There will be no codes around here. I'll not get in trouble on account of you lot. Ready for your medication, Mr. Cannon? That's a good boy."

"I don't want any more medicine, nurse. I feel just fine the way I am. The drugs make me too sleepy."

"Now, now, Mr. Cannon. This won't hurt a bit." She jabbed him with a needle and quickly injected some medication into his buttock. In his paralyzed condition, he was powerless to resist her.

She glowered at me, "Who are you anyway. What are you doing here without permission?"

"I dinna know I needed anyone's permission to visit a friend. What is this, some kinda prison? The Texas Hospital Board'll probably want to investigate this. They call it elder abuse." I had no idea if there was a "Hospital Board," but it sounded good, and there should be one if there wasn't already. I did know about tort law concerning elder abuse, one of the hottest fields for plaintiffs' attorneys these days.

"Look, mister, I don't want trouble, and I don't want to have to call security. It's just that unauthorized visitors to this patient aren't allowed."

"Who says so? He's just a sick old man; aren't visitors supposed to be good for him?"

"Mr. Randall Cannon says so. He's got power of attorney over Mr. Grant."

"All right, don't trouble yourself further on my account. I'm leaving."

Grant wailed, "Teddy, don't leave me here. I need your help to get out. See what I mean? I'm a prisoner held in this rat hole against my will. They're keeping me so drugged up I can't see straight. The day you arrived in America..."

"The day I arrived in America? What's that got to do with anything?" I asked him.

His eyelids fluttered, and he mumbled some gibberish. Then, with superhuman effort, Grant struggled against the effects of the drug and, for a moment, forced himself awake. He leaned forward and held my wrist in an iron-like grip with his one good hand and spoke with a sudden, savage vehemence. "The code, the code number, I remember it now. It's the day you and my Da' arrived in this country." Exhausted, he fell back onto the bed and drifted off.

And a blessed day it was too. Thank you Jesus, Mary, and Joseph. Saints preserve us all. I'd have to do a little research to ascertain Grant's grandmother's birthday, but I felt sure I could find it. That information would complete the account number, and now I had the pass code too. "Don't you worry, Grant. I'll take care of everything. That son of yours will never get a dime nor the Church neither."

Despite what he'd done to my family and despite probable numerous other misdeeds in his life, I didn't like the idea of Grant's own son keeping him a chemical prisoner, drugged up in a foul nursing home against his will. He seemed to be trying to make amends. Then again, this nursing home might be better than what he really deserved, which was to rot in prison. I added this to the mental list of grievances I intended to discuss with Randall Cannon.

I backed out of the room, keeping a wary watch on Cannon's belligerent nurse. I could feel her eyes burning into my chest. In the hallway, I leaned against the wall and paused for a huge breath of air, which I immediately regretted. The odors of urine and feces could not be avoided, like an overripe diaper. I quickly made for the elevator.

Along the way, through the open door, I saw the corpse still shrouded in its room. The nursing staff had settled into the routine of caring for the thirty or so patients populating this ward. I wondered how many of them were kept in chemical narcolepsy like Grant Cannon. As I reached the elevator, I looked up. There, emblazoned above the adjoining doors was inscribed, "The Randall Cannon Family Memorial Wing."

I should've known.

CHAPTER
25

GRANDMA KATE'S HOUSE
DALLAS, TEXAS
SATURDAY, AUGUST 2, 2008

I drove the Beemer through the tree-lined beauty of Grandma's Preston Hollow neighborhood once more. At her spacious, flagstone driveway, I entered the code, waited while the iron gates groaned open, pulled through, and parked.

Someone had already noticed my arrival. Her brown face peeked from behind the drapes. Nothing much escaped the watchful eye of Grandma's trusted housekeeper, Faye Rudolph. As I reached for the doorknob, the door swung open as if on cue.

"Why, Mister Frank! Ain't you a sight for sore eyes? To what do we old people owe the pleasure of your company on this fine day?"

"Miss Faye. You just love to lie in wait for me behind that door, don't you? Can't a devoted grandson visit his Grandma now and then without enduring the third degree? I do love to see you too, of course, especially when you're making fried chicken." I'd timed my arrival for the lunch hour in case there might be some leftover chicken lying around unattended.

"Since you put it that'a way, 'course you can. C'mon right in and set yourself down in the living room. I'll go fetch your Grandma; then I'll look-see if we got some of that fried chicken and a nice cold beer too."

"Miss Faye, you always did know the shortcut to my heart was through my stomach. Thank you."

I plopped into an overstuffed chair in the oak-paneled living room and perused the leather-bound books crammed onto the bookshelves. I couldn't escape the guilt I felt enjoying the comforts of this place, now knowing the source of the money used to buy it. One day in the near future, I'd own the house and all its contents. I would make amends to certain Hispanic Dallasites who'd had their American dream shattered by wealthy people's fear and greed. 'Til then, Grandma and Faye could live out their lives undisturbed.

I had a different plan for today's agenda, though, and it didn't involve Grandma Kate's money at all. She held the key to a puzzle that had vexed me since I'd first discovered the Cortez murders. The squeaky wheels of her wondrous walker announced her presence well before she actually honked and wheezed her way into the room.

She stooped over the walker even more than before. Her torso had become twisted, forcing her to stare at the floor. I greeted her as usual, but this time she accepted my help settling into an armchair. The awkward spinal position compressed her lungs so severely she panted with the effort.

"Grandma, you're looking well."

"Go on with 'ya. I'll be dead in a few days at this rate."

"Seems to me I've heard that line before, and you always manage to pull through. If you're going to die, I wish you'd get it over with. Make things easier on everyone."

She laughed until she began to choke so harshly I thought she might really keel over then and there. When she'd recovered her wits, she said, "No joking this time, Frankie. The doctors say that the lungs are OK and I'm good for a long time, but I don't believe 'em. The deceiving so-and-so's never wanna look you in the eye and give you a straight answer." She had to pause to catch her breath. "Truly, I'm not long for this world. An' I'm glad of it, Frankie, glad of it."

"Don't talk like that, Grandma. What would Faye and I do without you?"

"Maybe you'll understand when you get to be my age, Frankie. This ain't no way to live; can't get enough wind, always looking at the floor, needing someone to feed me and wipe me arse. And when I take me last breath on God's green earth, you'll inherit everything I got, including this house. There's plenty put away for Faye, but I want you to promise me something."

"Of course, Grandma, what is it?"

"Promise that Faye can live here long as she wants to. Don't kick her out into the street or an old folk's home. Grant an old woman's last request."

She began to weep, tears cascading through the deep furrows of her face. She grabbed a Kleenex from the basket affixed to her walker and honked a couple of good ones. Scrawny, bent, and wizened she might be, but I hoped she wouldn't be dying anytime soon.

"Grandma, of course I'll take care of Faye; I love her as much as you do. She can live here as long as she likes, at least as long as she remembers how to make fried chicken."

She wanted to laugh again but thought better of it. "Don't make me laugh, or I'll choke and die even sooner than we thought.

How rude of me! I got so wrapped up in me own problems, I forgot to ask after you and Danny."

"We're both doing well, thank you. I'm all healed up. They reattached Danny's ear, and he's recovering nicely."

"Thanks be to Jesus. I hope the bastards who done this get theirs in spades."

"They will, Grandma, they will. I've got a plan to make things right. Already taken care of part of it, in fact. The information you gave me back in April helped quite a bit too. Now I wonder if you could tell me something more personal. Let's reminisce a little, since you're at death's door and all. I'd like to learn about my family heritage and our connection to the Cortezes before you pass on."

"There you go again, Frankie, making fun of an old woman in her last days on this earth. What wouldja like to know?"

"For starters, tell me about your Pa and your brothers, William and Michael."

She didn't need much coaxing. Faye arrived with a plate of cold chicken and a Heineken. She placed them on a small serving table in front of me and sat down across from us on the sofa. Like a baseball pitcher winding up, Grandma hawked some phlegm out of her throat, sneezed, and blew her nose a couple more times. "There be no secrets here between me and Faye. That OK with you?"

"No problem. I bet Faye knows the details anyway."

"She sure does. Maybe she can correct me flagging memory if I make a mistake." The story flooded out of her. "Me Pa, he was a hard one. Rough and ready as they come, he was. Came from the old country when he was just sixteen; met me Ma on the boat coming over. That was in the twenties. They was both poor as church mice, come to America for a better life. Pa worked construction in New York, then in the coal mines of West Virginia, then on the railroads. That's how he come to Dallas." Her brogue thickened as she spoke, and her eyes turned wistful as if she'd been transported back to another age.

"When he got here, there was a buncha Irish folk in Dallas already, so he fit right in. At first he did a lotta odd jobs, some of it kinda unsavory work, I'm afraid. But once he'd earned enough money, he bought the pub. Kilgore's Tavern he called it, hoity toity like. That gave him a much better living; Irish people gotta drink, ya know. There, let me catch me breath a minute."

She gulped the air down into her compressed lungs and continued. "Pretty soon me Ma was pregnant; first William, then Michael, then me, and all of us born at home. There was a couple stillborns between us last two and another one after me. Ma got an infection and nearly died from that last pregnancy. After that she couldna get pregnant no more. God's will, you know; all for the best. When the boys got big enough, they helped Pa run the tavern."

She told me the story of what happened at the tavern that night. This part, I had already pieced together.

"I know about the dishonest real estate deal that occurred back then, Grandma. What I'm most interested in is what you can recollect about the girl in the back room and her relationship to Michael."

"She were a mystery all right. But they finally figured out who she was. Pretty soon everyone knew."

"Who are 'they'?"

"Why, my boyfriend, Johnny Harrigan, and his buddies. He were only sixteen too. Supposed to be too young to drink in a bar, but he hung out there regular. He told me the whole story. Wonder what ever become of him?"

I tried to imagine Grandma as a pretty young girl with a cocky boyfriend full of swagger named Harrigan. To look at her now, all bent and wizened and breathless, the thought of a beautiful, young Grandma seemed impossible. Aging is inexorable; eventually it steals your appearance and vitality. I wondered how she ultimately ended up with McNamara, my grandfather, instead of Johnny Harrigan, but that story would have to wait for another time. "Go on."

"Johnny said Mikey and that Mexican girl had a fling that summer. He used to entertain her in his office at the back of the bar while Willie took care of business out front, when things was quiet. I expect you can guess what were going on in that back room."

"I can imagine. Young hormones gone wild."

"Exactly. I heard she got herself pregnant. Mikey didn't know. Not until Canuto and Ramón come into the bar, that is. They discussed the beef he had about the price of his land; then Canuto demanded Mikey marry his daughter on account she were pregnant. You remember her name, Faye?"

"Carolina, I think. She was supposed to be a beautiful young woman."

"Carolina, that's it. Anyways, Mikey knew Carolina were in the back room, but he wouldn't admit to it. He said he were too young to get married; said it must be someone else's. He basically told Canuto that his daughter was a tramp, slept around with other men so no one could really tell who the father was."

"What happened then?"

"That's when all hell broke loose. The Cortezes attacked me brothers. They defended themselves, that's all. And the Cortez boys ended up dead. Such a shame too; they wasn't bad Mexicans. Oh, one other interesting thing. That girl in the back room, Carolina, she started hollering an' shooting wild like, all over the bar. Never hit much, though."

"Whatever became of her?"

"Don't know, Frankie. I lost touch with them folk after Mikey died. You remember he got killed the next week. I do know the baby girl survived."

The exhaustion clearly showed on her face; she'd run out of gas. Grandma's nap was long overdue, and Faye escorted her away to the bedroom, shuffling and wheezing. When she returned, Faye said to me, "She really ain't so good, Frankie; won't see the doctor and wouldn't listen to his advice even if she did. She perks up a lot when you visit all right, but in between she's no good at all. Come again by and by unless you want her to go sooner rather than later."

Faye sure knew how to lay on the guilt. I promised I would.

❖

Javier's Gourmet Mexicano would be an ideal place for implementing the next phase of my plan. Located in midtown, Javier's is an eclectic combination restaurant, cigar bar, and internet café. The place is frequented by upper middle-class men and women just like me, offering the anonymity I sought. It was already crammed at 8:00 p.m. on a Saturday night. I made my way to the cigar bar and internet café at the back.

For a couple of bucks, a person could order up a margarita, smoke a cigar, and rent time on a computer. The patrons comprised an assortment of middle-aged Hispanics and Caucasians, some with very young girlfriends dressed revealingly. No one paid me any heed.

I purchased a Pacifico long-neck, chips and salsa, and a computer password from the bartender, then took a seat at a computer terminal. A few couples danced to the music emanating from an old Wurlitzer jukebox. It played a song called "If Dallas Was in Tennessee": *True love is a treasure that's very seldom found, But you can't stay together if there's no common ground.*

Others drank and debated and smoked; there seemed to be more partying than computing going on. So much the better for me. The easiest way to go unnoticed is to get lost in a noisy crowd.

I chomped on chips and salsa and washed them down with my cerveza. I entered the password into the computer and then filled in a URL code and e-mail address. I typed the first message quickly, for I had rehearsed it many times in my mind over the past week. It needed to sound both authentic and intriguing enough to arouse the recipient's concern. Done and sent.

I settled back for another swallow of beer and composed my thoughts. The other patrons still ignored me. I entered a different URL and e-mail address for the second message. This one was directed to Mr. Quincy Stanbury, President of the International Bank of the Caribbean, and explained my situation. I requested a meeting with him three days hence, on the morning of Tuesday the 5th, in the offices of his bank. I sent the message and drained the last of my still ice-cold Pacifico.

I stepped outside to escape the din in the bar and dialed Tracy's number on my cell phone. She answered on the third ring.

"Hello, Frank. How are you?"

"Better and better, Tracy. Thanks for asking. Say, what are you doing tomorrow?"

"I'm off tomorrow, but I've got to be in the office first thing Monday morning. Arthur Shapiro and I have work to do on the Cannon/Chandler case. Why do you ask?"

"I thought we might meet in Miami tomorrow night."

"Miami? It's impossible this weekend. I'd never get back to DC in time."

"You might want to reconsider when you hear what I have to say."

"Really? Convince me."

I told her about my experience with Chandler but not about his secret offshore account. I described my visit to Grant Cannon in the nursing home and how I'd lucked into obtaining his account number and pass code. Then I outlined my plan to recover Grant's money, but it required a quick trip to the Cayman Islands via Miami.

"You know, Frank, I think my schedule just got changed. I'm sure Shapiro won't mind waiting. I'm checking the airline schedule right now. OK, I've got it. I'll be on the 3:00 p.m. flight from DC to Miami tomorrow; it arrives at 5:00 p.m. I'll be staying at the Biarritz Hotel on Lincoln Avenue. See you there."

The valet brought my car around, and I jumped in. I had a lot of organizing to do before tomorrow's flight to Miami, where I would rendezvous with a certain very attractive IRS agent. I knew her assistance could prove invaluable in repatriating many millions of illicitly obtained and untaxed dollars and incidentally fattening my wallet at the same time.

It's not wise to keep the IRS waiting.

CHAPTER
26

GEORGE TOWN, GRAND CAYMAN ISLAND
MONDAY, AUGUST 4, 2008

Unfortunately I ended up having drinks and dinner alone at a marvelous restaurant in the Biarritz Hotel. Tracy didn't make the 3:00 p.m. flight from Washington, or the 6:00 p.m. flight, or the 10:00 p.m. one either. She met me at the airport the next morning, looking frazzled. She had taken the early flight from Reagan International to Miami and arrived barely in time to join me for the 11:00 a.m. flight to George Town, capital of the Cayman Islands.

The words flooded out when she saw me. "I apologize, Frank. I tried so hard to get here last night. Arthur had me reviewing a bunch of crap from the Cannon-Chandler file before I left, stuff I already knew better than he did. When big money's at stake, he just doesn't trust my instincts even though we've done this routine before."

"Take a deep breath, Tracy, and try to relax. The main thing is to clean out Cannon's bank account without his knowledge. We can review the details on this flight instead. Give Shapiro a break; he does what he thinks is best for the IRS, that's all. Besides, I need the so and so to make a deal for me that'll wash my share of the money clean."

The two-hour flight from Miami to George Town passed amiably enough. I tried to remember that Tracy Park was an IRS agent first and foremost; an attractive one to be sure but an "unsavory revenuer" just the same. Her first loyalty lay with the IRS. For my part, the idea of a government with its hand in my back pocket is abhorrent, even if a necessary evil. Yet I needed her at that moment and she needed me, so I lay any negative sentiments aside.

My intuition proved correct too. As soon as we were seated, she tried to get me to divulge Cannon's account number and secret pass code. "C'mon, Tracy," I said, "please don't take me for a fool. I know you're just doing your job, but there is no possible way I'm going to give you those numbers. If I do, and the IRS takes possession of all the money in Cannon's account, how long do you think it'll be before I get my share?"

"Right away, of course. Shapiro told me to expedite things for you."

"Don't be naïve. I don't trust the government to have my best interests at heart, especially not the IRS. I could be tied up in court for years trying to claim what's rightfully mine if the IRS gets its hooks into that money. No chance. Let's talk about something else, like what you meant when you said Shapiro doesn't trust you."

"All right. Even though I'm the one who developed all of our contacts in the Caymans, Shapiro doesn't think I have the savvy to carry out an undercover operation of this magnitude. Truth is, he thinks I got my job because of affirmative action. To get Shapiro to send me on this trip, I had to convince him you wouldn't deal with anyone else. Was that OK?"

"That's the truth, Tracy. I don't trust Shapiro, which is why I appreciate you staying in DC long enough to get him to sign that contract I negotiated before you flew down here. Even if I did miss you last night, I wouldn't do this deal without getting it in writing first."

"Just part of the superior service we provide for our taxpayers. If Cannon's account is worth what we think it is and if we pull this off, Frank, you'll make enough for a lifetime and I'll be in for a big promotion. It would be a huge feather in my cap."

"Tracy, I want this to work as badly as you do. Tell me, what did you mean when you said you got your job because of affirmative action?"

"When I applied for the job several years ago, there were numerous other applicants, most of them white. I think I got the job because I was the most qualified, but some people felt I was hired because I'm black. I have a degree in accounting from NYU, but after I graduated, I made a lot more money as a runway model. After four years of that, I decided to return to accounting, first with a Big Eight accounting firm, then with the IRS. I know I'm qualified because of my training and experience, not favoritism, but some people still hold my race and past life against me."

She still looked every bit the consummate professional, though her fashionable business suit was rumpled. I wasn't surprised to learn she'd been a successful runway model. "How do you feel about that?"

"Pissed, excuse my language. If the entire system must be rigged for me to win, I'd be saying I'm inferior, that I can't play the game without special rules to give me a fighting chance. I reject that idea. I'm not blind. I know that racism still exists. But part of overcoming it is learning how to work the system rather than overturning it entirely. It's all too easy to rely on minority set-asides, affirmative action, and, worst of all, welfare.

"We blacks don't need alibis, Frank. We need education and success in business, achieved by ourselves, to really earn self-respect. But whatever opportunities black people have will be wasted if we keep blaming everyone else for what we lack and keep accepting government handouts. Right now, affirmative action just perpetuates the notion that we aren't as capable as everyone else."

"So we should get rid of it?"

"I don't think blacks will feel truly equal until we do. Maybe we needed it at one time, but not anymore."

"What about the idea that blacks need affirmative action to compensate them for past injustices?"

"If we ever did, that time has come and gone. I'm not a victim. I can compete with anyone even if the playing field is tilted against me. Despite the horrors of slavery, my color doesn't make me feel different—promoting affirmative action does."

When we stepped off the American Airlines jetliner at George Town's ultra-modern airport, great puffy billows of strato-cumulus greeted us. The instant the plane's door opened, I could smell the bougainvillea. The distant sound of steel drums and laughter wafted from the terminal building. Gentle ocean breezes whisked away the humidity from the warm air.

We made our way out of the airplane onto a motorized ramp and into the building. Since the Cayman Islands aren't known for trying to keep people out, clearing Customs was a mere formality, executed efficiently by black officers in starched white uniforms. We grabbed a taxi from an orderly lineup and gave the driver the address of our hotel, the Grande Caribe Royale, on Seven Mile Beach.

Tracy stared casually through fashionable dark sunglasses out the window of the cab at the exquisite sights of this tropical paradise. In the course of her duties, she'd been here many times. The experience was brand new for me, though, so I soaked up the exotic panorama and the azure blue ocean.

Immediately after Grant Cannon's revelation of the secret Cayman Island bank account, I'd made plans to journey here to empty it. I wanted to bring Randall Cannon to justice too, if possible, but the money came first. I needed to launder the money; I didn't want to live the rest of my life looking over my shoulder.

The only way I could legally accomplish those goals involved the IRS. I had Cannon's pass code and account number; the IRS held the means to wash the money clean and make the transaction legal. All they had to do was agree that the money represented "compensatory" damages rather than "punitive" damages. Legally speaking, compensatories aren't taxable since they represent a recovery for previous injuries; they're not considered income, like punitives. And I had plenty of injuries. I'd willingly give up a portion of the proceeds in order to make the balance of it legal. So I struck a deal with the IRS, and Tracy had just handed me the signed contract.

As an attorney, I was well acquainted with "Whistleblower litigation." In these cases, a member of the lay public can share in the recovery of funds rightfully belonging to the United States government if his information proves vital to the case. So I had filed a lawsuit against Cannon and Chandler at the federal courthouse in Dallas under the appropriate *Qui Tam* Statute, the official Latin phrase. Qui Tam lawsuits are kept highly secret until the government decides if it wants to take part in the case. That way, the wrongdoer will not be warned and flee the country.

Because I knew of their interest in Cannon's dealings, I notified Arthur Shapiro and Tracy of the lawsuit. Shapiro was chief of the Abusive Tax Shelter and Offshore Banking Section or ATSOBS. Tracy told me the agents there called him "the chief SOB," but not to his face. Shapiro leapt at the opportunity to enrich the Treasury Department.

Normally a person who brings information to the government's attention, resulting in a monetary recovery, may obtain up to 25 percent of the proceeds. I negotiated a deal for 33 percent, plus legal expenses, and insisted I be a part of the recovery team in order to protect my interest.

Can you believe that Shapiro initially balked at that, insisting he would protect my rights? But I knew the IRS would probably have kept all the money for itself, and not informed me of any possible bonanza, had I not already known the law. So I insisted on going along. Good thing I'm such a cynical bastard.

We arrived at the Ritz Carlton Hotel and were escorted to our rooms by neatly dressed bellboys with clipped British accents. Tracy suggested we meet for dinner in two hours in the hotel's renowned Silver Palms Lounge. Tomorrow we would meet Mr. Quincy Stanbury, manager of the International Bank of the Caribbean, to claim the funds and set up a sting operation to trap Randall Cannon.

I took a hot shower, changed into casual clothes, and called Danny on my cell phone. He stayed at his grandparents as usual. Raquel's team of doctors had deemed him well enough to have his ear reattached, and the operation had taken place last week. So far, it was successful. The doctors were optimistic that both Danny and his ear would make a full recovery.

I called Raquel too. She seemed glad to hear from me. She said she had just bought another gun from Keith; we agreed to test it when I returned. I made my way downstairs to the restaurant's bar, a little before the appointed dinner hour. I'd sworn off alcoholic beverages during this trip, at least until the conclusion of tomorrow's business. But I figured just one little martini couldn't hurt.

By the time Tracy arrived, somewhat late, I was halfway through my second. She still wore a business suit though this time with a skirt instead of trousers and some magnificent perfume. "Black Orchid" by Tom Ford, she said. I'd remember that for Raquel.

"Frank, you're looking more relaxed. I see you've got a head start on me with the cocktails. You hungry?"

"Famished. How about you?"

"Me too. Dinner's on the IRS tonight. May I suggest a bottle of wine?"

"That's strange; usually I'm paying the IRS, not the other way around."

"Then let's take advantage of your good fortune. How about a chilled French Chablis? I have a feeling we'll be ordering one of the outrageously good seafood dishes; they make delicious mahi-mahi and grouper. And there's a fabulous duck on the menu as well. Chablis would go perfectly with any of those."

"Fine by me. You seem awfully familiar with this place, Tracy, and a wine connoisseur too. It's good to know that all the money we paeans pay dear Uncle Sam doesn't go to waste."

"Let's just say I've been here before but always in the line of duty to catch the tax cheats who force the rest of us to pay more than we should. You wouldn't believe the assets hidden overseas and the greed; people worth millions of dollars, hundreds of millions even, coveting more by not paying their proper taxes. The government money spent investigating fraud in these islands is outrageous, but it's money well spent, believe me. We make a tremendous return on our investment."

"Touché. It's not really the tax collectors I dislike; I know they're only doing their jobs. The tax code itself, that's the problem. It's practically unintelligible and just begs for chicanery."

"Believe it or not, most IRS employees feel likewise. We fill out the exact same tax forms, and we hire accountants like everyone else. In fact, we've got to be more careful than anyone else because we get audited automatically every year. Blame Congress, blame the special interests, blame whoever you like for the tax code, but not the IRS. Care to review our plans for tomorrow's meeting with Mr. Stanbury?"

"We meet him at 10:00 a.m., correct? I'll give him the proper account number, pass code, and some identification. He'll wire a check for the entire proceeds of Grant Cannon's account to my bank in Dallas. After deducting my one-third share of the money and my legal expenses, I will send the IRS the balance. You've given me the account information for that transaction."

"Haven't you got that part ass-backward? Mr. Stanbury is supposed to wire the money to the IRS's bank account, and we'll distribute your share of the proceeds within two weeks."

"Tracy, Tracy, Tracy. I might've been born at night, but not last night. Even after two martinis and some wine, I still know enough to see right through that ploy. Once the IRS gets hold of the money, it'll take its own sweet time about disbursing it. I might get my share in two weeks or two years, who knows? I might even have to sue to get it back and be tied up in court for years. No thank you. At most, I might be convinced to have the appropriate amounts wired to our accounts simultaneously."

"Right. Then just give me the account and pass code, and I'll wrap up the whole deal for you in a nice red bow and cut you a check immediately."

"That was a joke, wasn't it? Otherwise I better get you to a psychiatrist right away; you're off your rocker."

"I wasn't laughing. OK, have it your way. Thought I'd give it a try."

"You know the definition of psychosis, don't you? It's engaging in the same dysfunctional behavior over and over again yet expecting a different result each time. You keep asking the same question from different angles, and you get the exact same answer every time. There's no way I'll give out those numbers 'til we meet Stanbury at the bank. Please don't get psychotic on me, at least not until after tomorrow."

"All right, all right. Just make sure we get our money quickly. Otherwise Shapiro will not be happy. He'll slap a tax lien on everything you own so fast it'll make your head spin."

"First, let me say that I don't like to be threatened, even by a woman as beautiful as you. Second, you already know my attitude: never mess with the IRS. I pay my taxes, as happily as one can do with taxes, and I pay right on time. I definitely don't need an irritated IRS boss or a lecture from you."

"Well then, you're to be commended, Frank. If everyone obeyed the law and paid what they owe, we wouldn't need IRS agents at all. I didn't mean to threaten you; we really don't want to mess with you anyway. After all, you're helping us. Much more fun to go after big shots like Randall Cannon and much more profitable too. That's where the money is, and that's why they pay me the big bucks."

"Then let's call a truce, at least until after tomorrow."

The maitre d' escorted us to a cozy table for two in a corner of the restaurant. Tracy chose the wine, and the Chablis paired perfectly with my grouper and her duck. We ordered another bottle. After all, the IRS was picking up the tab, and I wanted to make certain it got good value for its investment.

My eyes began to droop with the time change and my over-served condition. But Tracy, still bright and alert and sensing my disadvantage, couldn't resist one last attempt to pry the account and pass code numbers from me. As I rose from the table to wobble to my room, I nonetheless had the resolve to resist her. Mumbling something about psychotic IRS agents, I said goodnight and left her there, nonchalantly drinking Chablis.

I forgot to request a wake-up call for the next morning and woke up late. I dashed half dressed through the hotel lobby, down the steps to Tracy's waiting taxicab, mere seconds before she'd have left for the bank without me. She sat in the back seat, tapping her wristwatch and enjoying my discomfort. I practically flew into the cab, shirt-tails flapping under my suit jacket, socks sagging around my ankles, and tie draped unknotted around my neck. I clutched my briefcase in one hand and a to-go cup of coffee in the other.

"You could've called to wake me up," I said testily.

"Here I am, cab already organized, waiting for you to deign to show up, and you blame me for the lack of a wake-up call? You're a big boy, Frank, or so I thought. You must know how important this meeting is to both of us and how wise it would be to arrive on time. Just like a child; it's always someone else's fault."

"Look, Tracy, at least don't treat me like one of the enemy. Do I need to remind you that your precious Internal Revenue Service wouldn't have a penny of these millions without me? So let's work together on this, please; then you can go your way, and I'll go mine, hopefully as friends. How were you going to get into Cannon's account without the proper pass codes anyway?"

"I always have a backup plan."

I didn't doubt it. She'd probably hypnotized me last night and made me divulge them. We spent the remainder of the short ride to the International Bank of the Caribbean offices on Commerce Street in oppressive silence. I licked my palms and patted my chaotic hair into position. She stared out the window, crossing and re-crossing her long legs and fastidiously examined her fingernails. She had chosen a pinstriped gray business suit with an ultra-short skirt for the occasion. Despite my annoyance, her great legs were a distraction, which, I suppose, was her intention.

At the bank, a female assistant guided us into a tastefully decorated private office and left us there to wait, all without saying a word. The sign on the door read "M. Quincy Stanbury, President." From sumptuous sofa to antique bookcase to elegant desk, it was quite obvious that the International Bank provided Mr. Stanbury with a lavish lifestyle. The time on his elaborate Louis Quatorze desk clock showed precisely 10:01 a.m.

"Good of you to arrive so promptly," said a cultured voice from behind us. I hadn't heard the concealed door open or close. Tracy poked me in the ribs as if to say *told you so.* "I trust you had a pleasant flight to our tropical paradise."

He stepped around our chairs and extended his hand, first to Tracy, then to me. "Quincy Stanbury, at your service. I've previously had the pleasure of Miss Park's acquaintance. You, sir, must be Mr. Frank McNamara, Esquire of Dallas, Texas. May I offer you something to drink?" He spoke in a patois mixture of a clipped British accent and Caribbean lilt.

Tracy politely declined his offer but I answered, "A pleasure to finally meet you, Sir. Black coffee, please."

"You Americans and your morning coffee, eh? I believe I'll have some tea myself. Are you sure you won't join me, Miss Park?"

"No, thank you, Sir Quincy. I've breakfasted already." She glanced reprovingly at me, as if I were about to do or say something unspeakably vulgar. Sir Quincy was far less arrogant—most gracious, in fact.

He looked incongruously un-knightlike, though. His owl-shaped head showed tufts of gray wool at the sides, and his bald dome was topped with a few long strands combed back and forth to give the futile impression of scalp coverage. I wondered what would happen to the careful arrangement on a windy day. He peered quizzically through thick, horn-rimmed spectacles, and he was impeccably dressed in a tan linen three-piece suit.

"Let's get right to it, shall we? No sense knocking about the bush as you Yanks like to say." I briefly thought about correcting his flawed attempt at American idiom, but I glanced at Tracy and thought better of it. We sat back down as his assistant arrived with the tea, coffee, and some biscuits too, which I eyed ravenously. He'd never really ordered the refreshments; the young woman just seemed to know his mind. "I understand you're here on a most delicate matter." He poured coffee for me and tea for himself. Tracy reluctantly accepted a cup.

"Yes, sir. As we discussed on the phone, our business concerns the account of Mr. Grant Cannon, a close family friend of mine.

Mr. Cannon entrusted me with his private account number and the pass code so that I could transact some business for him." I handed over a sheet of paper containing two items: the bank account number—GMC-4995 for Grant Michael Cannon and his grandmother's birthday, April 9, 1895—and the pass code of 9226, for September 2, 1926, the date on which Earl Cannon and Teddy O'Boyle arrived in America. I'd retrieved those dates from archives available over the internet.

"Please keep those numbers confidential for the time being. You may be aware that Mr. Cannon has suffered a major stroke and now resides in a nursing home. He asked me, as his dying wish, to transfer the full balance of the account to certain charities he has designated in the US, in an effort to make himself right with the Lord before he passes. He especially wanted his son, Randall Cannon, to be kept as far away from the money as possible."

"Yes, so you explained to me." He glanced at the paper. "The account number and pass code seem to be in order. The problem I have with your request is that this same Mr. Grant Cannon signed notarized affidavits many years ago stating that in no event should his funds be released to anyone other than himself, no matter what the circumstance. I have them here for your perusal if you wish. He did this when my father held the position of president, but as managing partner of the bank, I was well acquainted with the man and his wishes. Possibly he did it to prevent his son from accessing the funds as you say. I've researched the matter thoroughly, and because of those documents, I'm afraid I cannot grant your request without further consultation. We have very strict banking laws here in the Cayman Islands."

I reviewed the proffered documents; they looked authentic. "Mr. Stanbury, I thought we had discussed these details and ironed out all the problems last week. Now, at the last minute, you've managed to create a hitch in the proceedings. Since I wasn't apprised of the need to obtain a written nullification of his previous instructions, surely he must have provided for another person to act as Power of Attorney in the case of his incapacity."

"He did. Unfortunately both of those designees have predeceased Mr. Cannon, and I'm afraid you were not amongst them. He has failed to nominate anyone else."

We seemed to be at an impasse. All that money so close yet so far away. My face reddened in anger and frustration. I grabbed a biscuit to distract myself. In fact I took two and managed to drop some crumbs on the expensive carpet, to hell with good manners. Tracy remained impassive, listening and sipping the tea she didn't really want. She chose that moment to place her cup on the coffee table between us, lean toward Stanbury, and uncross her amazing legs. Stanbury stared lecherously at them.

She fixed him with the most malevolent stare, one I didn't think possible in such an attractive woman. I should have known better; she was, after all, a highly experienced IRS field agent. "Mr. Stanbury," she said, "do I detect a note of reticence to part with such a large sum of money? I suppose it will reduce the bank's profits to some extent when you can no longer lend it. I understand that, and I sympathize. But, what *you* must realize is that it's not your money to manage any longer. It's our money now." She indicated herself and me with a nod of her head.

"Ah, Miss Park, but I do understand. The money isn't yours or Mr. McNamara's yet, is it? It still belongs to Mr. Grant Cannon until such time as I obtain official instructions from him to the contrary. Until then, I will decide the disposition of the money, and for now, it will stay in my bank."

She continued, "Apparently you don't fully comprehend the peril of your uncooperative position, Sir Quincy. You are acquainted with my superior, I assume. Mr. Shapiro is not a man to be trifled with, at least not when it comes to funding the United States Treasury. He's a most aggressive enforcer of our tax code, and he sent me down here to pick up my government's share of Mr. Cannon's ill-gotten money. Now you are attempting to prevent me from doing my job. I thought we had already settled any conflicts, including your exorbitant fee."

"Indeed we did, Miss Park. But I didn't anticipate finding Mr. Cannon's instructional letter in the file when I reviewed it yesterday. Unfortunately my hands are tied by my country's banking laws."

"Banking laws? More like tax avoidance schemes." Her steely voice rose an octave higher. "You are, of course, aware of my country's grave distaste for offshore tax havens such as those found in the Cayman Islands. Some of them have a legitimate purpose, no doubt, but it is common knowledge that most are set up to avoid US taxation. As such, we intend to stamp out all the abuse in the system, and that includes any unofficial "understandings" with certain governments like yours. We've even created a special department for the purpose, and we will squash any puny bank such as yours, Sir Quincy, which attempts to hinder us. Believe me, we will grind you into dust."

He hesitated. He had obviously no desire to run afoul of the American IRS. That might spoil his lucrative offshore banking business. Still, he wouldn't easily part with the enormous profits to be obtained from such a large account as Cannon's. "I understand your position, Miss Park. Allow me to consider your request in the light of this newly acquired information. Shall we meet again in say two days' time, at the same hour?"

"No, Sir Quincy, we shall do no such thing. We'll settle this right now."

The two of them ignored me as they hurled verbal daggers at each other. I felt like a spectator at a prizefight; they closed on one another, stabbing and parrying, probing for a weakness. I felt glad it wasn't me on the receiving end of Tracy's barbs.

"I think you'll see the light in a moment, Sir Quincy. I anticipated having a hard time prying that much money from your clutches, so I created a contingency plan."

"Have you now? A plan I'm sure will fail before our impartial banking laws."

"Not likely. As I said, Mr. Shapiro doesn't take kindly to interference with the enforcement of the American tax code."

"Then we have your income tax law in opposition to my banking law, do we not? And I hope you've not forgotten we're in the Cayman Islands at the moment, Miss Park, not Washington, DC. My laws will doubtless prevail."

"Can you be so certain? Did you know that my boss has a close personal and professional relationship with a highly placed minister in your country's government?"

That statement stopped him for a moment. His eyes flickered, and he paused to sip his tea and regroup. "You don't say? And who might that be?"

"Does the name Sir Percival Hastings mean anything to you?"

"Sir Percy, the Chancellor of the Exchequer?" He nearly choked on his biscuit.

"Yes. In fact he's expecting your call right now if you please."

He blanched. "Right now? I'm to call Sir Percy right now? That will never do; he's a busy man, no time for trivial matters such as this. Never, it couldn't possibly be." He clearly realized he was trapped.

"There are exceptions to every rule, Sir Quincy. Go ahead, he's waiting. Shall I dial the number for you?"

"You know his number by heart?"

"I do indeed. It's his personal cell phone number, in fact; he and I are on a first name basis. How shall I phrase this delicately? We're very close friends." She picked up the desk phone and dialed. A moment later a deep bass voice answered. Tracy's call apparently delighted the person on the other end of the line. He kept her talking for several minutes before reluctantly agreeing to speak to Stanbury. "Thank you so much for your help in this matter, Sir Percy. Mr. Shapiro will be most appreciative. And thanks for the invitation to dinner. If I can only settle this little dispute with Sir Quincy in a timely fashion, I'll call you later."

She handed the phone to Stanbury, whose right hand had apparently suffered an untimely palsy. He seemed unable to grasp the receiver due to the sudden tremor. She had to fold his fingers around it and clasp it to his ear. My respect for Tracy's skills increased exponentially.

"Hello, Sir Percy? Sorry, Sir Percival." A one-sided conversation ensued in which Sir Percy mostly talked and Sir Quincy mostly listened. The voice on the other end, so congenial with Tracy, sounded harsh and authoritative, even from across the desk. Once in a while Quincy stammered and mumbled assent to something he heard. He became pale and trembled; beads of perspiration appeared on his brow and receding chin. His arm flailed behind him to locate his chair. Finding it at last, he sank gratefully backward. When the conversation ended, he rested his head on the seat back and exhaled.

Thus properly rebuked, Quincy turned to us. "It seems Sir Percival would be most appreciative if I hand over the money you rightfully own with all due haste. I'm also to extend to you every possible assistance and courtesy. And I intend to do exactly that as he instructed. I apologize for any inconvenience." He knew when he was beaten.

"Thank you so much, Sir Quincy," she soothed him. "We know you were only doing your job, protecting your clients' interests. We admire that, don't we, Mr. McNamara? We'll be certain to inform Sir Percy and Mr. Shapiro of your exceptional cooperation." She glanced at me and winked.

I barely had time to nod assent before she continued. "Now, I believe the present balance in the account is $132 million plus. If you could prepare the two bank wires we require, one for me in the amount of $88 million made out to the IRS, and one to Mr. McNamara in the amount of $44 million plus whatever loose change is left over for his 'expenses.' We'll watch you wire them to our respective banks in the US and wait for confirmation that they've been received. And then we'll be out of your hair." After witnessing Tracy operate, I didn't dare quibble with her division of the spoils.

"Just one more thing, Sir Quincy," I added. "While we're at it, there's one other account in need of 'adjustment.'" I handed him another piece of paper with different account and pass code numbers on it. "Please divide the entire contents of that account the same way, two-thirds to the IRS and one-third to me, and wire the proceeds to the same two banks in the US." I turned to Tracy and winked back. A broad smile spread across her face.

CHAPTER
27

George Town, Grand Cayman Island
Tuesday, August 5, 2008

Grand Cayman Island is the largest of the three-island Cayman chain. Nature has endowed it with some of the most exquisite underwater scenery in the entire world. Old shipwrecks adorn otherwise pristine sandbars and reefs, attracting all manner of wildlife from green and hawksbill sea turtles to orange elephant ear and strawberry vase sponges. Placid angelfish swim alongside fearsome barracuda while vicious-looking moray eels thrust formidable jaws from crevices in the coral at unsuspecting prey.

Stingray City, a sandbar in the North Sound of the island, is the most famous aquatic site by far. It teems with hundreds of tame stingrays eager for food and human attention. Nowhere else on earth can humans interact with stingrays like this.

After the successful conclusion of our business with Sir Quincy, Tracy and I headed down to the docks. The concierge kindly referred us to the 'Big Bad Barracuda Bait Barn,' or B-5, the premiere location on the Sound to obtain nautical equipment and alcoholic refreshment. We rented a motor launch with an ice chest and some snorkeling equipment. With a six pack of Caribe Beer packed away in the cooler, we pushed off, and the surf eradicated our footprints. Warm gusts of wind flicked frothy foam skyward. I felt ecstatic; it's not every day that I bank $59.5 million.

We headed out to Eagle Ray Pass, smack dab in the middle of Stingray City. An underwater canal there meanders through the reef, allowing passage for the rays from the shallow, ten-foot-deep water of the Sound to the vast depths of the ocean on the other side. We decided to share the rest of our afternoon with the flotilla of friendly stingrays that usually hang about in the vicinity, begging for morsels of fish.

On the way there, we recounted the remainder of our meeting in Stanbury's office. Tracy's demeanor had changed entirely; previously brusque and businesslike, she became relaxed and sociable in a matter of minutes. "Who is Sir Percy Hastings," I asked, "that he could engender so much fear and respect from the likes of Quincy Stanbury? And how do you know him so well?"

"He's the Chancellor of the Exchequer here in the Caymans, comparable to our Treasury Secretary. He's a man with a lot of power because he has jurisdiction over all the financial institutions in the country. And because he also controls the money supply, he's not someone to trifle with. In other words, he could put any bank out of business if he had a mind to. As far as my relationship with him is concerned, that's a private matter and not for public consumption."

"Now that *is* intriguing. Does Mr. Shapiro know about it?"

"Again, not your business, but yes, he knows and approves wholeheartedly. It makes me more effective. If Shapiro cares about one thing, it's my results, not the means I use."

"Lovely. Remind me never to cross swords with him."

"Remember, you'd never have pried the money from Sir Quincy, the avaricious little man, without our help. And your $59.5 million is tax free because Shapiro himself approved the deal and deemed your share to be 'compensatory damages.' You'll probably never have to concern yourself with him again, after you thank him profusely, of course."

"From your lips to God's ears. Believe me, being rich makes me feel warm and fuzzy all over. And I do thank both him and you. But don't forget that the IRS wouldn't have recovered a penny without my input. Aside from making lots of money, I thought the best part of the day occurred later on when Randall Cannon walked into Stanbury's office, didn't you?"

"My God, yes. Your e-mail set him up perfectly. How'd you do that?"

"Not too difficult, really. I already had Randall's private e-mail address from my work at Shipwright and Chandler. I obtained Quincy's from a search of the International Bank of the Caribbean's web site. I used a phony URL on a computer at an internet café to send Randall a message he thought came from Quincy. The message stated that there had been some irregularities in Randall's account that could only be discussed in person due to his country's banking secrecy laws. It alluded to the IRS making inquiries about his transactions; just enough information to frighten him and lure him to the Caymans but not enough to answer any questions definitively."

"The fear of losing $132 million will do that to a person," she said. "When Randall barged into Quincy's office, I thought the dear old man would faint; but he played his part well, didn't he?"

"He sure did," I said. "Nice of him to allow us to observe from his secret hideaway."

"I really will give Percy a favorable report on the matter. Did you notice how relieved Randall became once he heard his money was safe? He plopped back into one of those armchairs sweating like a Trojan but managed to regain his breath when he heard the good news. I think Quincy actually enjoyed his role; he seemed most convincing when he presented Randall with that fake check for $132 million."

After observing how easily Quincy deluded Randall, I immediately called my bank in Dallas to ensure that my deposits had arrived safely. They had.

"Now tell me about Chandler."

"Ah yes, Chandler. We didn't get as much money from his account, but in some ways cleaning him out was even sweeter. I had my electronic wire on when he phoned Sir Quincy on my behalf from his office. It recorded the numbers he spoke into the phone, and after you softened up Quincy, I didn't think we'd have much trouble emptying that account as well. Another $31 million for the IRS and $15.5 million for me; that bastard was hiding $46.5 million even after he paid me $8 million. He'll probably want to kill himself when he finds out if he hasn't already."

"Our agents in Dallas are arresting him right now, hopefully before he does. Eighty-eight plus thirty-one equals $119 million. Shapiro will be pleased."

I slowed our boat as we approached the reef. "What happens next with Cannon?"

"When Randall arrives back in Miami, federal agents will be there to arrest him and haul him off to jail. Our lawyers will argue strenuously that he should not be granted bail due to the major risk he'd flee the country. I'm guessing he'll remain in jail pending trial, which could be years away. Since he never declared that he owned the account on his tax form, never paid tax on the money in the first place or on the interest earned, and never declared the money when he entered the country, we've got him cold on several counts of tax evasion, fraud, conspiracy, and money laundering. It'll cost him many millions of dollars, plus several years in prison. And do I understand correctly that you have other incriminating information about dear Randall?"

"Do I ever! How about failing to report profits on several different real estate transactions?"

"Oh, this is getting juicy. I get turned on just thinking about it."

"Well, hold onto your bikini. Wish I could be there to see Randall's fat face; the shock'll probably be enough to push him over the edge. But I admit I'd rather be here with you, snorkeling at Stingray City. Maybe he'll do the right thing and die of a sudden heart attack. It would save a lot of grief for everyone concerned. I'll cut the engine and drop anchor over there." I pointed to a lighter shaded patch of ocean where several other boats floated. "Get your gear on."

"You do have a mean streak, don't you? You should never wish ill health on another human being."

"Why not? He wished it on me and my son."

"Because if he dies, he'll never be able to pay off his debt to the IRS."

"Just when I thought you might have some compassion, it comes down to money. Always looking out for the company, aren't you?"

"Yes, and don't ever forget it. I believe in the virtue of my work. Shapiro said he'd call to notify me the moment they have

Cannon in custody, hopefully alive. In case you're interested, I'd rather be here too, snorkeling with you."

She stood up, balanced perfectly against the rocking of the boat, like a *Sports Illustrated* swimsuit model in her revealing aqua and beige bikini. She paused momentarily so I'd be sure to notice, looking like a bronze goddess. Then she jumped overboard, floated for a moment adjusting her snorkel and mask, and flutter-kicked slowly over the sand bar.

I donned my fins and mask and grabbed a small net full of sliced mackerel and jumped over the gunwale after her. A moment later, several hungry rays surrounded us. They paraded regally past, wheeling and banking for another run. We caressed them as they brushed against our legs. We fed them directly from our open palms, feeling the soft suction of their mouths until they had slurped up every last scrap of fish. But when our supply of mackerel ran out, the ungrateful moochers left us for nearby 'bluer pastures,' where other divers dangled yet more goodies.

We returned to the boat exhilarated. How often do you get to communicate with untamed, primordial creatures like stingrays, so gentle yet potentially so lethal? We lay side by side on the transom of the boat, absorbing the warm sun, drinking beer and rocking softly on a moderate swell. No words were necessary.

After a while, I clambered down, started the engine, and raised the anchor. We cruised to the north wall of the Sound and moored in front of the Tarpon Alley Bar. We strolled along the dock to the wharf where we took a shaded table with a panoramic view. A few stray ships anchored in the pale blue ocean and fluffy white clouds dotted the horizon, interlaced with dive-bombing pelicans. The busy bar served its patrons, and street vendors aggressively hawked their wares. A random halyard flapped against a ship's mast in the light wind, making a pleasant knocking sound. The romantic scene made me think of Raquel, despite Tracy's nearness.

We shared a dozen oysters, chased by crackers and more ice-cold beer, and watched the tourists on the strand. "You seem to have devoured seven of these little honeys to my five, Tracy. Does the IRS always take advantage of its taxpayers like this?"

"Couldn't help myself, and you're way too slow. Anyway, Uncle Sam's paying, remember? Careful though, they're aphrodisiacs."

"This time I'm buying. I've got to justify certain 'expenses' incurred working on this case. Didn't you love those stingrays? They seem so placid and friendly. But didn't somebody on a nature show get stabbed in the heart by a stingray's tail and die while filming?"

"Yep. But I heard he grabbed the tail trying to play with the beast; best not to rile 'em up, just like the IRS." She slurped down the last oyster. That first dozen turned into a second as we whiled away the idyllic afternoon of a very productive day. But somehow, I could never quite catch up to her oyster consumption. We returned to the boat and cruised back to the beach, where I hailed a taxi to our hotel.

There she headed to the La Prairie Spa for some sort of makeover while I returned to my room to shave and shower. I checked in with Danny, whose ear improved daily, and he continued readjusting well to school. I felt proud of him; the kid seemed tougher than I'd thought. And I called Raquel who said she missed me and couldn't wait for me to return. She wanted to talk.

I met Tracy in the lobby for dinner. She had transformed herself once again. No more stuffy business attire or revealing bikini; instead, she wore a fitted blue cocktail dress, its lines showcasing her curves. I'm not quite sure what the spa people had done to her face, but her cheeks glowed and her eyes sparkled.

"You're sure Sir Percy won't miss your company tonight? Didn't you have an appointment to meet him?"

"I come to the Caymans quite a lot these days, so I can see Percy anytime. Right now I'd rather have dinner with you."

"Your attitude toward me sure has changed since this morning."

"Was I too rough on poor Frankie? I'm sorry; business before pleasure I always say. I had to have my game face on earlier, but I'm off the clock now. I'll make it up to you, I promise."

I couldn't argue with that philosophy, but I reminded myself never to interfere in her business. We took a taxi to the Bamboo restaurant at the Reef Resort, on the far eastern end of the island. Heads swiveled in our direction as we were seated on the veranda. A white jacketed waiter served the Martinis straight up and ice-cold with pimento olives. Mine was vodka, hers gin.

She said, "Did you notice those people staring? You'd think they'd never seen an interracial couple before. Guess I'm just too used to New York and Washington where nobody really cares anymore."

"They care in Dallas, believe me. Where I live, there's an uneasy truce between blacks, Hispanics, and whites, who are no longer the majority by the way. People are much more conservative there, and you rarely see whites with blacks; Hispanics with blacks or whites maybe. But it surprises me that the black people here in the Caymans seem to gawk at us just as intently as the whites do. I thought blacks, at least, were more tolerant than that, especially in the islands."

"Not necessarily. Blacks have the same stupid prejudices as other people."

"Live and learn."

Her cell phone rang, and she took a moment to answer it. "Sorry for the interruption, I've been waiting for that call; it was Shapiro. Now I can turn it off and give you my full attention. He said federal marshals arrested Randall Cannon the moment he arrived in Miami and bundled him off to jail. He's facing so many charges it'll make his head spin for years. He'll be cleaned out, with not even a pot to pee in, which might be a worse fate for a man like Cannon than going to prison, though I imagine he'll get to enjoy a lengthy stay at 'Club Fed' too."

"I know he deserves whatever's coming to him, but I can't help feeling sorry for the guy. Losing everything you've got and going to prison for perhaps the rest of your life sounds appalling. I think I'd find a way to commit suicide."

"He should've thought of that before he bilked his country out of millions and nearly killed you and your son. The arrogant bastard thought no one could ever take him down. Come now, Frank, don't waste another ounce of sympathy on a man like Cannon. In my opinion, his crimes warrant the death penalty. Today, though, fines and imprisonment is all we can do to the likes of him, so we'll have to take what we can get."

"I know you're right. I'll try to put it behind me." So I forgot about Randall Cannon and tried to focus on healing my family and on my new-found wealth. But stunning, intelligent Tracy Park kept short circuiting my thought processes.

The sun began its inexorable descent into the ocean behind us. Soaring royal palms cast exotic shadows over the harbor, and we watched sea birds floating and wheeling in the dusk. Twilight segued into inky black tropical darkness, illuminated by a few twinkling lights from distant ships. I wished Raquel could have shared the romantic scene with me. Everything, the birds, the trees, the clouds, and especially the ocean, reminded me of her. But she was in Dallas, and there was beautiful Tracy right beside me.

The air chilled dramatically, and she drew closer. Steamed, salted edamame accompanied our second cocktail. The Bamboo restaurant is known for its sushi, so we sampled almost everything. We had tuna with beer; yellowtail with sake; snapper with more beer; and scallops with more sake. By the end of dinner, I felt stuffed and drowsy and guilty at feeling aroused by Tracy's nearness.

I paid the check, hailed a cab from the line of taxis, and escorted Tracy into the back seat. I slipped in beside her. When I mentioned I had a slight headache, she produced two Advil and insisted I rest my head on her lap. She massaged my temples, and the stress of the past days and months began to dissipate. The tender rocking of the cab combined with the warm softness of her lap lulled me to sleep.

⁕

Next morning we sat on the tarmac awaiting clearance for our flight to Miami. We sat beside each other but spoke little. We had accomplished a great deal in the past forty-eight hours, but something had changed since last night, and now there seemed to be an uncomfortable tension between us. We received clearance to take off and taxied down the runway. I broke the silence first.

"Tracy, thank you for all you've done to see this deal through. No doubt about it, I never would've been able to convince Sir Quincy to give me the money without your help. I'm grateful, and I'm going to write Shapiro, telling him what a topnotch agent you are. If there's ever anything I can do for you, please don't hesitate to ask."

"Thanks for the kind words, Frank. You're a wonderful man; I just wish we'd met each other sooner."

I stared through the porthole as the plane lifted into the air, wondering what she meant by that but hesitant to ask. It accelerated to cruising altitude, sweeping past acres of open ocean, dotted by whitecaps and an occasional ship. "What do you mean by 'sooner'?"

"Sometimes men can be so dense," she replied harshly, "you in particular."

"Was I not a gentleman last night? Did I offend you?"

"That's exactly the problem, Frank. You were entirely too gentlemanly last night. I've been searching for a reliable man like you for a long time. Then, out of the blue, you fall right into my lap, literally. So I tried my damnedest to seduce you, and believe me, my damnedest is usually pretty good. But all you could do was repeat Raquel's name over and over again in your sleep."

"I am so sorry. The last thing I'd ever want to do is hurt you; you've been a good friend. I did tell you about Raquel, didn't I? I didn't try to lead you on?"

"No, you didn't. You were perfectly honest about her. It's just that—oh, never mind. Obviously you two were meant to be together. Don't be sorry, Frank; be happy. Still, if you ever change your mind, you know where to find me."

The 727 began its lumbering descent into Miami International Airport. God help me if I'll ever be able to understand women!

EPILOGUE

Rough Creek Lodge
Glen Rose, West Texas
Friday, August 15, 2008

The day began overcast, but the summer sun quickly chased the clouds away. While the rest of the city worked, the two of us stole out of town for a weekend alone, a guilty pleasure shared with someone special. We were on our way to the exclusive Rough Creek Lodge in West Texas. Raquel had to organize residents and associates to cover for her, but leaving town was much easier for me; I still had no job to worry about. Then again, I no longer needed one.

I guided the Beemer south through downtown and took the ramp for Highway 67, west toward Cleburne. After a leisurely drive of about an hour, we arrived at Fossil Rim Park, a state preserve dedicated to the conservation of the bones and habitat of prehistoric creatures.

We inspected authentic dinosaur tracks and plant fossils, preserved for millions of years in the hardened clay soil of dried creek beds in the parched landscape. An entire Triceratops skeleton had been recovered from this same region in 1976, and is now displayed in the Dallas Museum of Natural History. Afterward we lunched at the nearby Safari Lodge, a rustic resort populated by all manner of African game and other exotic animals.

We continued on to the rural town of Glen Rose, the county seat of Somervell County, situated smack dab in the middle of the Barnett Shale geological formation. Here impoverished ranchers became wealthy overnight from the discovery of a natural gas bonanza fortuitously located directly beneath their property. Gas wells dotted the landscape everywhere.

Another seven miles past Glen Rose, we crested a hill and entered a well-manicured private driveway leading to the lodge. A breathtaking panorama greeted us. Rough Creek Lodge, built by an eccentric multi-b'jillionaire, is a magnificent log cabin resort blended harmoniously with the surrounding harsh beauty of the West Texas plains. Almost nothing disrupted the monotonous flatness of the landscape. From the lodge you can see for many miles in every direction, your gaze interrupted only by scrub brush, the odd arroyo, and an occasional coyote loping along, marking his territory.

The bellman conveyed us to a huge log cabin suite overlooking an enchanted valley forested by dwarf trees. A thin ribbon of a stream meandered through the hills and rocky outcrops. The place was decorated in a Western motif: large fireplace with hammered andirons and logs ready for lighting; heavy leather bedspread; spurs, branding irons, and ranching pictures covering the walls. The price included an extravagant dinner for two in the adjacent five-star dining room.

No one disturbed us on our balcony all afternoon while we drank in the glorious view and sipped on the martinis I prepared. A gentle breeze raised the hairs on our forearms and ruffled Raquel's blouse, accentuating her breasts. With each deep draught of desert air, the stress dissipated from our tense muscles.

I felt reluctant to interrupt the tranquility of the moment, but she turned to me and said, "It doesn't get any better than this, Frank. This place is so remote, so elegant and rustic, I'll have no choice but to forget about work and relax for a while. Thanks for inviting me."

"And now I get your full attention for an entire weekend. And Danny's doing well. Hell, even Josue Fuentes is hanging in there. I'm even beginning to let go of my hatred for Cannon and Chandler. It certainly helps that I have most of their money and that they'll be locked up for a long time. The best part is that the Latinos displaced by the construction of the original Regency building are going to be compensated out of Forestglen funds."

"Thanks to Josue Fuentes and his Latin American Fund for Equal Rights and all the lawsuits they filed. Who says lawyers are good for nothing?"

"We have our moments; I knew you'd come around eventually. I'm trying hard to forget those two and what they did. My psychiatrist says that clinging to hate destroys a person faster than any other emotion. It eats away at your insides until it consumes you."

"Me too. I won't lie to you; I still have nightmares about Brunelli but less often. I simply won't allow that man to ruin the rest of my life. I'm glad I killed him, though. Is that wrong of me?"

"I don't think so, considering what he did. And I know Brunelli's where he deserves to be, roasting in hell. Besides, if you hadn't killed him, I'd have had to do it."

"I guess you and the IRS fixed Cannon and Chandler good, didn't you?"

"Oh, we only started the ball rolling. Once Josue took over, the media had a feeding frenzy. After we got through with him in Grand Cayman, Cannon's pockets were $132 million lighter, and I was personally $44 million richer. Adding that to the $8 million I wheedled out of Chandler and the third of his Cayman Island stash makes a total of $67.5 million. Not too shabby; I can do some real good with that money. Maybe I'll even be able to afford dinner tonight."

"If not, I'll float you a loan as long as you don't eat too much. Doctors don't make the big fat salaries people think we do."

"You're right, they don't. So here's what I'm planning to do: I don't want you to ever again have to worry about money. So I'm going to give you $5 million. You ought to have a reward for all you've done and all you've suffered on my account."

"Five million dollars! Are you nuts? I don't need it. I don't deserve it."

"Yes you do; you most definitely deserve it. Give it away if you like, but you're getting it regardless. If it'll make you feel any better, you won't be alone on the receiving end of my largesse. I'm giving away a lot more. Five million to a trust fund for Danny's education, and the same to your Uncle Alfredo. I know it won't bring his family back, but maybe he'll feel somehow vindicated. Maybe he'll even learn to like me.

"There's also $5 million for Josue, providing he sets aside enough on which to live comfortably for the rest of his life before giving the balance away to his LAFFER organization. And I'm giving a million each to Nestor Guzman and Connie Nevils for their exceptional help in rescuing Danny. Besides, I owe Nestor a little something for the loss of his crack house."

"I wondered if you had a hand in that."

"We lawyers like to say, 'I neither admit nor deny anything.' Though things do seem to have a way of working out in the end, don't they?"

"Yes. What goes around comes around. At least Nestor can take up a legitimate line of work now or go back to Mexico a rich man."

"I hope so; he's a loyal guy. Oh, speaking of loyalty, I can't forget Tracy. There's a million for her. And Sheila Redfern. I've got a million for her too and a job indefinitely as long as she wants it. I'm going to need a good personal secretary. And I gave another million to Keith Glenn, except that he claimed he and Jan didn't need it, so he donated it to the National Rifle Association. What do you think of that?"

"I like my guns; that's for sure. Where would we law abiding citizens be without them? I'd be dead, and you'd never have been able to rescue Danny. You seem to enjoy throwing those multi-million-dollar checks around, don't you? Be careful; you're spending your windfall like a drunken sailor. At this rate there won't be anything left over."

"Don't worry; there'll be plenty left. Sixty-seven million is too much for one person anyway, but it does give me a lot of latitude to do the right thing. I've never felt like this before, Raquel. I feel almost like when I used to take Vicodin. I'm one attorney who's determined to be a part of the solution, not the problem. You're right, though. Giving money away feels great; there's really nothing like it. I think I feel better than the recipients. And I've been saving the best part for last. Want to know what it is?"

"Who's the lucky person this time?"

"Methodist Hospital, in your name, to start that Indigent Clinic you've always wanted. I hope someone like your grandmother,

Carolina, never again has to die in childbirth for lack of funds. Now you'll be able to treat your patients as you see fit, according to your medical training, not because of some government mandate."

"Yes, the meddling has become absurd. I spend a big chunk of every day coding and filling out forms instead of treating patients. We sure will put that money to good use. Thank you for myself and on behalf of the hospital."

"My pleasure." I squinted into the imperceptibly descending sun.

"I can hardly explain how much I'm enjoying myself with you, Frank. Just the two of us, here at the lodge. It's not the money at all. This place is so romantic. Thanks for practically forcing me to take a weekend off."

"I was hoping you'd think that way." I pointed skyward. "Have you noticed that red-tail hawk floating back and forth way up there? I bet he's scoping out a tasty morsel somewhere down below; his circuit is becoming tighter and tighter. Watch."

A warm wind rippled through our patio. We stared transfixed for another minute or two as the hawk continued to track his prey. Round and round and round he hovered, gliding on invisible draughts of air above us, while the meal he sought undoubtedly scurried about below, mindless of its peril. And suddenly the hawk was gone. Not actually gone, just transformed into a hurtling missile. The raptor folded its wings about its sturdy aerodynamic body and plummeted several hundred feet down before we could distinguish him again.

A scant few feet above the earth and its own certain destruction, the hawk suddenly parachuted his wings wide like Dracula snapping open his vast cape, and lurched to a halt, talons extended. It flapped violently for balance for a few seconds as it sank those razor-sharp talons into the soft, yielding flesh of a young rabbit.

Within a few seconds, it rose ponderously into the sky, wings beating furiously with the added weight of its kill clutched tightly within its claws. This time the predator looked more like a Huey helicopter laboriously lifting off than the streamlined jet plane it had been moments before. The doomed rabbit struggled in vain to extract itself from the hawk's death grip as its life blood slowly drained away.

After a moment in awed silence, Raquel blurted out, "My God, nature can be violent. I guess some creatures must die so that others might live. It's the universal order of things."

"That it is. Seems like that hawk just found his evening meal. Maybe it's time for us to head out to the restaurant for our dinner. You hungry?"

"Famished."

So we showered and dressed. She wore an ivory sheer-lace blouse with delicate ruffles in front, hinting at a black demi-bra underneath, paired with a silk, black, mid-calf skirt slit modestly up the left side and gathered at the hip. I never imagined such a serious academic could look so glamorous. In that outfit, she would not have looked out of place on a *Vogue* magazine cover.

I dressed in a black Pal Zileri tuxedo with a pinstripe twill shirt open at the neck and no tie. With my newfound wealth, I'd splurged on the outfit at Sebastian's Closet, a trendy men's store in North Dallas.

The moon disappeared behind some threatening clouds, and a breeze blew through the screened porch. Twilight approached as we strolled from our cabin to the expansive, enclosed verandah of the main building. She snuggled closer, and I enveloped her in my arm. Neither of us spoke; we communicated via the intertwined fingers of our clasped hands.

The maitre d' led us through the lobby to the dining room. He seated us side by side at a candle-lit table, facing an enormous, room-length window furnishing a unique vista of the darkening valley below. The brooding sky looked ominous as the dying sun peeked from behind tall black thunderheads. A sudden, violent squall blew across the plain, accompanied by jagged bolts of lightning that now and then illuminated the darkness outside.

We enjoyed a glass of Opus One Cabernet Sauvignon as rain began pouring from the heavens, slanting sideways and pelting the window panes. Thunderclaps interrupted the steady thrumming of the downpour. Everywhere on those wide open plains, I knew that West Texas ranchers thanked their various deities for the desperately needed rainfall.

Raquel swirled the wine around inside her mouth and licked her lips with an impish grin. Her piercing blue eyes held my gaze, as if I were under her hypnotic spell. But underneath the cloth-draped table she shifted her leg until it caressed my own. Dinner arrived. She ate her entree of beef rib-eye voraciously. She said she preferred maintaining herself with demanding Zumba workouts three times a week, rather than by denying her robust appetite. I ate my Tasmanian salmon with fingerling potatoes rather more slowly.

Torrents of rain fell from the sky, but we lingered over a shared dessert of chocolate angel food cake with macadamia ice cream, snug and contented. Neither of us appeared eager to leave this charmed place, yet we were both also impatient to return to our room. Finally I signed the check, and we rose to go.

By the front door, a valet provided us with an enormous umbrella, the words *Property of Rough Creek Lodge* boldly imprinted on it lest we forget and accidentally take it home. We cuddled underneath and made our soggy way under a covered walkway back to the cabin. Powerful winds roiled the waters of the small lake into snowballs of foam and spray and pressed us onward to the cabin door. Under the portico, we shook ourselves off, grinning and laughing while I fumbled for the key.

When I turned the knob, a forceful blast thrust the door open, and we hurried through. Closing it against the wind was another matter entirely. Inside the room, the blaze of a romantic fire inflamed us further as the rain pounded our windowpanes.

We kissed urgently, and then were at each other, hands everywhere. We embraced, kissing and caressing without speaking a word. Our clothing fell to the floor by the front door. I had never touched any woman the way I touched her body that night, discovering her most secret places. We were so totally engrossed in each other; no other living soul even existed.

Her nipples hardened as they flicked against my bare chest. She gasped in delight. Unashamed, she posed seductively for me and caressed the hairs on my chest and stomach. She smiled when she noticed my erection. I carried her gently to the duvet-covered bed and laid her on it. She sank into the luxury of the silk sheets, lounging against the soft down pillows.

She loosened her hair and let it spill down her back in a wave, tossing her head to force the crimps and curls out. I stood at the side of the bed, silhouetted by the red embers and yellow flicker of the cozy fireplace. Then I lay down beside her.

At first I worried that I would be clumsy or worse, quick. But Raquel guided my movements expertly; her hands cool on my fevered flesh. She took out a small bottle of scented oil she had concealed in the bedside table. I watched as she poured a few thick drops onto her palms. It had a musky fragrance that filled my lungs, intensifying my desire as she released my erection and straddled me. She rubbed the oil onto my chest, making me gasp, while grinding her pelvis on my abdomen.

I took some of the oil from my chest and reached upward to her breasts, remembering the first time I had seen the soft swell of them in her gown at the Dallas Country Club many months ago. I pressed my mouth gently against one, then the other, tasting her perfumed skin. She panted and gasped and opened her mouth to lick dried lips with her tongue; then she stiffened, arched her back, and finally shuddered in release. She collapsed quivering onto my chest.

My nostrils smelled the musk, whether from her or from the scented oil, I couldn't tell. I lay her on her back and tasted her. This time the orgasm was more subdued. A soft mewling sound rhythmically rose and fell from her, accompanied by thrusts of her insistent pelvis, followed by uncontrollable trembling.

Even then, I could not sate her. When I plunged inside she groaned frantically, thrashing her head side to side. Every portion of our bodies yearned for each other. Finally months of pent-up sexual tension released itself in one long, strenuous, orgasmic climax.

We collapsed together in a tangled heap of exhausted limbs, straining for air. Silence filled the room for a long while. Each of us savored the moment privately. Propping my head up on one elbow, I turned to her, staring in wonderment at her nakedness. Her eyes fluttered; she smiled and clutched me desperately. She placed a finger over my parted lips in a silent plea to maintain the perfect quietude. We snuggled closer and fell asleep.

I awoke several hours later and stared outside the cabin, where it was pitch black and silent. The storm had passed and a half moon slid from behind the remaining scraps of cloud to cast a dim silver light over the reeds and lilies of the shallow, wind-rippled lake. Raquel lay there, still in my embrace. I marveled at my good fortune. The unpredictable twists and turns that had led me to her, though certainly painful, had also been exhilarating. If the future is truly already set, I guess it's good that we can't know every detail, otherwise life would quickly devolve into a dull, gray sort of limbo. And, for all the pain it brought, I wouldn't have had it any other way.

She stirred beside me. "You awake?" she whispered. "What're you thinking?"

"I'm thinking what a lucky guy I am to have found you. Who'd have ever thought our chance meeting at a cemetery would end up like this?"

"If I tell you something, will you promise not to hold it against me?"

"I can't promise that. I'd like to hold it against you every time I get the opportunity, if it's all the same to you."

She laughed. "OK, hold it against me then. What I want to say is that I liked you from the moment I first saw you. But I've been burned before in relationships, believing in promises which were never really made. I seem to fall for the wrong sort of guy, the narcissistic types who have no time for the give and take of a long-term relationship. That's why I couldn't commit. But I believe you're different, Frank."

We burrowed our still naked bodies even closer together. "I understand. Waiting this long for the right person just made it all the sweeter, for me anyway."

"Me too. This sure has turned out to be an amazing night, hasn't it? We must always remember the first time."

"Now that I know what I've got, I'm never letting you go."

"What a beautiful thing to say. You just try looking at another woman; you won't know what hit you, mister." It was my turn to laugh.

"There is something we've got to figure out, though." She fidgeted and looked over at me, nervously twisting the bed sheets into a long silk pretzel. She was obviously worried that something would gum up the works, even now.

"And that is?"

"The question of consanguinity."

"What do you mean?"

"Remember the fight at the Kilgore Tavern I told you about, the one that resulted in the deaths of Canuto and Ramón? Grandma Kate told me the whole story, and it very much concerns the two of us." Her eyes widened in disbelief and tears welled up as I related it to her.

"Was that true? Did my grandmother really sleep around?"

"No. As far as anyone can tell, the child was Michael's, and his refusal to marry Carolina must have infuriated Canuto. That's what started the brawl. I know it's tardy, but I apologize on behalf of the Kilgore family. In any case, the question of Michael ever marrying Carolina became moot the next day when he was murdered by your other great uncle, Ricky Cortez."

"What a horrible waste! That stupid Latino machismo strikes again. What became of Carolina?"

"It turns out she was the girl in the back room who fired off a couple of shots to try to warn her family. When she couldn't save them, she fled the scene. You already know what happened next, don't you?"

"I think so. Sadly, she delivered her baby at home; there were no hospitals for indigents in those days. I think she must've died of what we doctors call 'puerperal sepsis,' a post-partum infection of the uterus. There were no antibiotics back then either. That's why I'm so grateful for the money you donated to my clinic, Frank. It'll go a long way toward ensuring that kind of situation doesn't happen again."

"I hope so. And I'm sure you figured out that the baby turned out to be your mother, which makes both of us one-eighth descendants of Henry Kilgore. That's why I raise the question of consanguinity. We're third cousins once, or is it twice, removed. Legally, I think it's fine though. You know what the prophet Obadiah says, don't you? 'Life is short and then you're dead for a long time.' So let's not waste any."

"Medically it's fine too. But honestly, Frank, who cares anymore? Not me, that's for sure. And right now you seem a bit too far removed. Could you please come a little closer? Frank . . . Frank, what are you doing down there? Oh, don't stop now. There's a good cousin."

We laughed, and soon our naked bodies lay entwined once again. Fate is surely a strange, unforgiving taskmaster. He mocks us in our futile efforts to alter our destinies, so I decided to go with the flow. The joyous sounds of our second intense union wafted tenderly away on the softening breeze outside and lost themselves in the eerie solitude of a mystical West Texas night.

We dozed off, locked in each other's arms, with wicked smiles on our faces. I understood her reasons; I smiled for those and for a whole lot more.

The Kilgore Curse had been lifted at last.

ACKNOWLEDGMENTS

One afternoon about five years ago, Chris Meadows recounted a bizarre story to me. While visiting her family's gravesite, she came upon another family visiting their own ancestors' graves. They insisted that her relatives had murdered theirs in a barroom brawl back in 1948, and Chris' research proved the truth of the matter. That tale formed the nidus of an idea which led, ultimately, to *The Kilgore Curse*. So thank you for that, Chris, for reviewing an early version of the book, for permitting the use of family photos, and for being a friend.

With many thousands of manuscripts submitted daily, getting a publisher to notice an author's work is unusually difficult. Thankfully, I found the Brown Book Publishing Group. The professional staff at Brown knows its business intimately and functions seamlessly to create books worthy of the reader's time and money. I am indebted to publisher Milli Brown, editors Tim Boswell and Janet Harris, project manager Kathy Penny, and art director Omar Mediano for their exceptional contributions to *The Kilgore Curse*.

There actually was an attorney in Dallas named Frank Hernandez, who really did successfully argue the case of *Hernandez v. Texas* (no relation) before the US Supreme Court in 1954. He and I shared breakfast together at a "little Mexico" restaurant in Dallas several years ago just like El Taquito's, right down to the seriously spicy salsa. He provided me with considerable insight into the Latino culture and history of Dallas. The character of

Josue Fuentes in the book is based on Frank, who died in 2012. Thanks also to Hugh Aynesworth, a longtime newsman, patient, and friend, for referring me to Frank, for reviewing the manuscript, and for offering encouragement.

Understanding complex real estate transactions and zoning laws was also problematic for me, and for schooling me on those issues, I have another friend to thank: Sam Kartalis, President and COO of Henry S. Miller Real Estate here in Dallas. And thanks to Javier Gutierrez, proprietor of Javier's Gourmet Mexicano, the premier restaurant of its kind in Dallas, for providing the setting of an important chapter in the book and for many a delicious meal.

I owe much of my knowledge of firearms and most of my guns to Shawn Nelms, owner (with his wife, Shirley) of the Bachman Gun Store on Northwest Highway. Thanks for all you have taught me and for your friendship. The character of Keith Glenn in the book is loosely based on Shawn, an old Marine to the core.

There were many others, family and friends, who offered support and constructive criticism of this project. They are too numerous to mention here, but y'all know who you are, so *gracias*. I can't let this moment pass, however, without acknowledging my children, Jillian Forrester and Robert Pivnick, for providing me with such wonderful grandchildren and for making me proud to have sired them.

ABOUT THE AUTHOR

The Kilgore Curse is Larry Pivnick's first published novel, but he's been writing all his life. In medical school (MD, Toronto, 1971), he wrote scientific papers and short stories for amusement. During law school (JD, SMU, 1993), he wrote court briefs and tinkered with novels. Then he graduated from SMU's Creative Writing Program in 2007. *The Kilgore Curse* is the culmination of his multifaceted education, extensive experience, peripatetic travel, and unfettered imagination.

Born and raised in Toronto, Dr. Pivnick has practiced family medicine in Dallas for the past thirty-six years and law for twenty. He has received numerous "Patient Choice" awards and "D" magazine recognition for outstanding medical practice. He recently retired in order to dedicate himself to writing fiction full time and lives in Dallas with Linda, his devoted wife of forty-three years. Together they have two grown children and four extraordinary grandchildren. They love to travel and play golf though, to his eternal bemusement, she is the better golfer.